Ante Nazor

The Croatia[n] War of Independence:

Serbia's War of Conquest Against Croatia and the Defeat of Serbian Imperialism 1991-1995

HEALTHY EYE SERIES

The Croatian War of Independence: Serbia's War of Conquest Against Croatia and the Defeat of Serbian Imperialism 1991-1995
by Ante Nazor

Project coordinator: Julienne Eden Busic

Editor: Andrea Cetinic

Translator: Janko Paravic

Cover photo by: Zeljko Gasparovic

Cover design by: Mladen Bradvica, mladen.bradvica@icloud.com

Healthy Eye design by: Boris Ljubicic, boris@studio-international.com

Ante Nazor

The Croatian War of Independence:

Serbia's War of Conquest Against Croatia and the Defeat of Serbian Imperialism 1991-1995

HEALTHY EYE SERIES

Table of contents

The National Anthem of the Republic of Croatia

"Our Beautiful Homeland"

Our beautiful homeland,
Oh, dear heroic land,
Our fathers' ancient glory,
May you be blessed forever!

Beloved for your glory,
Beloved as our one and only,
Beloved you are in your plains,
Beloved in your mountains!

Flow on, Sava and Drava,
Flow on, you mighty Danube,
Blue sea, tell the world,
That the Croat loves his people,

Whilst the sun warms his fields,
Whilst winds lash his oaks,
Whilst the graves harbor his ancestors,
Whilst his heart beats!

[Decree on the Promulgation of the Law on the Coat of Arms, Flag and National Anthem of the Republic of Croatia, and the Flag and the Sash of the President of the Republic of Croatia; *Official Gazette*, 55; 21 December 1990]

"Our Beautiful"
The Croatian national anthem begins with these two words. The Croats have dedicated it to the beauty of their country and to the heroic, millenary struggle of their ancestors for their home, freedom and survival. Home and freedom are the meaning of life and inspiration in the struggle of all people denied these values. Even in the most difficult moments of its history, the proud people dream of freedom, sing of it, and live for it:

O beautiful, o beloved, o sweet freedom,
God has given us all the treasures in you,
(…)
All silver, all gold, all human lives,
Cannot repay your pure beauty!

(Ivan Gundulić, Croatian poet)

This is why, lest one forget the most valuable of treasures, the pledge carved into the stone fortress of freedom, Croatian Dubrovnik still admonishes:

Non bene pro toto libertas venditur auro!
(Freedom is not sold for all the gold in the world!)

Introduction

In the early Middle Ages, the Croats settled the area which had since ancient times been the link between the East and the West but also the boundary of civilizations, great empires and religions, and the scene of their conflicts. Given the geo-strategic position of this territory, in which the Croatian state was established no later than the ninth century, the Croats experienced a history full of ordeals. The borders of the Croatian state are also the outcome of such an eventful history. They are largely due to the Ottoman onslaught towards Western Europe and the many centuries of anti-Turkish wars in the late Middle Ages, and of aggressive Serbian policies in the former Yugoslav states. The present-day borders of the Republic of Croatia were confirmed in the defensive and liberating Homeland War* [*see Note*] after a new period in Croatian history was ushered in with the democratic changes in 1990, and the establishment of the new, independent and sovereign Croatian state in 1991. Of course, just like all previous historic periods, it was also a result of major social changes in Europe, especially Eastern Europe.

This book intends to present a brief chronological survey of the historic process which included the creation of the modern Croatian state, Serbian aggression against the Republic of Croatia and the defense of its territorial integrity, as well as draw attention to certain stages and important events in that process.

* *The Homeland War* is the generally accepted name for a recent period in Croatian history in the 1990s, when the modern Republic of Croatia was established and then defended in the imposed war. According to the legislation of the Republic of Croatia (Act on the Rights of the Croatian Homeland War Veterans and Members of Their Families), the Homeland War covers the period between 5 August 1990 and 30 June 1996. (Although, in legal terms, the state

of war ceased on 23 August 1996 with the signing of the Agreement on Full Normalization and Establishment of Diplomatic Relations Between the Republic of Croatia and the Federal Republic of Yugoslavia.)

The term Homeland War refers to the following:

- Final preparations of the Serbian aggressor for their war of aggression and the annexation of sizeable parts of Croatia and Bosnia & Herzegovina to Serbia (creating "Serbian republics" in these areas) to achieve the main goal of Greater Serbian policy: "All Serbs in one state," as conducted by the Serbian leadership and Slobodan Milošević;
- Unconstitutional and terrorist actions, and the armament and armed insurgency of part of the Serbs in Croatia after mid-1990 (in military terms, a creeping or latent aggression);
- Organization of Croatian defense and armed forces, a process that began in August 1990 and ended with the cessation of war;
- The beginning of the war and open aggression of Serbia and Montenegro, i.e., the Yugoslav National Army (JNA), and territorial defense and police forces of Serbia, Montenegro, and part of Bosnia & Herzegovina, including various Serbian paramilitary troops against Croatia, since the summer of 1991 (immediately following the Croatian Parliament's adoption of the Constitutional Decision on the Sovereignty and Independence of the Republic of Croatia on 25 June 1991);
- Defense of the territory of the Republic of Croatia starting in 1991, and the military liberation of the greater part of its provisionally occupied territory in the period between late 1991 up to the end of 1995.

Therefore, according to the laws of the Republic of Croatia, the term *Homeland War* also comprises the period immediately preceding the war in Croatia, i.e., the open Serbian aggression against the Republic of Croatia, and the period immediately following the end of war operations in Croatia and Bosnia and Herzegovina.

Given that the final part of the occupied territory of the internationally recognized Croatian state was returned through political agreement and not military action, from a political perspective the date 15 January 1998 can be considered the end of the Homeland War. This date marked the conclusion of the peaceful reintegration of the Croatian Danubian Area (Baranja, part of Eastern Slavonia and Western Srijem) into the constitutional system of the Republic of Croatia.

Among the Croats in Bosnia & Herzegovina who participated in large numbers in the defense of Croatia, the *Homeland War* is also the widely accepted name for the period from 1991 (the attack of the JNA and Greater Serbian forces in October 1991 on the village of Ravno <majority Croatian population> in eastern Herzegovina) up to end of 1995, including the defense from Serbian aggression, territorial war initiated by the Bosniak-Muslim forces, and participation of the Croatian Defense Council (HVO) and Special Police Units of the Ministry of the Interior of the Croatian Republic of Herzeg-Bosnia (SP MUP HRHB) with the Croatian Army and Army of BH in final liberation operations of southwestern and western Bosnia.

Historical Foundations of the Constitution of the Republic of Croatia (1990)

The millennial identity of the Croatian nation and the continuity of its statehood, confirmed by the course of its entire historical experience in various statal forms, and by the perpetuation and growth of the idea of one's own state, based on the Croatian nation's historical right to full sovereignty, manifested itself:

- in the formation of Croatian principalities in the seventh century;
- in the independent medieval state of Croatia established in the ninth century;
- in the Kingdom of Croats established in the tenth century;
- in the preservation of the subjectivity of the Croatian state in the Croatian-Hungarian personal union;
- in the autonomous and sovereign decision of the Croatian Sabor (Parliament) of 1527 to elect a king from the Habsburg Dynasty;
- in the autonomous and sovereign decision of the Croatian Sabor to sign the Pragmatic Sanction of 1712;
- in the conclusions of the Croatian Sabor of 1848 regarding the restoration of the integrity of the Triune Kingdom of Croatia under the power of the Ban, on the basis of historical statal and natural rights of the Croatian nation;
- in the Hungarian-Croatian Compromise of 1868 regulating the relations between the Kingdom of Dalmatia, Croatia and Slavonia and the Kingdom of Hungary, on the basis of the legal traditions of both states and the Pragmatic Sanction of 1712;
- in the decision of the Croatian Sabor of 29 October 1918 to dissolve state relations between Croatia and Austria-Hungary, and the simultaneous affiliation of independent Croatia, invoking its historical and natural right as a nation, with the State of Slovenes,

Croats and Serbs, proclaimed on the theretofore territory of the Habsburg Monarchy;
- in the fact that the Croatian Sabor had never sanctioned the decision of the National Council of the State of Slovenes, Croats and Serbs to unite with Serbia and Montenegro into the Kingdom of Serbs, Croats and Slovenes (1 December 1918), subsequently (3 October 1929) proclaimed the Kingdom of Yugoslavia;
- in the establishment of the Banovina of Croatia in 1939 by which Croatian state identity was restored within the Kingdom of Yugoslavia;
- in laying the foundations of state sovereignty during the Second World War, through decisions of the Antifascist Council of the National Liberation of Croatia (1943), as counter to the proclamation of the Independent State of Croatia (1941), and subsequently in the Constitution of the People's Republic of Croatia (1947) and several later constitutions of the Socialist Republic of Croatia (1963 – 1990), during a historical turning point of rejecting the Communist system and changes in the international order of Europe, in their first democratic elections (1990), the Croatian nation free willingly confirmed their thousand-year statehood.

Appendix (from the "Revised" version of the Constitution of the Republic of Croatia, 25 April 2001):
"By the new and revised Croatian Constitution (1990) and victory in the Homeland War (1991-1995), the Croatian people expressed their will and inclination to create and preserve the Republic of Croatia as an independent, sovereign and democratic country."

THE REPUBLIC OF CROATIA AND THE HOMELAND WAR

(A Chronology of Political and Military Developments in the Process of Establishment of the Modern Croatian State, Serbian Aggression Against the Republic of Croatia, and the Struggle for its Freedom and Integrity, 1990, 1991 – 1995/98)

The Second Half of the 1980s

The "Greater Serbian" Policy – the Main Reason Underlying the Collapse of the SFRY

The fall of the Berlin Wall in November 1989 symbolically marked the beginning of a new period in European history in which the one-party communist regime in communist countries in Europe (Poland, Hungary, East Germany...) was replaced by multi-party systems and democracy. As democratic anticommunist movements emerged in communist countries, the process of democratization also swept Croatia, then one of the six republics of the Socialist Federal Republic of Yugoslavia (SFRY). Initiatives for political pluralism appeared in Croatia in early 1989. Because of past differences in terms of standards and freedoms in Croatia as compared to countries of the former Eastern bloc, certain specific features characterized the process of democratization within the country. However, a civilized and in the first place peaceful development of democracy in Yugoslavia in the 1990s was opposed by Great Serbian projects conceived in the nineteenth and twentieth centuries, according to which the western boundary of the Serbian state – the so-called

Greater Serbia – was planned deep in Croatian territory along the Virovitica-Pakrac-Karlovac-Ogulin line, including parts of Gorski Kotar – Karlobag. That was approximately the boundary of Ottoman conquests between the fifteenth and seventeenth centuries. A media campaign focused on mobilizing Serbian population for a nationalist, actually imperialist policy, and creating conditions for its implementation, was set in motion with the publication of part of the draft Memorandum of the Serbian Academy of Sciences and Arts in the Belgrade daily *Večernje Novosti (Evening News)* late in September 1986. Serbian nationalists stressed the allegedly endangered condition of the Serbs and Serbian culture in Yugoslavia, especially in Kosovo and Croatia, while actually aspiring for a greater centralization of the state and Serbia's domination over other Yugoslav republics. A comment highlighted in the same paper (24 September 1986), in which the Memorandum was compared to "a new call for new bloodshed," was extremely significant, and unambiguously pointed to the culprits for the tragic war which took place in Croatia in 1991, and later on in Bosnia and Herzegovina. Along with the media, the systematic promotion of Greater Serbian ideas was also supported by part of the leadership of the Serbian Orthodox Church and part of the Serbian intellectual elite, led by some members of the Serbian Academy of Sciences and Arts, and writers whose chauvinistic books enjoyed a high circulation. Individuals in Serbia who publicly opposed the Greater Serbian policy were unable to change the course of events. In Serbia, the voice of reason was smothered by the war cries of supporters of the Greater Serbian idea.

Such circumstances marked the rise of the "Balkan Butcher" Slobodan Milošević (as of January 1986 the President of the Presidency of the League of Communists of Serbia). Milošević became popular in Serbia after a TV camera recorded his words to a Serbian worker, "No one must dare beat you!" spoken in Kosovo Polje on 24 April 1987. The statement received tremendous publicity, and Milošević, promising to resolve the crisis in Kosovo, became a hero fighting for the "Serbian cause" in the eyes of the Serbian public. The 8th Session of the Central Committee of the League of Communists of Serbia, held in late September 1987, was decisive for his political rise and progress of the Greater Serbian conquest. Milošević's people came to power in Serbia, and on 8 May 1989, he became President of the Presidency of the Socialist Republic of Serbia. The former President, Ivan Stambolić, actually Milošević's political mentor who because of Milošević' policy stepped down from office in mid-December 1987, wrote on the occasion: "The eighth session was actually the bugle call to arms which roused the Serbian nationalists to destroy Yugoslavia. Yugoslavia was at that time already sentenced to death. All that was left were its dreadful death throes smothered in blood…" (From the book *The Road to Wilderness* by Ivan Stambolić, former President of the Presidency of the Socialist Republic of Serbia; Belgrade 1995, 19).

After taking over power in Serbia, the followers of Milošević's policy resorted to violent methods – rallies and the so-called Anti-Bureaucratic Revolution – in order to take over power in the autonomous provinces of Vojvodina and Kosovo and the Republic of Montenegro (late 1988 and early 1989, respectively). By decision of the Assembly of the Socialist Republic of Serbia on 28 March 1989, Vojvodina and Kosovo were (de facto) deprived of their status of constitutive units of the Yugoslav Federation, but retained the votes of their representatives in the collective SFRY Presidency (8 members: 6 representatives of the republics and 2 of the autonomous provinces). The annulment of the autonomy of Vojvodina and Kosovo was not in accordance with the federal 1974 Constitution, according to which Yugoslavia consisted of six republics and the mentioned two autonomous provinces, but the federal bodies did not respond. This state of affairs was defined by the new Constitution of the Republic of Serbia enacted in September 1990. Since the pro-Serbian representatives of Montenegro, Vojvodina and Kosovo were elected into the SFRY Presidency, Milošević secured control over half of its members, and Serbia gained preconditions for political domination over the other Yugoslav republics. The developments in Serbia provoked a reaction in the western Yugoslav Republics (Croatia and Slovenia).

Along with these political developments, the restructuring of the SFRY military was also initiated in the mid-1980s. Since 1969, it consisted of two legally equal components: the Yugoslav People's Army (JNA) and the republican Territorial Defense (TO). The JNA was the federal army, and the mission of its peacetime component was to prevent any strategic surprise; the TO was the wartime army with only small peacetime core units and commands. However, according to the Unity Plan, the SFRY military was centralized in terms of organization and command. The scope of the JNA's military territorial organizations was expanded, and instead of the previous six armies with zones of responsibility which partly matched the boundaries of the republics, after late 1988 the JNA had three ground army commands (military districts), one military-maritime district, and the air force and air defense. The reorganization excluded the republican leaderships from the command of TO units, which contrary to the 1974 SFRY Constitution, were now subordinated to JNA commands, while the territory of Croatia was divided into several commands. Thus the 5th military district (according to the peacetime organization), with headquarters in Zagreb, covered north-western Croatia, Istria, Gorski Kotar, Lika, Kordun, Banovina, and Slovenia. The remaining part of Croatia was divided between the 1st military district with headquarters in Belgrade (Slavonia), and the military-maritime district with headquarters in Split (Adriatic Coast and northern Dalmatia).

The preservation of Yugoslavia as a strictly centralized state with the predominance of the most numerous (Serbian) people in it (based on the principle of "one man, one vote"), and the reduction of the rights of the republics but greater authority of federal bodies, were the reasons why part of the JNA leadership was drawn to the Serbian leadership and why the JNA was transformed into a Serbian army. Of course, owing to circumstances, first of all because of the armed resistance of the Slovenians and especially the Croats, followed by the Bosniaks-Muslims, the goal was reduced to the occupation of "Serbian" areas in Croatia and Bosnia and Herzegovina, to be later on annexed to a rump Yugoslavia, actually (Greater) Serbia.

In line with the Greater Serbian policy controlled from Belgrade, the Serbs in Croatia organized an anti-Croatian rally in Knin as early as 28 February 1989. The religious (Orthodox) feast held by the Lazarica church in Kosovo Polje near Knin on 9 July 1989 also turned into a political, anti-Croatian rally of Serbs from Croatia and other republics. The mentioned event was sharply censured as a manifestation of Serbian nationalism by the Presidency of the Central Committee of the League of Communists of Croatia and by the Presidency of the Socialist Republic of Croatia. The Serbian media used the arrest of 14 people at the rally as a propaganda message claiming that Serbs in Croatia had no ethnic rights. These rallies in Knin and the surrounding area were actually the launch of Serbian insurrection in Croatia.

1990

Multi-Party Elections and the Collapse of Communism in Croatia

A new attempt by the Serbian leadership to impose its option of a centralized and unitary state by convening the 14th Extraordinary Congress of the League of Communists in Belgrade failed in January 1990. The Slovenian delegation, followed by the Croats, walked out of the congress, and the League of Communists of Yugoslavia fell apart. Thus ended, after the death of the Yugoslav President for Life, Josip Broz Tito (1980), the second major factor for the preservation of the Socialist Federal Republic of Yugoslavia. The third remaining factor was the JNA.

The disintegration of the League of Communists of Yugoslavia coincided with the introduction of the multi-party system in the Yugoslav republics. The process of democratization in Slovenia and Croatia could no longer be stopped. In Croatia – then the Socialist Republic of Croatia – the liberal-reform stream in the communist leadership enacted legislative changes required for the legalization of new political parties and the carrying out of direct multi-party elections by secret ballot. The long-awaited multi-party election campaign could finally start when the Speaker of the Parliament (Sabor) of the Socialist Republic of Croatia promulgated the Decision on Elections for the Members of the Parliament of the Socialist Republic of Croatia. Already in early February, the political parties in Croatia were formally legalized, and by 9 April, the Republican Secretariat (Ministry) of Public Administration and Justice registered a total of 33 parties.

In early 1990, the supporters of Greater Serbian policies tried to stop the process of democratization in Croatia by means of new incidents and organizing mass rallies ("events of the Serbian people") – on 4 February in Karlovac and on 4 March on Petrova Gora *(Peter's Mountain)*. Pictures of the President of the Presidency of the Socialist Republic of Serbia, Slobodan Milošević; Serbian, Yugoslav and Communist Party flags; and Greater Serbian and anti-Croatian slogans dominated the rally. The crowd shouted threats against Croatian politicians (even against Ivica Račan, President of the Central Committee of the League of Communists of Croatia), calling them "ustashe." On 7 March, the Presidency of the Socialist Republic of Croatia denounced the Petrova Gora rally as an attack on the Socialist Republic of Croatia. Following this, on 18 March 1990, a Serbian extremist attempted to assassinate the President of the Croatian Democratic Union (HDZ) Franjo Tuđman during an election rally in front of the Asseria Hotel in Benkovac. On 21 March, the Presidency of the Socialist Republic of Croatia condemned this attack as well. All these events provoked reactions by the Croats and further strained the political relations between Croatia and Serbia. Eventually this caused the break-up of Yugoslavia.

Although strained by deteriorating Croato-Serbian relations, on 22-23 April and 6-7 May 1990, Croatia held free multi-party elections, won by the Croatian Democratic Union (HDZ) led by Franjo Tuđman. During its election campaign, the HDZ based its message on the markedly anticommunist mood of the majority of Croats and on the awakened national enthusiasm, which was also the reaction to the growing Serbian nationalism since the mid-1980s, and the insistence on the centralization of Yugoslavia, that is, the domination of Serbia over the other Yugoslav republics. The SFRY military responded to the results of the Croatian elections in mid-May 1990 by seizing almost all weapons stocks of the Croatian Territorial Defense (according to estimates, about 80,000 to 200,000 "barrels") and removed them to warehouses controlled by the JNA. The weapons were seized in agreement with the Serbian leadership and based on an order illegally signed on 14 May 1990 (without the knowledge and agreement of the SFRY Presidency) by General

Blagoje Adžić, Chief of the General Staff of the SFRY Armed Forces. Three days later, Borisav Jović, Slobodan Milošević's associate and Serbian member of the SFRY Presidency, and as of 15 May 1990 its President, noted in his book (*The Last Days of the SFRY: Excerpts from the Diary;* Belgrade, 1995, p. 146): "We have practically disarmed them. In formal terms, this was done by the Chief of the General Staff, but as a matter of fact it was done at our command. The Slovenes and the Croats reacted sharply, but they had nowhere to go."

By disarming Croatia, the JNA secured complete superiority in the case of an armed resolution (the certainty of which appeared to be growing) of the political crisis in Yugoslavia, as threatened by the President of the Socialist Republic of Serbia Slobodan Milošević, on St. Vitus Day (28 June 1989), in his speech at the giant Serb rally on Kosovo Polje near Priština. "Today, six centuries later, we are again in the midst of battle and confronting battles. This time they are not armed battles, though that cannot yet be excluded..." It is more than obvious that Milošević had already planned to carry out the "armed battles" he announced on the occasion, with the help of the JNA, relying on the support of its mainly Serbian command cadre and prevailing communist character (most of the highest officers were members of the League of Communists of Yugoslavia).

Results of the elections for the National Parliament 1990

1	2	3	4
HDZ	42.30	68.75 (55)	57.58 (205)
SKH-SDP, SSH	35.30	25.00 (20)	30.06 (107)
KNS	15.00	3.75 (3)	5.90 (21)
Independent candidates	4.10	1.25 (1)	3.65 (13)
Others	1.70	0.00 (0)	1.40 (5)
SDS	1.60	1.25 (1)	1.40 (5)
Total	100.00	100.00 (80)	100.00 (356)
	Socio-Political Council (DPV) in Parliament	DPV mandates in Parliament	Total mandates in Parliament

The constituent assembly of the new democratically elected multi-party Parliament (*Sabor*) of the Socialist Republic of Croatia was held on 30 May 1990. Franjo Tuđman was elected President of the Presidency of SR Croatia; Žarko Domljan was elected Speaker, and Stjepan Mesić President of the Executive Council of the Parliament of SR Croatia (i.e., Prime Minister). The HDZ assumed power and became the leading party in the country. Refusing to accept democratic changes, the Serbian party in Croatia – the Serbian Democratic Party (SDS) – boycotted the assembly. Its leadership staged an attack on their own activist in Benkovac, Miroslav Mlinar (president of the local SDS chapter), presenting it as an "ugly, callous, ustashe act" (*Politika*, Belgrade daily, 21 May 1990), and used the "Mlinar Case" as a reason for suspending relations with the Parliament of SR Croatia.

Despite deteriorating interethnic relations and serious disturbance of public order, the previous leadership of the Republic ensured a peaceful and democratic implementation of the process of democratization and change of power in Croatia. After a civilized transfer of power with former President Ivo Latin, and in accordance with election results, Franjo Tuđman became the first democratically elected President of the Presidency of SR Croatia – and essentially, the first President of modern, democratic Croatia.

The Unconstitutional Activity and Armed Insurgency of Part of the Serbs in Croatia

The insurgent Serbs in Croatia instigated a process of unconstitutional activity and redrawing of the territorial-administrative boundaries of Croatia already in June 1990. On 27 June 1990, the assembly of the Municipality of Knin enacted the Decision on the Foundation and Constitution of the Association of Municipalities of Northern Dalmatia and Lika. The Association was the forerunner of the future Serbian Autonomous Regions (SAOs) in Croatia: SAO Krajina (Knin, 21 December 1990), SAO Western Slavonia (12 August 1991), and SAO Slavonia, Baranja and Western Srijem (Beli Manastir, 25 September 1991). By decisions of its Assemblies, the mentioned regions would be united in the Republic of Serbian Krajina (Knin, 19 December 1991). Naturally, the Constitutional Court of the Republic of Croatia annulled all the decisions of the leadership of the Serbian insurgents that did not conform to the Croatian Constitution, and which were enacted with the intention of jeopardizing the integrity and sovereignty of the Republic of Croatia.

The democratic changes also implied amending the names of government bodies, offices, and symbols that reflected the previous ideological, communist totalitarian climate, and introducing names and titles more suitable to the democratic and modern government structure. Accordingly, on 25 July 1990, the Parliament of SR Croatia adopted a number of amendments to the Constitution of SR Croatia: the adjective "socialist" was removed from the name of the state, and the new (historical) coat of arms and flag defined. The names of several offices were changed: the former president of the presidency became President, the executive council of the Parliament became the Government of Croatia, and republican secretaries became ministers.

It was also decided to start the process of adoption of a new Constitution of the Republic of Croatia.

On the same day, the Serbian National Council (founded at the Serbian Diet in the town of Srb (in Croatia) as the Diet's executive body), adopted the Declaration on the Sovereignty and Autonomy of Serbs in Croatia. A plebiscitary statement of the Serbian people regarding all issues essential for its position in Croatia and Yugoslavia was also announced. The date for this plebiscite of the Serbian people in the Republic of Croatia on Serbian autonomy was later set to be conducted from 19 August to 2 September 1990. The leadership of the insurgent Serbs in Croatia claimed that "people secede, not states." On the contrary, the Croatian position was that republics and not ethnic groups were entitled to self-determination, that the borders of the republics were state borders, hence, international, and that the Serbs in Croatia therefore had no right to secession. Such a conclusion was based on Article 5 of the 1974 Constitution of the Republic of Croatia according to which the "borders of the Socialist Republic of Croatia could only be changed by decision of the Parliament of the Socialist Republic of Croatia." The Croatian position was also supported by Opinion No. 2 of the International Arbitration Commission of the Conference on the Former Yugoslavia of 11 January 1992, which established that whatever the circumstances, the right to self-determination must not involve changes to existing frontiers at the time of independence (*uti possidetis iuris*) except where the states in question agree otherwise. The intention to carry out what was practically a referendum brought the political situation in Croatia to a head.

On the eve of the announced Referendum on Serbian Autonomy, in his speech at the traditional ring-tilting tournament *(Sinjska Alka,* 5 August 1990), the President of the Republic of Croatia, Franjo Tuđman, appealed to the Serbs in Croatia "to democratically resolve all prerequisites for a peaceful coexistence with the Croats."

Several days later on 9 August 1990, in an interview for TV Slovenia on developments in Knin, President Tuđman stated that they were not an expression of democratic trends among the Serbian people in Croatia because the eleven municipalities involved in the insurgency only accounted for 26% of the Serbian population in Croatia with a 22% Croat population. He also stressed that Croatia would grant the Serbs "all civil and ethnic rights that can be guaranteed in any free democratic community" and that "the Serbs will have to accept the fact that the Republic of Croatia is the sovereign state of the Croatian people."

The Croatian leadership became increasingly concerned by the disturbance of public order and disregard of the Constitution and law in parts of Croatia with a majority Serbian population, especially because of the questionable loyalty of part of the police (militia) to the lawfully elected Croatian authorities. Namely, according to official records in 1984, less than 50% of the employees of the Secretariat of Internal Affairs of SR Croatia were Croats, while as many as 49.9% were Serbs (in some more "delicate" services the percentage was even higher). The ethnic structure of the Ministry of the Interior (MUP) of the Republic of Croatia did not change significantly until mid-1990: (in late September 1990, 50.3% were Croats, 30.1% Serbs, 15.6% Yugoslavs, and 4% others), although at the time Croatia had about 12% Serbs and about 78% Croats. Because of that, the Croatian leadership decided to increase the police force in Croatia in order to bring the ethnic structure in the Croatian MUP in line with the structure of Croatia's population, and so as to recruit and arm as many people as possible willing to acknowledge the legally elected Croatian government. Of course, such a decision had to be enforced in accordance with existing federal and republican laws, taking due account of the fact that the layoff of "surplus" Serbian police officers could be used by Serbian extremists as a pretext for conflicts. Article 25 of the Internal Affairs Act provided grounds for the increase of the number of police officers, and permitted the formation of new, special units in situations involving the deterioration of social or political conditions. Accordingly, in line with the need to arm a greater number of people ready to defend Croatia, the first two-month training course for new police officers, entitled the First Croatian Police Officers, began on 5 August 1990. About 1700 candidates were enrolled, and a police brigade formed. That was the first armed unit of the Croatian MUP, which the Croatian authorities could fully rely on in confrontations with Serbian extremists. Selected course trainees who met high mental and physical criteria replenished the Lučko Antiterrorist Unit on 7 September 1990, and later on other elite Croatian MUP units and the National Guard Corps (ZNG). Thus, the First Croatian Police Officers were the core which developed into the Croatian armed forces during the Homeland War. Of course, the police officers who had remained loyal to the Ministry of the Interior of the Republic of Croatia also took part in the defense of their country.

Because of the arrival of armed Croatian Serbs on the eve of the illegal Referendum on Serbian Autonomy, the Ministry of the Interior of the Republic of Croatia decided to seize the weapons intended for the MUP reserve in police stations in Dalmatia and Lika, which in fact was the very area where the Serb armed insurgency was being prepared with the support of Serbian state services and the JNA. The Serbian extremists used this decision as a direct motive for proclaiming a "state of war." Thus, on 17 August 1990, armed insurgents blocked the main road and rail routes from the interior of Croatia to Dalmatia with logs and boulders. The JNA, however, stopped the attempt of the Croatian police to establish order and peace in the area. After that, in the evening hours of 20 August 1990, in Civljani (between Sinj and Knin) Serbian extremists opened fire from infantry weapons on Croatian police officers who had come to remove the barricade. The so-called "Log Revolution" marked the beginning of the armed insurgency of part of the Serbs in Croatia against the democratically elected Croatian government. Its ultimate objective was the annexation of part of the Croatian territory to the Republic of Serbia and the creation of an integral Serbian state, which could only be achieved by the aggression of Serbia and the JNA on the Republic of Croatia.

In August and September 1990, the Serbian insurgency spread to other parts of Croatia as well. According to available information, a person of Serbian nationality (M.B.) was killed in Karlovac County on 18 August 1990. He was murdered by his compatriot (M.G.), with the objective to misrepresent it as a Croatian crime and thus alarm the Serbian population and motivate it for insurgency against Croatian authorities (Ivan Strižić, *The Battle for Slunj,* Slunj-Zagreb, 2007, 131-132). In order to arm the police reserve but also in order to gain better control of weapons, on 28 September 1990, the MUP decided to withdraw 60% of weapons of the police reserve units from police stations. The Serbian population opposed the act, and extremist Serbs rioted and attacked police stations in Petrinja, Glina, Dvor na Uni, Obrovac and Donji Lapac. In the night of 28/29 September, one Croatian policeman suffered a firearm wound as police endeavored to establish law and order in Banovina.

At the same time, there was a particular increase of the number of terrorist actions by Serbian extremists and terrorists, including persons infiltrated from Serbia. Behavior involving elements of armed insurgency and actions which could be characterized as felonies – theft, robbery, threats to security, terrorist acts (sabotage of industrial plants and infrastructural facilities, mining of roads and rail links, stealing of weapons from JNA warehouses, armed attacks on Croatian policemen and civilians, interception of vehicles and mistreatment of citizens) – took place in almost every community with a majority Serbian population (Knin, Lika, Kordun and Banija). In November 1990, Serbian terrorists even killed one of their own compatriots near Obrovac, a police officer who after the armed insurgency began, returned from Biograd where he was on duty to the Benkovac police station and to his comrades-in-arms in soon afterwards the self-proclaimed SAO Krajina. At the time, the MUP and Croatian authorities did not *de facto* control the area. On 29 November 1990 at Dvor na Uni, Croatian police arrested several armed persons from Serbia who patrolled around Croatia in order to set up a "War Council" of Serbs in Croatia. Obviously, all these actions were promoted by the Serbian leadership, and organized and implemented by Serbian services.

In spite of such circumstances, the Parliament of the Republic of Croatia enacted decisions guaranteeing equality to all the citizens of Croatia. Thus, at its extraordinary session on 24 August 1990, Parliament adopted the Resolution on the Protection of the Constitutional Order and Ethnic Rights in Croatia. It clearly highlighted the intention of the Croatian Parliament "to protect the constitutional order and laws of the Republic of Croatia with all means of a law-governed state," but also its resolute "intent to guarantee all human, political and ethnic rights." For that purpose, "the European Parliament and other qualified public and private organizations studying and monitoring the state of human, political and ethnic rights worldwide were invited to send their monitors or envoys to verify on the spot, freely and unimpededly, the condition of such rights in Croatia, especially with regard to the Serbian and Croatian population in areas involved in the insurgency." In an attempt to defuse the situation and achieve a Croato-Serbian agreement, in late August and early September, representatives of Croatian authorities and the HDZ organized a number of meetings with representatives from the Serbian Democratic Party (SDS). One of the topics was defining the cultural autonomy of Serbs in Croatia. With that objective in mind, the mixed Croato-Serbian Parliamentary Working Group for the Drafting of a Project on Serbian Cultural Autonomy in Croatia met on 24 October 1990. However, the SDS turned the group down as "illegitimate," deeming the Serbian National Council the exclusive negotiator with Croatian government bodies and institutions.

At the time, the Serbian leadership had already abandoned the idea of preserving Yugoslavia, and the Greater Serbian ideologists determined the border of future Serbia in which all the Serbs in the territory of the former Yugoslavia would live. Borisav Jović noted in his diary, after talking to one of the most important ideologues, Dobrica Ćosić, of the new attempt at creating "Greater Serbia":

> There is no longer any serious reason for the existence of Yugoslavia (...) Therefore, there is no force that can unite us. Such circumstances leave open the question of the destiny of the Serbs and of Serbia in the collapse of Yugoslavia as the main political issue. At least for us. That is why he [D. Ćosić] does not want to deal with the power struggle in Serbia but rather with the struggle for the state of the Serbs, which should include, in the distribution of territory with Croatia, the number Croats in Serbia matching the number of Serbs left in Croatia. In this sense, he is closely cooperating with Serbian parties in Croatia, Bosnia and Herzegovina and Croatia. He has personally urged Jovan Rašković to found the Serbian Democratic Party [in Croatia]. (...) An ethnic map of the Serbian space is being drawn up, especially in Bosnia and Herzegovina and Croatia, in order to clearly identify the territory where the Serbs are in the majority: the Serbs are the majority from Šibenik, across Lika, Bosanska Krajina, and along the Sava to Bijeljina. The Muslims are in the center of Bosnia. The Serbs cut across Sandžak along the Drina, and the Muslims cannot unite. That is the future space of Serbia. (From B. Jović, The Last Days of the SFRY: Excerpts from the Diary; Belgrade, 1995, p. 193).

The course of events and especially the brutal Serbian aggression against Croatia in 1991 confirm that Croatian authorities did not agree to a partition of territory with Serbia.

Taking advantage of its domination in the collective SFRY Presidency, the Serbian leadership itself engaged in criminal actions at the expense of the other republics, especially in the financial sector. Thus, by borrowing 18.2 billion dinars (then about USD 1.4 billion) on 28 December 1990 from the National Bank of Serbia, the Socialist Republic of Serbia actually carried out a "pirate" attack on the Yugoslav monetary system and brought down its integral financial policy in what actually amounted to a financial coup d'état.

Because of substantial threats to public law and order in areas of the Republic of Croatia with a predominantly Serbian population, and danger of an open insurgency of Serbs in Croatia, the MUP began forming new, battalion-strength special units. After the Lučko Antiterrorist Unit (ATJ) was brought to full complement, special purpose units were established in October at Tuškanac (Zagreb),

Rakitje (near Zagreb) and Valbandon (Pula). Additional units were formed in Kumrovec in November 1990, Pionirski Grad (Dubrava) in December, ATJ Sljeme in February 1991, and Vinica (Ivanec) and Erdut in April 1991.

Additionally, special police units – regular formations with a full complement of 100 to 150 active members – were established within each police administration. Their purpose, organization, equipment and training were specified in the Special Instruction of the Minister of the Interior on 5 March 1991. In mid-1991, the units were reorganized into special police units. Every unit had a reserve complement of the same size in terms of personnel.

Proclamation of the New Croatian Constitution (22 December 1990)

The anti-constitutional activity of the insurgent Serbs in Croatia reached a climax on 21 December 1990 with the proclamation of the Serbian Autonomous Region of Krajina with Knin as the "seat of the highest bodies of SAO Krajina and its capital." SAO Krajina comprised municipalities with a substantial share of Serbs (Croatian citizens) in Dalmatia, Lika, Banovina and Kordun. The contents of the Statute of SAO Krajina showed that if the SFRY were to be reorganized into a confederation of sovereign states or if the Republic of Croatia proclaimed independence, the leadership of the insurgent Serbs intended to annex Krajina to Serbia as a "historically and ethnically Serbian space."

It was amidst such political and terrorist actions of Serbian extremists that the Parliament of the Republic of Croatia promulgated a couple of days before Christmas (22 December 1990) the new Constitution (entitled the "Christmas Constitution"). The Constitution promoted human rights and freedoms, the equality of all citizens before the law, and multi-party democracy, market economy, and private property rights. The Republic of Croatia was defined as an integral and indivisible democratic and welfare state. One day earlier, Parliament adopted the Act on the Coat of Arms (the historical Croatian coat of arms in the form of a shield with 25 red and white/silver fields and crown consisting of five smaller shields with historical Croatian coats of arms); Flag (red, white and blue tricolor, with the coat of arms in the middle); National Anthem ("Our Beautiful Homeland"), and Presidential Flag and Sash (the symbol of the presidency).

The representatives of the insurgent Serbs in Croatia cited the new Croatian Constitution as one of the main reasons for the continued deterioration of their relations with the Parliament of the

Republic of Croatia and cause of the armed insurgency of part of the Serbs in Croatia. With its promulgation, they pointed out that the new Croatian authorities "expelled the Serbs from the Constitution," i.e., deprived the Serbs "of their status of a constituent people" and thereby turned the Serbs in Croatia into "second-class citizens." However, a comparison of previous Croatian Constitutions adopted in Yugoslavia with the new Constitution of the Republic of Croatia confirms that this is not true. For example, the part of the 1974 Constitution of the Socialist Republic of Croatia according to which "SR Croatia is the national state of the Croatian people, the state of the Serbian people in Croatia, and the state of other nations [peoples] and nationalities [ethnic minorities] living in it," does not allow for the unequivocal interpretation that the Serbs were then elevated to the level of a constituent people in Croatia. In the 1974 Constitution of the Socialist Republic of Croatia, they were only separately highlighted with respect to other nations and nationalities, while the equality of all Croatian citizens was also guaranteed by the 1990 Constitution of the Republic of Croatia. The Historical Foundations of the 1990 Constitution of the Republic of Croatia read as follows: "The Republic of Croatia is hereby established as the national state of the Croatian nation and a state of members of other nations and minorities who are its citizens: Serbs, Muslims, Slovenes, Czechs, Slovaks, Italians, Hungarians, Jews and others, who are guaranteed equality with citizens of Croatian nationality and the realization of ethnic rights in accordance with the democratic norms of the United Nations Organization and free world countries."

At any rate, since the new Constitution of the Republic of Croatia (Articles 3, 14, 15) emphasizes the equality of all citizens regardless of nationality, religion, race or sex, it cannot be claimed that the Serbs – after the promulgation of the new Croatian Constitution – no longer enjoyed equality with other Croatian citizens, or that they were "expelled from the Constitution." Analogously, regardless of the contents of the new Croatian Constitution of December 1990, its historical sources, incidents, and the terrorist actions of Serbian extremists in the second half of 1990, including the anti-constitutional decisions of the leadership of the insurgent Serbs from mid-1990 (when the new Croatian Constitution was not even drafted up), show that the armed insurgency of the Serbian extremists in Croatia cannot be justified by the contents of the Croatian Constitution of December 1990, that is, by the attitude of the Croatian authorities toward the Serbs in Croatia.

1991

The Communist JNA Threatens to Enforce a "State of Emergency" – The First Armed Conflicts

The beginning of 1991 brought new threats to the Croatian leadership and the continuation of anti-constitutional actions by insurgent Serbs in Croatia. On 4 January 1991, the leadership of SAO Krajina in Knin decided to stop recognizing the authority of the Ministry of the Interior of the Republic of Croatia (MUP RH). The decision only institutionalized the state of insurgency that prevailed since the summer of 1990, when a number of police officers of Serbian nationality refused obedience to the MUP RH in Zagreb. The Croatian authorities responded immediately on 10 January 1991 with a decision whereby the employees of the Ministry of the Interior could only retain employment and receive their pay after signing a statement of loyalty to the Republic of Croatia. The leadership of the Secretariat of the Interior (SUP) of SAO Krajina called it a "provocation" which deprived their officers of their "dignity."

Having seen that it would be impossible to impose their will by political means, the leadership of Serbia and the JNA were forced to resort to a more aggressive approach. Of course, the main objective was the overthrow of the democratically elected authorities in Croatia. Accordingly, on 9 January 1991, the SFRY Presidency ordered "all paramilitary armed formations, and armed formations which were not part of the integral armed forces of the SFRY or of bodies of interior affairs, and the organization of which did not conform to federal regulations, to be disarmed and disbanded within 10 days." Actually, the paramilitary force in Croatia was the breakaway SUP of SAO Krajina, that is, the units of the Krajina Militia, also known as Martić's Militia. However, the true intention of the pro-Serbian members of the SFRY Presidency was to prevent, if necessary even by force, the fortification of the Croatian police, although it was carried out in conformity with Yugoslav and republican laws.

On the day of expiry of the ten-day ultimatum, 19 January 1991, the President of the SFRY Presidency and co-creator of Milošević's "Greater Serbian" policy, Borisav Jović, spoke with JNA generals Veljko Kadijević and Blagoje Adžić about possible options in resolving the problem in Croatia. They concluded, "...a radical variant, conflict with the Croats, and overthrow of the Croatian government by force would not suit them, as it did not offer a good prospect of getting out of such a situation." Instead, they decided to "apply a special variant of exposing HDZ policies and weakening the HDZ government," and within such actions "take every step to discredit the Croatian government because of its illegal arming and anti-Yugoslav policy." (From B. Jović, *The Last Days of the SFRY: Excerpts from the Diary,* Belgrade, 1995, p. 255.) Two days later, on 21 January, Jović and Milošević agreed to accept secession if the Croats proclaimed it, and keep the Krajina municipalities (municipalities in Croatia with a majority or considerable Serbian population) "militarily" until a plebiscitary decision was made on where they wanted to live. Unlike them, Veljko Kadijević sought an "uncompromising approach until the final collapse of the Croatian government." Already on 15 January, Kadijević confirmed to Jović that "the military was prepared to apply a radical option until the overthrow of the HDZ government" (B. Jović, *op. cit.,* pp. 247, 257).

On 23 January 1991, the Presidency threatened to use the JNA unless "all mobilized armed units in the area of the Republic of Croatia were disbanded immediately." On the same day, Serbian "leader" Slobodan Milošević insisted that the JNA "cover Serbian areas in Croatia," and Veljko Kadijević then presented the Serbian leadership with a program of military steps which he had taken (higher combat readiness, unit redeployment, and additional mobilization). The competent body for decisions regarding such steps was the collective SFRY Presidency as the commander-in-chief of the JNA, which meant that such decisions were made without the knowledge of the other republics and contrary to the Yugoslav Constitution to which the military referred repeatedly (B. Jović, *op. cit.*, p. 264).

On 24 January, the Fifth JNA Military District with headquarters in Zagreb was put on full combat readiness. On 25 January 1991, when the national television broadcasted the program "What is the Truth About the Arming of the HDZ in Croatia," prepared by the security service of the armed forces of the SFRJ, publicly known as the JNA Counter-Intelligence Service (KOS), the enforcement of a state of emergency in Yugoslavia seemed to be inevitable. All the more so as the attention of the world was focused at the time on the Iraqi occupation of Kuwait and the Allied military intervention in Iraq. The psychosis of tension and insecurity grew worse when JNA soldiers arrested several Croats, JNA (and HDZ) members (the so-called "Virovitica Group"), and after the Military Court in Zagreb issued on 30 January a warrant to detain the Minister of Defense of the Republic of Croatia, Martin Špegelj "for investigation purposes upon reasonable suspicion of having committed the offense of armed revolt."

Nevertheless, the state of emergency was not declared in January 1991. The leadership of the insurgent Serbs continued to explore options for annexing Croatian territory to Serbia. In late January 1991, SDS President and distinguished Serbian intellectual and academy member Jovan Rašković, gave the following message to his party members: *The national movement of the Serbian people in Croatia is a movement for national equality, civil rights and the democratic, residual and federal Yugoslavia. There still remain some options which will become topical in no later than a few months: independent Serbia, the Serbian state of Krajina as part of Serbia or its autonomous province, or ultimately, ethnic Serbia, to use an old-fashioned or deceitful name, Greater Serbia...*

In such circumstances, and having received the Resolution of the Assembly of the Republic of Slovenia regarding the proposal for an agreed dissociation of the SFRY, on 21 February 1991 the Croatian Parliament adopted the Resolution on the Acceptance of the Proposal for the Dissociation of the SFRY and Possible Association into a Confederation of Sovereign Republics. On 28 February, the leadership of the insurgent Serbs in Croatia adopted the Resolution on the Dissociation of the Republic of Croatia and SAO Krajina.

In late February 1991, the military leadership (JNA) and Serbian leaders coordinated their plan of joint future action:

- Firm reliance required on forces favoring Yugoslavia in all parts of the country, and combined political and military steps to be taken in order to overthrow the government first in Croatia and then in Slovenia;
- In Croatia, the Serbian Krajina needs to be strengthened institutionally and politically, and its secession from Croatia supported, but in effect rather than publicly;
- Mass rallies against the HDZ to be organized in Croatia, "pro-Yugoslav" actions promoted throughout Bosnia and Herzegovina, and protests organized in Macedonia for the overthrow of the pro-Bulgarian leadership;
- Improve combat readiness of armed forces (JNA), and prepare for decisive action in Croatia

(From the book *The Last Days of the SFRY: Excerpts from the Diary,* by Borisav Jović, the President of the SFRY Presidency: Belgrade 1995, 276-278).

At the same time, the insurgent Serbs in Croatia continued to destabilize Croatia in order to claim parts of its territory. In February and March, new anti-Croatian rallies took place in Croatia (in Knin, Vukovar, Beli Manastir, Dalj, Bobota, Mirkovci, Trpinja, and Borovo Selo), and on 18 March 1991 the Decision on the Separation of SAO Krajina from the Republic of Croatia was adopted in Knin.

The Croatian police also became the target of more serious attacks by Serbian terrorists. In Pakrac on 2 March 1991, the first armed conflict between the Croatian police and Serbian terrorists (a day earlier Serbian police forces overtook the police station), and in Plitvice Lakes National Park on Easter Sunday, 31 March ("Plitvice Bloody Easter"). The Serbian extremists intended to annex Plitvice Lakes National Park (under UNESCO protection), known all over the world for its beautiful landscape and an important source of tourist revenues, to the self-proclaimed SAO Krajina. With that objective in mind, on 25 March, the Serbian Democratic Party (SDS) organized an anti-Croatian rally at Plitvice. Luckily, nobody was killed in Pakrac (some Croatian police officers were wounded), but the Plitvice conflict claimed the life of Croatian police officer Josip Jović (the first Croatian defender killed in the Homeland War) and one armed Serbian terrorist. The determined intervention of the Croatian special units in Pakrac and Plitvice showed that Croatia had highly motivated and well-trained military forces prepared to defend every inch of their country. These actions uplifted the morale of Croatian citizens who had accepted the democratically elected authorities, and reinforced their belief that Croatia would preserve its territorial integrity.

The day after, 1 April 1991, in Titova Korenica the leadership of the insurgent Serbs in Croatia adopted the Decision on the Unification of SAO Krajina with the Republic of Serbia and ordered the mobilization of the territorial defense of SAO Krajina. This practically exposed the main objective of the Serbian insurgency in Croatia. It was precisely in early April that the Serbian leadership (Slobodan Milošević and Borisav Jović) decided to "cross the Rubicon" and completely ignore the collective SFRY Presidency. According to a note in Jović's aforementioned book (p. 317), they had the promise of JNA generals that the army, even if it had to resort to armed action, would not permit Croatian police "to take Knin and other 'Serbian' towns now under Serbian authority."

The JNA had already intervened during the conflicts in Pakrac and Plitvice, formally – to separate the "conflicting parties," and practically – to protect Serbian terrorists in moments when the

Croatian police had defeated and threatened to arrest them. In fact, the JNA deployed itself in areas planned by Greater Serbian strategists as parts of the new Serbian state. The Serbian leadership expected the JNA to engage in armed conflicts with the Croatian police, which could provide a motive for the enforcement of a state of emergency in the country, but the Croatian leadership would not be provoked. At the same time, anti-Croatian sentiment grew stronger in Serbia due to the fact that the Serbian media was spreading false rumors about the suffering and massacre of Serbs in Pakrac. Although JNA representatives denied such rumors, the SFRY crisis deepened.

The events in Pakrac also marked the failure of the Serbian leadership's plan whereby the JNA would be granted approval at the meeting of the SFRY Presidency to enforce a state of emergency in the country. Croatian, Slovenian, Macedonian, and Bosnian and Herzegovian representatives thwarted the plan after a dramatic ballot in which the Bosnian and Herzegovian representative, a Serb (to boot!) – Bogić Bogićević, cast the crucial vote. After that, and in order to achieve a compromise and peaceful resolution of the crisis in the country, the six presidents of the Yugoslav republics met in Croatia (Split, 28 March 1991), Serbia (Belgrade, 4 April), Slovenia (Brdo near Kranj, 11 April), Macedonia (Ohrid, 18 April), Montenegro (Cetinje, 29 April), and Bosnia and Herzegovina (Sarajevo, 6 June 1991).

Unfortunately, none of the meetings offered a final solution, primarily because of the exclusive position of the Serbian leadership. Even after the democratic changes in Slovenia and Croatia, the Serbs resolutely turned down all proposals regarding an agreement on a new arrangement for Yugoslavia, including the Slovenian-Croatian suggestion on restructuring Yugoslavia as a confederal state.

Serbian politicians continued to incite the Serbs in Croatia against the democratically elected Croatian government. On 2 May 1991, Serbian extremists in Croatia ambushed and killed 13 Croatian police officers – 12 in Borovo Selo and one in Polača in the Zadar hinterland.

Moreover, more than 20 Croatian police officers were wounded at Borovo Selo. The situation was also extremely dramatic in the village of Kijevo, which was blocked after the establishment of the Croatian police station on 29 April 1991 by the Krajina militia and JNA.

Such a high number of casualties in a single day provoked the revolt of most Croatian citizens and caused a war psychosis in Croatia as well as vengeful acts of individuals against citizens of Serbian nationality. In protests against the JNA, which were held in Split (May 5) because of the blockade of the village of Kijevo, the first regular young soldier, Saško Gešovski, a Macedonian from Kavadarci, was killed under mysterious circumstances. All this additionally aggravated the security situation in parts of Croatia affected by the crisis, especially the Municipality of Vukovar, where a state of war prevailed. Creating chaos and uncontrolled conditions in Croatia was precisely the objective of the Greater Serbian strategists because it could provide motive for the enforcement of a state of emergency and JNA intervention in Croatia. Nevertheless, Croatian authorities succeeded in preventing the escalation of the conflict. They, however, could not secure public order and safety in areas under control of the insurgent Serbs because the activity of the Croatian police had been thwarted by the JNA, under threat of an armed conflict, as early as August 1990. The simultaneous murders of Croatian police officers in different parts of the Croatian state – in Slavonia and Dalmatia – demonstrated that preparations for the aggression against Croatia had entered their final phase.

The Serbs and the JNA used the events at Borovo Selo as a repeated request for military intervention. At new dramatic sessions of the SFRY Presidency on 8 and 9 May 1991, attended also by the presidents of all the Yugoslav republics, the Croatian leadership was forced to accept the decision on the deployment of the pro-Serbian JNA in crisis-stricken parts of Croatia. The JNA thus began to deploy, formally as a "buffer zone" between Serbian terrorists and Croatian armed forces, but actually in order to occupy an advantageous position for the attack on Croatia. Thus, the JNA openly assumed the role of protector and ally of the insurgent Serbs in Croatia.

In mid-May, the political situation in Yugoslavia took a dramatic turn for the worse. After the Serbian-Montenegrin bloc in the SFRY Presidency by means of regular procedure on 15 May 1991 refused to confirm the Croatian representative Stjepan Mesić as President, the work of the Presidency was blocked. At the same time, after the illegal Referendum for Unification (12 May 1991), the leadership of the insurgent Serbs in Croatia proclaimed SAO Krajina, that is, part of the territory of the Republic of Croatia, "an integral part of the united state territory of the Republic of Serbia." (16 May 1991, by the new Decision on the Unification of SAO Krajina with the Republic of Serbia.) As in the decision of 1 April, the territory of SAO Krajina was to be comprised of the municipalities of Knin, Benkovac, Obrovac, Gračac, Donji Lapac, Korenica, Kostajnica, Vojnić, Vrginmost, Glina, Dvor na Uni, parts of the municipalities of Petrinja, Sisak and Pakrac, and "all Serbian settlements unified with one of these municipalities, as well as settlements that later opt for unification in the demarcation process." Then, on 29 May 1991, the Assembly of SAO Krajina claimed that "SAO Krajina was defined as a form of political-territorial autonomy within federal Yugoslavia." Due to international circumstances, the Serbian leadership could not officially accept such a decision, but it continued to support the Serbian insurgency in Croatia militarily, economically and politically.

Given that Croatia was part of Yugoslavia, and was not permitted formally or legally to have its own army, and due to the fact that the JNA had seized the weapons of the Croatian territorial defense already in May 1990, Croatia's defense was based on the units of the Ministry of the Interior (MUP). Of course, many volunteers were ready to defend their homeland. However, the main problem was the lack of weapons and ammunition, especially heavy weaponry. The police units formed up until that time could protect Croatian citizens from the attack of Serbian terrorists and from the insurgency of part of the Serbs in Croatia. But the threat of using the JNA in order to preserve the SFRY forced the Croatian leadership to start forming military-police components of the armed forces, entitled the National Guard Corps (ZNG) in April 1991. By the end of May 1991, the first four active ("A") ZNG brigades were formed. Members of the later Guards Brigades were recruited from their ranks. The ZNG was also designed as an active and a reserve component. The ZNG reserve was organized on the basis of the number of reserve police members – about 39,000 on 11 April 1991 – and divided into brigades and independent battalions. In order to improve the morale of Croatian citizens but also to deter possible aggression, a review of ZNG units was held at the stadium of the Zagreb Football Club on 28 May 1991. Along with the special units subordinated to the Croatian General Staff and special MUP RH units, the Guards Brigades played an exceptional and indeed crucial role in the struggle against Serbian terrorists and in the defense and liberation of the Republic of Croatia.

Along with the formation of professional armed forces, the organization of National Protection Units also began on 15 March 1991. It was actually the continuation of a process focused on the formation of unarmed volunteer units as a form of defense against the threatening aggression of the JNA and insurgent Serbs in Croatia. By the end of June 1991, the National Protection Units had more than 50,000 members, of which 20,000 in Zagreb. The mass and voluntary enrolment in volunteer National Protection Units confirmed the determination of the Croats, but also of Croatian citizens of other nationalities, to stand up against the threatening aggression of the JNA and Serbian-Montenegrin forces.

Of course, the Croatian leadership continued to pursue a peaceful solution to the crisis in negotiations with the leaderships of the other Yugoslav republics. Considering the balance of forces and the increasingly open cooperation of part of the JNA with the Serbian leadership, it was precisely Croatia – disarmed and without its own armed forces – who was vitally interested in seeing no JNA involvement in the resolution of the crisis, and avoiding or at least postponing an armed conflict as long as possible.

Extract from the speech of Ivan Šreter held on 30 May 1991 in Pakrac on the occasion of the National Day (Translation by Ana Perišić Mijić)

We have gathered today in front of the Municipal Assembly in Pakrac in order to show, here in our town, in our beautiful Croatia and worldwide, that Pakrac can never be a one-track community, and that it belongs to nobody in particular, but to all of us. In order to show that we Croats, Czechs, Italians, Hungarians, our Serbian brothers, also want peace, equality and happiness in the Municipality of Pakrac. We are here to show that we do not agree with recent developments. We do not agree with the way our municipal bodies operate. We are not, and neither is the vast majority of us in this Municipality, satisfied with the results of the election. But we are here to say that we respect legality and legitimacy. We do not want guns of any kind; we do not want the army. We want to be left alone by the careerists who are ready to sell us for the sake of their careers to the so-called Krajina and Serbia to which Pakrac will never belong. We have asked ourselves what any Krajina would bring us. We have never been part of the Knin region in territorial, cultural, or civilizational terms. We have always been here. We welcome everybody. Last year we celebrated the 300th anniversary of the flight of the Serbian people from oppressed areas to this region. They were received in a kindly and friendly manner. And we have lived with them relatively well. Here and now, we invite them to continue our peaceful coexistence. Let them turn to work. Work goes along with good living. Give up your Knin and Belgrade tutors. False tutors will sell you for a small sum, yet you will still continue to live here with us. We have never threatened you and we never will. Stay away from madness. Elect your representatives in all bodies and we shall discuss every problem in a democratic fashion. Guns can achieve nothing, nor can blowing up buildings, or desecrating our holy places. We could also blow up your homes but the thought does not even cross our mind. It is truly an ineradicable disgrace for Pakrac that we live together and you blow up the door of the church you do not attend. You have destroyed St. Joseph's which weathered the First and Second World Wars. Disavow the extremists! We will never respond in kind, and you can show us who they are and disavow them.

Desist from annexation and from the redrawing of frontiers. If you want to see the villages around Okučani or the distant islands all the way to Stara Gradiška within the Municipality of Pakrac, we could also pursue to claim Garešnica and Kutina. You cannot overrule our own will, our coexistence, or our democracy regardless of the number of villages you annex to the Pakrac Municipality. And even then you would have to communicate with us. You cannot go on without us, and we do not want to go on without you. We want to be together under the Croatian flag, the Czech and the Italian flags, and your own Serbian flag, but do not put up chetnik symbols on the municipality building by force. None of us approved, collaborated with or promoted the ustashe movement. Disavow the chetniks and we will live together in peace.

My friends, you have seen what happened recently in Pakrac. These developments only brought us ills. Our companies lost contracts; our hospitals lost outpatients. We also suffered the loss of tourists, although there were not many to begin with. We shall lose everything there is to lose. We do not sow fear here but call for peace and coexistence. If something is wrong, let us say it openly, but let us remove the dynamite, guns, and tanks in the streets, because they are not going to solve anything. This has always been and will always be Croatia!

(In August 1991, Serbian terrorists abducted Dr. Šreter and took him to a camp at Bučje; his fate is still unknown.)

The Proclamation of the Sovereign and Independent Republic of Croatia (25 June 1991)

The Greater Serbian policy of the Serbian leadership and the refusal of Serbia to restructure Yugoslavia into a confederal state encouraged Croatia and Slovenia to embark on the process of independence. In order to strengthen the Croatian position in the process, on 25 April 1991, the President of the Republic of Croatia, Franjo Tuđman, decided to call a referendum with questions regarding Croatia's independence or its remaining in Yugoslavia. At the referendum held on 19 May 1991, almost 94% voted for an independent Republic of Croatia and about 92% against remaining in Yugoslavia (the turnout was about 85% of the 3,625,225 Croatian citizens with voting rights). Based on the report of the Republican Commission for the Implementation of the Referendum, the President of the Republic of Croatia, Franjo Tuđman, announced on 23 May 1991 that the citizens of Croatia had decided as follows:

1) The Republic of Croatia, as a sovereign and independent state guaranteeing cultural autonomy and all civil rights to Serbs and members of other nationalities in Croatia, can enter into a confederation of sovereign states with other republics.
2) The Republic of Croatia will not stay in Yugoslavia as an integral federal state.

The results of the referendum unequivocally confirmed the commitment of the majority of Croatian citizens to the creation of an independent Croatian state. However, the question is still left open of the reaction of leading world powers. In that respect, the visit to Yugoslavia by U.S. Secretary of State, James Baker, is considered as highly significant. On 21 June 1991, he met in Belgrade separately with each of the presidents of all the Yugoslav republics, ministers of the federal government, and members of the SFRY Presidency. It is believed that he warned his collocutors that "the U.S. supports the unity of Yugoslavia but at the same time opposes the use of force for the purpose of maintaining that unity."

Immediately after that, the European Community decided not to recognize the independence of Croatia and Slovenia if the two republics unilaterally decided to leave the Yugoslav federation.

In spite of that, given that no agreement on the restructuring of Yugoslavia was possible with the Serbian leadership, based on the referendum of the Croatian citizens, on 25 June 1991 the Parliament of the Republic of Croatia (Sabor) enacted:

- The Constitutional Decision on the Sovereignty and Independence of the Republic of Croatia
- The Constitutional Act on Amendments to the Constitutional Act for the Implementation of the Constitution of the Republic of Croatia
- The Declaration on the Establishment of the Sovereign and Independent Republic of Croatia
- The Charter on Rights of Serbs and Other Nationalities in the Republic of Croatia.

The first Speaker of the Croatian Parliament, Žarko Domljan, could enthusiastically close the historic session of Parliament with the words: *The State of Croatia is born, may she live long and happily!* The event is marked in Croatia as Statehood Day, although we are really dealing with a revival of the independence of the Croatian state, which already existed in the early Middle Ages, by the 9th century at the latest.

On the same day, Slovenia also proclaimed independence. Thus began the process of Croatia's dissociation from the other republics and the SFRY, and the course of its international recognition. However, at the request and through the involvement of the European Community and the U.S., on 7 July 1991, on the Brioni Islands, Croatia and Slovenia accepted a three-month moratorium on independence entitled the "Brioni Agreement" so that negotiations on a peaceful resolution of the Yugoslav crisis could continue.

The discussion about the importance of 25 June 1991 in Croatia's recent history and its appraisal with regard to other dates confirms the necessity of an interdisciplinary scientific approach. Namely, different dates are being mentioned as to the beginning of the war, aggression against Croatia, and even occupation of Croatia (all of course referring to individual events), for example:

- Mid May 1990: the seizure of Territorial Defense weapons
- 17 August 1990: armed insurgency of Serbs in Knin and its surroundings (the so-called Log Revolution)
- 25 January 1991: arrest of the Virovitica Group (prominent HDZ members from Virovitica)
- 2 March 1991: events in Pakrac (first armed conflict of Croatian police with Serbian terrorists)
- 31 March 1991: "Bloody Easter" at Plitvice Lakes National Park; Croatian policeman Josip Jović was killed in a conflict with Serbian terrorists (first Croatian defender killed in defense of the sovereignty and territorial integrity of the Republic of Croatia)
- 2 May 1991: murders of 13 Croatian policemen – 12 at Borovo Selo and one in the Zadar hinterland.

Therefore, when we speak of international conflict and the character of the war, it is important to note that according to international law, war is a conflict between two states, and that on 25 June 1991 the Croatian Parliament proclaimed independence.

On the night of 25/26 June 1991, literally immediately after the Sabor's decision proclaiming the independent and sovereign Republic of Croatia, the insurgent Serbs launched an attack on the police station in Glina and on Croatian forces and settlements in Banovina with the aim of expelling Croats from the area. Obviously, the attack had already been planned earlier, and the proclamation of Croatian independence only served as a motive. On the same day, special MUP RH forces succeeded in restoring control over the police station in Glina, but not over the whole town, because an armored JNA unit had deployed there under the guise of establishing and maintaining a "buffer zone." Having thus allowed Serbian extremists to retain control over the greater part of Glina, the JNA continued, even after the proclamation of Croatia's independence, to interfere directly in the conflict of legal Croatian forces with the units of the insurgent Serbs. Actually, as the army of another state, the JNA had thereby initiated an open aggression against the Republic of Croatia. Encouraged by the presence and support of the JNA, the insurgent Serbs occupied part of Banovina, and maintained their anti-constitutional actions and armed attacks on legal Croatian forces in both Banovina and the whole of Croatia.

In such a situation, on 27 June 1991, the leadership of the insurgent Serbs from Croatia and representatives of the Serbs from Serbian Krajina issued the Declaration on the Unification of SAO Krajina and the Association of Municipalities of Bosnian Krajina. The contents of the Declaration disclosed that the ultimate goal of the revived Greater Serbian policy and Serbian insurgency in Croatia – expressed through the principle of "all Serbs in one state" – as "the creation of an integral state of all the Serbs in the Balkans."

On the same day, in the Republic of Slovenia, the JNA and the federal police clashed briefly with the Slovenian territorial defense – officially in order to retain control of border crossings, but actually to thwart Slovenia's bid for independence. At the time, Croatia did not get militarily involved and did not attack the barracks in Croatia as suggested by Lieutenant General Martin Špegelj, then Minister of Defense of the Republic of Croatia. In fact, Croatia had no armed forces of its own at the time. Commenting this period in his book *My View of the Collapse* (Belgrade, 1993, p. 129), the Secretary of the Federal Secretariat for National Defense – the then Yugoslav Minister of Defense – General of the Army, Veljko Kadijević, wrote that the JNA would have fared better if Croatian President Franjo Tuđman had decided to attack the JNA then and not later ("time was more against us than in our favor"), and that at that stage of the conflict the JNA was forced "to wait for the attack rather than attack first."

As they observed the conflict in Slovenia, in early July 1991, the Serbian leadership (S. Milošević and B. Jović) asked General Kadijević to respond fiercely to Slovenian actions, and take up positions in Croatia with the main JNA forces in order to ensure the implementation of Serbian requests and expel Slovene and Croatian officers from the JNA.

1. Respond fiercely to Slovenian actions with all available means including the air force, and put an absolute stop to their harassment of the JNA. Then withdraw from Slovenia. A proper decision will be made in due time. This will raise the army's morale, alarm Croatia, and calm the Serbian people.
2. Concentrate the main forces along the following lines: Karlovac – Plitvice in the west, Baranja – Osijek – Vinkovci – Sava in the east, and Neretva to the south. This would cover all territories inhabited by Serbs until the full resolution and final free commitment of the people at the referendum.
3. Total elimination of Croats and Slovenes from the military.
(Borisav Jović, The Last Days of the SFRY, p. 349).

General Kadijević accepted the requests; actually, the JNA was already proceeding in line with them: on 26 June 1991, JNA units helped Serbian paramilitary units occupy the greater part of Glina, and on 3 July 1991, launched offensive operations in Baranja. Given the fact that the JNA had already begun to deploy in the crisis areas in Croatia as early as May, by early July 1991, the JNA controlled all the bridges on the Danube between Croatia and Serbia. (On 7 May the bridge between Ilok and Bačka Palanka, on 2 July the bridge between Erdut and Bogojevo, and on 2/3 July the bridge between Bezdan and Batina.) Having taken important strategic positions, in early July 1991 the JNA was ready to attack the Republic of Croatia. The open aggression of Serbia and the JNA on the Republic of Croatia was not prevented even by the aforementioned Brioni Agreement of 7 July 1991, according to which the JNA was supposed to withdraw to barracks, and based on which Stjepan Mesić finally became the President of the SFRY Presidency.

At the same time, by decision of the President of the Republic of Croatia of 2 July 1991, Dr. Onesin Cvitan was appointed Minister of the Interior, replacing Josip Boljkovac. On 31 July 1991, he was replaced by Ivan Vekić, member of the Government of Democratic Unity.

On 15 April 1992, Ivan Jarnjak became Minister of the Interior and held the post until the end of the war. There were also changes in the Ministry of Defense. On 2 July 1991, Dr. Šime Đodan replaced Martin Špegelj. On 31 July 1991, Luka Bebić was appointed to the office, followed by Gojko Šušak (after 18 September 1991 until the end of the war).

As the war broke out, the rosary became the emblem of the Croatian defenders, and praying the rosary a testimony of their religious and national identity. The message "God is our Faith" pitted belief in love and readiness to sacrifice against hate, total destruction and crime.

Cardinal Franjo Kuharić marked the moral activity of the Croatian Catholic Church during the defense of the Homeland and creation of the Croatian State. His sermons in August 1991, at the very beginning of the aggression by JNA and Serbian-Montenegrin units, in which he called for the respect of moral values even in wartime conditions, struck a highly responsive chord among the Croatian defenders:

Love of God is necessarily love of man, and love of man is also patriotism! Therefore, our patriotism must not be poisoned even by a drop of hate or wish for revenge. The defense of freedom and peace is our right and duty, but always within the rule of law. (...) Hence, our patriotism must not be racist or imperialist or chauvinistic. Our patriotism is Christian. (...) If my enemy has burned my home down,

I will not burn his! If he has destroyed my church, I will not even touch his; on the contrary, I shall safeguard it. If he has left his home, I will not even take a needle from it! If he has killed my father, my brother, my sister, I will not retaliate in the same manner, but respect the life of his father, his brother, his son, his sister.

The massacre of Croatian policemen at Borovo Selo, followed by the first displaced persons and first torched villages in Slavonia in July 1991, alarmed everyone in Croatia and set off a series of protest rallies, including of course fierce reactions. Along with defense preparations, peace initiatives were also promoted. Already on 17 and 18 January 1991, Croatian women collected the signatures of citizens on Zagreb's Jelačić Square in an attempt to use their influence to bear on the generals of the Yugoslav army to desist from their criminal designs. United in the organization called *Bulwark of Love* (Mothers for Peace), in late August 1991 the mothers of JNA conscripts set off on a "peace march" to Belgrade to request the release of their children and prevent them from being used in attacks against their own homeland. *Bulwark of Love* organized many rallies issuing appeals for peace and against hate and killing. At one such rally held on 29 August 1991 in front of the then Headquarters of the JNA Fifth Army District, Croatian poet and humanist Vlado Gotovac delivered an address with a terse message from the Croats to the Yugoslav officers, highlighting moral principles which ought to guide people in the struggle for freedom and independence:

I love you and I am proud of you! And if I was to choose between dying with you or living with these scarecrow generals, I would choose death... If the generals had families, if the generals had children, if the generals had any kith and kin, they would not be entrenched in this building. But the generals have no children I am sure, for whoever kills someone else's children has no children! Whoever aggrieves someone else's mother has no mother! Whoever destroys someone else's home has no home! And the generals must know that there are no mothers, no children, no homes for them in this land! They will die in the wilderness of their own dead hearts! Their children will be ashamed of having such fathers! Their wives will be ashamed of them because they murdered someone else's children! Their families will be ashamed of them because they destroyed someone else's families!

And at last, you, the mothers and women who have assembled at this unique rally, the like of which has never been held in Europe before, have demonstrated that deep in her heart, Croatia, be it with the educated or uneducated, men or women, is imbued with the same sublime principle of love and dignity! And that is why I started out by telling you that I loved you, that I would rather die with you than live with the generals. And I know, I am positively certain that even once I am gone I will live in this love and with this love, in this dignity and with this dignity – and that is my joy and my strength, and the strength of all of you!

Let this love, this strength, this courage guide Croatia, whether armed or unarmed, because even unarmed we are no less brave, no less proud, no less in love with our homeland! If we have no weapons, we have the strength of what brought us here, the strength of our love, the strength of our dignity, the strength of our readiness to die if we cannot live like human beings. And that is something we are not prepared to relinquish! That is why I am not afraid! Croatia lives and will continue to live!

(Speech of Vlado Gotovac in Zagreb, in front of the Headquarters of the JNA Fifth Army District)

Open Aggression of Serbia and Montenegro, i.e., of the JNA and Serbian-Montenegrin Units Against the Republic of Croatia

The Croatian leadership tried to avoid an armed conflict with the vastly superior JNA. However, instead of seeking a peaceful resolution of the crisis, in July 1991 the terrorist actions of the Serbian extremists in Croatia developed into an open and merciless aggression of Serbia and Montenegro (JNA and Serbian-Montenegrin forces) against the Republic of Croatia (Slovenia was spared new attacks). In the first two weeks of July, at the very beginning of the open aggression against Croatia, at least 26 guardsmen and 14 policemen were killed, and 95 members of the Croatian armed forces wounded. At the same time, at least 5 civilians were killed and 18 wounded.

After mid-July, in areas designated by the Greater Serbian ideologues as parts of Greater Serbia, the attacks of Serbian terrorists and members of Serbian paramilitary units on Croatian citizens, and especially on ZNG members and Croatian policemen, became everyday events. The tragic series of events and the number of members of the Croatian armed forces killed and wounded in attacks by Serbian paramilitary units and the JNA increased daily. After the murder of Croatian defenders and civilians in Banovina in late July, the process culminated on 1 August 1991 with the massacre at Dalj, which wholly exposed the character of the launched war. This was not a conflict between two armies, but a war against the Croatian people, its faith and culture. The police station at Dalj was destroyed with tank shells, while the brute force of the JNA and Serbian paramilitary forces also struck Erdut and Aljmaš, expelling the population from their homes. Our Lady of Refuge (her statue was removed to safety in Osijek) was also expelled, whose sanctuary in Aljmaš was regularly venerated by thousands of Croatian Catholics.

Because of the blockade of traffic routes, (Serbian terrorists did not even let ambulances pass) wounded and displaced persons were transported to Osijek by riverboats and barges.

In the attacks of Serbian extremists and JNA armored units on Dalj, Erdut and Aljmaš, and following the occupation of these villages, more than 110 persons died or were killed, among them 39 Croatian defenders (20 policemen, 15 guardsmen, and 4 members of the Civil Defense). Croats and other non-Serbian residents were expelled from these villages, and religious buildings (Catholic churches) blasted with explosives (the church of St. Joseph in Dalj, the Church and Sanctuary of the Visitation /"Our Lady of Comfort"/ in Aljmaš, and the Church of All Saints in Erdut). Serbian extremists applied this pattern of action – murder, persecution, torching and demolition of homes owned by Croats and especially Catholic churches – in almost every conquered town and village in Croatia. Of course, these events affected the overall security situation in Croatia because individuals on the Croatian side also embarked on extremist actions against citizens of Serbian nationality.

In a period of escalating crisis, on 24 July 1991, Sabor Speaker Žarko Domljan promoted an initiative as one of the attempts of the Croatian authorities to resolve the Serbian issue peacefully and discourage insurgent Serbs from participating in the already initiated aggression against Croatia. The Speaker invited the leaders of all the parties to a meeting focused on democratic dialogue, exchange of views, and developing a political consensus concerning the rights of nationalities resulting from constitutional provisions and the Charter on the Rights of Serbs and Other Nationalities in the Republic of Croatia. The meeting was held on 30 July 1991 in the Sabor building, and resulted in the appointment of the Parliamentary Commission for the Protection and Promotion of Equalities of Nations and Nationalities. The working group of the Commission had already produced in July 1991 a draft of the document entitled Starting Positions in the Realization of Cultural Autonomy, Local Government and Self-Government and Proportional Representation of the Serbian

Nationality in the Government of the Republic of Croatia. The basic determinants of the document highlighted the values of ethnic communities, the anti-assimilation policy of the state, the need for the state to ensure ethnic communities everything that does not question democratic order and sovereignty of the state, and the need to determine the political relations between the Republic of Croatia and Serbian people in Croatia by means of a constitutional act which would ensure cultural autonomy, local self-government (territorial autonomy), and proportional representation (political autonomy). Along with freedom of expression, the Serbs in Croatia were guaranteed voting rights, free use of their own symbols, coat of arms and flags, and the flying of the Serbian flag on municipal or county halls in municipalities with a relative or absolute Serbian majority. The use of both Cyrillic and Latin names of streets in municipalities or counties with a relative or Serbian majority population was also guaranteed. Unfortunately, the leaders of the Serbian political structures in Croatia did not accept the offer of the Croatian authorities, most likely due to their confidence in the JNA's certain victory and in the achievement of the main goal, "the unification of all Serbs in the Balkans in one state."

The objective of the JNA's attack on Croatia, as described by JNA General Veljko Kadijević in his book *My View of the Collapse* (Belgrade 1993, p. 135), was the following:

- *totally block Croatia from the air and the sea;*
- *intersect Croatia along the Gradiška – Virovitica, Bihać – Karlovac – Zagreb, Knin – Zadar, and Mostar – Split lines;*
- *gain control over Eastern Slavonia and then advance rapidly towards the west, link up with forces in Western Slavonia and proceed towards Zagreb, Varaždin, and the border with Slovenia;*
- *concurrently break through with strong forces from Herceg Novi and Trebinje, and block Dubrovnik from the mainland, reach the Neretva Valley and thus operate jointly with forces advancing along the Mostar – Split line;*

- *secure and hold the planned border of the self-proclaimed Serbian Krajina in Croatia.*

The mentioned description of the then highest Yugoslav military official confirms that in 1991 the JNA operated as a Serbian army implementing Serbian policy interests. After all, Kadijević himself noted in his book that "the JNA was the basis for the formation of three armed forces: the Army of the Federal Republic of Yugoslavia (FRY), the Army of Republika Srpska (BH), and the Army of the Republic of Serbian Krajina." All three were geared towards Serbian conquest policies. The reasons why the JNA had not become the official Serbian army already in 1991 are outlined by a Serbian member in the SRFY Presidency and one of Milošević's closest associates, Borisav Jović, in his book *The Last Days of the SFRY: Excerpts from the Diary* (Belgrade, 1995, pp. 388-389). "That would have been unfavorable for Serbia and Montenegro in the future resolution of the Yugoslav crisis, and the Serbian-Montenegrin army would have been perceived as an 'aggressor' in Serbian areas outside Serbia." A similar explanation was provided in September 1991 by Serbian Minister of Religious Affairs Dragan Dragojlović in Valjevo, in his speech to demoralized members of a JNA brigade from Serbia who had suffered losses in Croatia during the battle for Vukovar: "We keep saying that Serbia is not at war with Croatia, but the Serbian people are. We cannot say that because of international public opinion, because Serbia would then be the aggressor. If a JNA soldier is in Croatia, we cannot say that Serbia is there. Because of that Serbia cannot have its own army in the JNA" (Dragan Todorović, *Let the General Apologize*; *Borba* daily, 26 September 1991, p. 3).

In the dramatic circumstances of the Serbian aggression, the Parliament of the Republic of Croatia (Sabor) formed the Government of Democratic Unity, which also symbolically confirmed the unity of Croats and all other citizens of Croatia who had accepted the legally elected Croatian authorities. Because of the "open aggression against the Republic of Croatia," on 3 August 1991, the Sabor invited "all international organizations dealing with the protection of human rights and the rights of ethnic minorities to send their representatives to Croatia to witness firsthand the condition of civil, human, and ethnic rights of Serbs and all other ethnic communities living in Croatia."

Croatia was attacked from Serbia, Montenegro and Bosnia and Herzegovina, as well as from its own territory settled by the insurgent Serbian population and from JNA barracks. Fighting was waged on battlegrounds in Slavonia, Dalmatia and Lika, and in Banovina and Kordun. Police units and the National Guard Corps, as well as poorly armed volunteer units resisted the first strike of the Serbian aggressor. It was only in mid-September 1991, with the formation of the General Staff of the Croatian Army and the adoption of the Defense Act, that conditions were created to provide an effective defense, lead a war, and the overall development of the Armed Forces of the Republic of Croatia. Of course, successful defense also depended on the blockade and overrunning of some barracks and JNA military equipment depots in Croatia (actually the taking over of weapons of the Croatian TO, seized in May 1990) after mid-September 1991. In this way, Croatian forces secured at least part of the armaments required for their defense. The Croatian expatriate community also provided substantial aid, and the entire Croatian economy was subordinated to defense requirements.

A portion of JNA members joined the Croatian armed forces (HV) along with professional Croatian soldiers in foreign armies, e.g., the French Foreign Legion. On 1 January 1990, the JNA had 46,293 persons on active duty: 25,101 officers, 19,165 non-commissioned officers, and 2027 professional contract soldiers. Altogether 3000 of them (or 6% of the total number – about 1700 officers and 1300 non-commissioned officers) left the JNA and joined the HV, while roughly 560 of them joined the HV after 31 December 1991. Of course, most of them were Croats (2648 or about 88%). This means that slightly under 50% of the Croats on active duty in the JNA in early 1991 joined the Croatian Armed Forces (the percentage is based on the number of 5362 persons of Croatian nationality on active duty in the JNA in 1991).

The number of generals and admirals active in the 1990-1992 period who left the JNA and joined the HV was much lower – only 26%. Among the 235 generals and admirals active in the JNA in the mentioned period there were only 27 Croats (11.5%). Of that number, 7 joined the HV (3 active and 2 retired generals, and 2 active admirals). Three more generals who had retired before 1990 also returned to active duty in the HV. The fighting during 1991 showed that the number of officers and non-commissioned officers was still too low for the efficient structuring and leading of the still nascent Croatian Army. The shortage of good non-commissioned officers was felt in particular, and the Croatian Military Academy was founded accordingly.

In late September and early October 1991, the Serbian aggression entered its most vicious phase. Ignoring the peace negotiations, namely, the attempts of the Croatian Government and international community to resolve the crisis peacefully, the JNA and Serbian paramilitary units launched maximum attacks on all battlefields in Croatia. The force of the onslaught was confirmed by estimates of some foreign military analysts that the Croatian defenders would not be able to hold out for "more than two weeks" – especially because in late September 1991 the UN Security Council banned all export of weapons and military equipment to Yugoslavia, which also meant Croatia and Bosnia and Herzegovina. Considering the huge ammunition stocks and pronounced superiority of JNA armaments over the Croatian armed forces, the UN embargo actually allowed the Serbian aggressor to conquer territories in Croatia more easily, and subsequently, in Bosnia and Herzegovina.

Amidst the most vicious aggression, on 7 October 1991, JNA aircraft rocketed the Viceroy's Palace, the seat of the Croatian Government in the center of Zagreb, capital of Croatia. The objective of the attack was to kill the President of the Republic of Croatia, Franjo Tuđman, President of the SFRY Presidency, Stjepan

Mesić, and President of the SFRY Federal Executive Council [Prime Minister], Ante Marković, who were meeting at the Palace right at that time and only avoided death by sheer luck. The attempted assassination showed that the Serbian leadership and JNA were not even considering a peaceful resolution of the Yugoslav crisis, nor did they shrink from any means to achieve their goal.

With the impact of the attack still fresh, as well as pictures and news on numerous casualties arriving from other attacked Croatian towns and villages, given the vicious aggression by Serbia, Montenegro and the JNA on the Republic of Croatia, on 8 October 1991, the Sabor adopted its final Decision on the Separation of the Republic of Croatia from the SFRY and its Independence. In Croatia, this date is marked as Independence Day. Because of the danger of possible attacks by JNA aircraft, the Sabor met in the basement of the INA Petroleum Company in Zagreb. Among other things, on that day the Sabor concluded that the Republic of Serbia and JNA had carried out an armed aggression against the Republic of Croatia, and that the JNA was an aggressor and occupying army, and urged the Republics of Bosnia and Herzegovina and Montenegro not to permit the use of their territory for waging war against the Republic of Croatia.

In accordance with the inalienable right of the Republic of Croatia to self-determination,
proceeding from the will of the citizens of the Republic of Croatia expressed at the referendum on 19 May 1991;
proceeding from the Constitutional Decision on the Sovereignty and Independence of the Republic of Croatia adopted by the Sabor at its session on 25 June 1991;
having established that the three-month moratorium on the implementation of the Constitutional Decision determined by the Brioni Declaration expired on 7 October 1991;
having established that within the term specified by the Brioni Declaration heightened terrorist actions have taken place against

towns and villages by so-called JNA and Serbian terrorists, with the ruthless destruction of hospitals, schools, churches, cultural monuments, and civilian buildings, culminating even with the bombing of Zagreb, resulting in the damage of the Residence of the President of the Republic, Government building, and the Sabor (while in session!) and in the attempt on the life of the President of the Republic;

having established that Yugoslavia no longer exists as a state community,

at the joint session of all its bodies held on 8 October 1991, the Sabor of the Republic of Croatia

HAS DECIDED AS FOLLOWS

1. As of 8 October 1991, the Republic of Croatia has severed all constitutional ties on the basis of which it made up, together with the other republics and provinces, the former SFRY.

(...)

4. The Republic of Croatia recognizes the independence and sovereignty of the other republics of the former SFRY on the basis of reciprocity, and is prepared to establish, maintain and develop friendly, political, economic, cultural and other relations with those republics with which it is not in armed conflict.

5. As a sovereign and independent state, which guarantees and ensures fundamental human rights and the rights of ethnic communities explicitly guaranteed by the UN General Declaration, the Final Act of the Helsinki Conference, OSCE documents and the Paris Charter, the Republic of Croatia is prepared, within the scope of European integration developments, to enter into interstate and interregional associations with other democratic states.

Soon after that, on 18 October 1991, at the Conference on Yugoslavia in The Hague, the European Community presented to the representatives of the former Yugoslav republics the so-called Carrington Plan for restructuring Yugoslavia into a community of sovereign states. All the republics except Serbia accepted the proposed plan, but under pressure of the Serbian leadership, Montenegro soon also withdrew its proposal. In this way, the exclusive position of the Serbian and JNA policy sealed the fate of Yugoslavia and provoked the continuation of the war in which many people died or were killed, or their fate still remains unknown (over 19,000 in Croatia and over 100,000 in Bosnia and Herzegovina). After the failure of the Carrington Plan, Croatia accelerated the procedure for its international recognition, basing it among other things on the provisions of the then valid Yugoslav and Croatian Constitution of 1974.

Croatia was forced to defend its newly proclaimed independence in a bloody war. The JNA and Serbian units furiously and simultaneously attacked many Croatian towns and villages: Dubrovnik, Šibenik, Zadar, Karlovac, Sisak, Gospić, Otočac, Ogulin, Duga Resa, Pakrac, Lipik, Grubišno Polje, Daruvar, Podravska Slatina, Slavonska Požega, Belišće, Valpovo, Novska, Nova Gradiška, Slavonski Brod, Osijek, Đakovo, Vinkovci, Županja, and especially Vukovar. Other Croatian towns were also hit periodically. The Yugoslav navy blocked ports and sea routes along the Croatian coast of the Adriatic Sea in an attempt to break Croatia's resistance in this way as well. The international public followed with particular abhorrence the attacks of the JNA and Serbian units on Vukovar, which was completely destroyed and occupied by 20 November 1991, as well as the destruction of Dubrovnik, a monument-city protected by the UNESCO Charter.

Because of the unexpectedly firm and almost three-month long resistance of the Vukovar defenders against a vastly superior enemy (between 25 August and 18/20 November 1991), and given an intensity of destruction such as Europe had not seen since the Second World War, in 1991, Vukovar became the symbol of Croatian resistance against Serbian aggression in the Homeland War. Its population, especially the defenders, became an example of incredible self-denial, inventiveness and courage – just as Ovčara, a farm near Vukovar and the site of a mass execution, became the symbol of the suffering and sacrifice of the inhabitants and defenders of Vukovar in their fight for freedom and independence of the Republic of Croatia. On 20 November 1991, two hundred of at least 266 wounded men and medical personnel were forcibly removed from the Vukovar Hospital by Serbian soldiers under the command of JNA officers and killed at Ovčara. The crime at Ovčara was one of the many mass crimes committed by Serbian aggressors (and the JNA), mainly during 1991, in their onslaught on Vukovar and Croatia.

On account of its military superiority, by the end of 1991 the JNA occupied almost one-third of the territory of Croatia. In the occupied territory, on 19 December 1991 in Knin, the insurgent Serbs proclaimed the "Republic of Serbian Krajina" (RSK) and adopted the Constitution of the Republic of Serbian Krajina. Among other things, the Constitution explicitly stipulated that the RSK "will continue to build strong state ties with other parts of the Serbian people in the territory of Yugoslavia and its states in order to create a common state for the Serbian people." (Art. 123) Amendment I of the RSK Constitution, proclaimed on 26 February 1992 in Borovo Selo, stipulated that "the territory of the RSK comprises the Serbian regions of Krajina, Slavonia, Baranja, Western Srijem and Western Slavonia." That marked the climax of anti-constitutional actions of the Serbs in Croatia in the process of separation of part of Croatia's territory and proclamation of the Serbian para-state in the territory of the Republic of Croatia. Non-Serbian residents in areas under Serbian control were almost entirely wiped out or expelled, and the same fate even befell Serbs who did not support the Greater Serbian policy. Likewise, the Croatian cultural and church heritage was looted and destroyed.

Nevertheless, Croatia was not defeated in 1991. On the contrary, in November and December 1991, Croatian military-police units succeeded in liberating over 2200 km^2 of occupied territory, and defeating the Yugoslav navy in the battle of the Split and Korčula channels (in a series of minor operations – Orkan 91, Otkos 10 [*Swath*] and Papuk).

In accordance with the democratic changes and decisions on independence, along with the introduction of new (actually historical) national symbols, Croatia also changed its personal identification cards and passports, and introduced the certificate of citizenship. In late 1991, it put its own currency – the Croatian dinar – into circulation. At the same time, within the circumstances of the insurgency of the Serbs in Croatia and the bloody Serbian aggression, in order to improve democracy and human rights, Croatia created democratic institutions and a modern legislation, as well as laws to ensure the equality of all its citizens before the law regardless of their ethnicity and religion, and consistent with the highest European standards. Thus, on 4 December 1991, the Sabor adopted the Constitutional Act on Human Rights, and Freedoms and Rights of National and Ethnic Communities or Minorities in the Republic of Croatia. The Act ensured the Serbian minority in Croatia all human rights and freedoms, cultural autonomy and other rights granted to ethnic and national communities or minorities.... (among other things, the official use of their language and script "in municipalities where they make up the majority of the total number of inhabitants"), and proportional involvement in the highest representative, administrative, and judicial bodies of the Republic of Croatia.... and the inhabitants are granted 11 municipalities with a majority Serbian population, and a special, higher level of self-administration. Furthermore, territorially connected municipalities with "special status" were afforded the possibility of association within their communities in order to more effectively "conduct activities of their own scope." The Arbitration Commission accepted the law, but obliged the Government of the Republic of Croatia to supplement it.

In spite of difficult economic conditions in Croatia caused by extensive destruction and disconnection of transportation routes throughout the entire war and even during the most vicious aggression, Croatia suffered no major shortage of staple foodstuffs and fuel thanks to the outstanding solidarity of all its citizens and successful organization of everyday life. Only Dalmatia felt a shortage of electric power due to the consequences of Serbian occupation. Of course, the overall economic situation was affected by the enormous cost of caring for numerous refugees and displaced person who longed to return to their homes. (By the end of 1991, Croatia cared for about 325,000 displaced persons, and just as many refugees from Croatia are assumed to have been abroad; *Croatian Displaced Persons*, Bulletin of the Community of Croatian Returnees, Osijek 2010, p. 65).

1992 – 1995

International Recognition of Croatia

Cyrus Vance, personal envoy to the UN Secretary General, brokered the ceasefire signed by representatives of the Republic of Croatia and the JNA in Sarajevo on 2 January 1992 (it was the fourteenth ceasefire agreement!). It was based on the agreement, brokered by UN representative Cyrus Vance and representative of the European Community Lord Peter Carrington, on lifting the blockade of JNA barracks and JNA withdrawal from Croatia, and the implementation of the UN Peace Plan (which envisioned the deployment of UN peace forces in Croatia), signed by the President of Croatia, Franjo Tuđman, President of Serbia, Slobodan Milošević, and JNA General, Veljko Kadijević, in Geneva on 23 November 1991. The Sarajevo Agreement, which entered into force on 3 January 1992 at 18:00 hours, for the most part put a stop to major war actions in Croatia. Soon afterwards, in the spring of 1992, UN protection forces – UNPROFOR – arrived in the occupied parts of Croatia in accordance with the Cyrus Vance Plan. They deployed in Eastern and Western Slavonia and parts of Dalmatia, Lika, Banovina and Kordun, in three UNPA zones: UNPA East (Eastern Slavonia and Baranja), UNPA West (Western Slavonia), and UNPA North and South (Krajina). (An UNPA zone is an area of 18 municipalities in which Serbs constitute the majority or a significant minority of the population, and in which reciprocal tension has led to armed conflict in the recent past.) The goal of the Vance Plan was the creation of conditions for the final agreement on the political resolution of the conflict in Croatia.

UNPA Zones

On 21 February 1992, the UN Security Council adopted Resolution 743 on the start of a peacekeeping operation and deployment of international peacekeeping forces in the Republic of Croatia for a period of 12 months (within the scope of the so-called Vance Plan for Croatia). The objective of the operation was accomplished only partly: the JNA left Croatia (after it had armed the rebel Serbs in Croatia and provided their logistic and manpower support), and the heavy weapons of the rebel Serbs were placed in storage under the joint supervision of UNPROFOR and the Serbs. But the other commitments were not fulfilled.

The UNPAs (without the "pink zones") comprised 12,554 km^2 of Croatian territory (22% in total); the "pink zones" (2208 km^2) brought the total to 14,762 km^2. In 1991, the population of that area was 536,370 – of which 258,298 (48.2%) Serbs, 205,075 (38.2%) Croats, and 72,997 (13.6%) others. They were divided into the following sectors:

Sector East, with headquarters in Erdut ("Eastern Slavonia" with Baranja and Western Srijem); 2153 km^2; population 188,184 (1991 census) – 49.1% Croats, 30.4% Serbs, 20.5% others; 4 municipalities – Vukovar and Beli Manastir, and parts of Osijek and Vinkovci.

Sector West, with headquarters in Daruvar ("Western Slavonia"): 2112 km^2; 99,452 inhabitants – 43.3% Croats, 35.4% Serbs, 21.3% others; 5 municipalities: Pakrac, Daruvar, Grubišno Polje, part of Novska (eastern part) and Nova Gradiška (western part).

Sector North, 3973 km^2, with headquarters in Topusko (Banovina and Kordun); 6 municipalities; Dvor na Uni, Kostajnica, Petrinja, Glina, Vrginmost, Vojnić and Slunj.

Sector South, 6524 km^2, with headquarters in Knin (northern Dalmatia and Lika); 5 municipalities: Knin, Benkovac, Obrovac, Gračac, Korenica and Donji Lapac.

Sectors North and South (UNPA "Krajina") comprised 10,497 km^2 (including the "pink zones"); population (1991) 248,734 – 66.7% Serbs, 28% Croats and 5.3% others.

The areas that did not enter the UNPA zones presented a special problem because they were not settled by a large number of Serbs and were under occupation of the JNA and the Serbian insurgents. According to the Vance Plan, they were to be restored "immediately and unconditionally" to Croatian authority, but the Serbian leadership opposed that. Thanks to the readiness of the Croatian leadership and President Franjo Tuđman to accept a compromise, these areas (the so-called "pink zones") remained outside Croatian control as a provisional solution. The international community undertook to reincorporate them "as soon as possible" into the constitutional system of Croatia. But that did not happen. Moreover, the international community did not succeed in opening communications, did not ensure the return of displaced persons (mainly Croats), and did not protect the remaining Croats and non-Serbian population in the UNPA zones. Actually, the UN forces in Croatia did not accomplish most of their tasks. During the UN mandate (under protection of the UN forces), several hundred Croatian civilians were killed in occupied parts of the Republic of Croatia (UNPA zones) – a figure that greatly exceeds the number of civilians killed by Croatian forces during *Operation Storm*. Moreover, several thousand civilians were expelled. In spite of that, nobody from the UN command structures was held responsible (nobody was even seriously taken to task) for omissions in the protection of lives and property of the citizens of non-Serbian nationality in the UNPA zones, or for having failed to fulfill the commitments under the Vance Plan.

During the same period, Croatia cared for more than half a million refugees and displaced persons from Croatia and Bosnia and Herzegovina, mainly Croats and Muslims (663,493 in late 1992), and the Croatian economy found it increasingly difficult to cope with the occupation of part of the country together with transportation isolation and blockades.

Along with its defensive war, Croatia also waged a diplomatic battle for international recognition. Its positive outcome was contingent on the opinion of the international Arbitration Commission founded to provide legal counsel to the Peace Conference on the Former Yugoslavia, which began operating in The Hague in September 1991. Also known as the Badinter Arbitration Committee (after its president, Frenchman Robert Badinter), in December 1991 and January 1992 the Commission established:

- that the Socialist Federative Republic of Yugoslavia is in the process of dissolution;
- that it is incumbent upon the republics to settle such problems of state succession as may arise from this process;
- that the Serbian population (…) in Croatia is entitled to all the rights concerning minorities and ethnic groups under international law and under the provisions of the Convention of the Conference on Peace in Yugoslavia of 4 November 1991 (…);
- that the republics must afford the members of these minorities and ethnic groups all human rights and fundamental freedoms recognized by international law, including, where appropriate, the right to choose their nationality;
- that all external frontiers must be respected in all cases (…);
- that the boundaries between Croatia and Serbia (…) may not be altered except by a freely made and mutual agreement;
- that except where otherwise agreed, the former boundaries become frontiers protected by international law (…);

that the alteration of existing frontiers or boundaries by force is not capable of producing any legal effect (…);

- that the Constitutional Act of 4 December 1991 (on human rights and rights of ethnic or national communities or minorities in the Republic of Croatia) does not fully incorporate all the provisions of the draft Convention of 4 November 1991 (…), and the authorities of the Republic of Croatia should therefore supplement the Constitutional Act in such a way as to satisfy these provisions, and subject to this reservation, the Republic of Croatia meets the necessary conditions for its recognition by the Member States of the European Community in accordance with the Declaration on Yugoslavia and Guidelines on the Recognition of New States in Eastern Europe and the Soviet Union, adopted by the Council of European Communities on 16 December 1991.

On the basis of these opinions, several member states of the European Community (Austria, Belgium, Denmark, France, Germany, Greece, Italy, Luxemburg, the Netherlands, Portugal, Spain and the United Kingdom) recognized the Republic of Croatia as an independent and sovereign state on 15 January 1992. Before that, Croatia had been recognized by Slovenia (26 June), Lithuania (30 July), Ukraine (11 December), and [UN members] Latvia (14 December), Iceland (19 December) and Estonia (31 December). On 13 January 1992, the Holy See followed suit. The Republic of Croatia attained full international renown and the climax of its diplomatic struggle for recognition on 22 May 1992, when it was admitted to the United Nations Organization as its 178th member. International recognition greatly encouraged the Government of the Republic of Croatia – together with the help of European and global diplomacy – to endeavor to peacefully reincorporate occupied parts of its territory.

Internally, the territorial structure of the Republic of Croatia was altered in late 1992 with the division into 20 counties and the City of Zagreb gaining county status. The Serbs as the largest ethnic minority in Croatia were offered two districts – Knin and Glina – with special status (Croatian Parliament, 8 May 1992: Decision on the Proclamation of the Constitutional Act with Amendments to the Constitutional Act on Human Rights and Freedoms and on the Rights of Ethnic and National Communities in the Republic of Croatia). In accordance with the Act of December 1991, the mentioned districts would merge regionally connected municipalities where the Serbs were the majority population, and receive a higher level of self-administration. The mentioned Constitutional Act “met the requirements of international law with respect to the protection of minorities” and the envisioned districts were to cover 11 municipalities. However, the leadership of the insurgent Serbs did not accept the offer, and intended to annex these areas to Serbia.

The next changes involved Croatian currency: on 30 May 1994, the Croatian dinar was replaced with a historical currency – the *kuna*, divided into 100 *lipa*.

The Beginning of the War in Bosnia and Herzegovina

After the war ceased in Croatia, at least temporarily and on part of the territory, it continued in Bosnia and Herzegovina. In fact, the state of war had already spread to Bosnia and Herzegovina in early October 1991 when the JNA and the Serbian-Montenegrin volunteer units torched the Croatian village of Ravno in the Municipality of Trebinje, southeast Herzegovina. Moreover, since the summer of 1991, the territory of Bosnia and Herzegovina had been the starting point from which the JNA and Serbian-Montenegrin units launched attacks on Croatia, naturally, with the exception of the parts of Bosnia and Herzegovina where Croats were the majority. Thus, on 7 May 1991, in the village of Polog between Mostar and Široki Brijeg in Herzegovina, the local population did not allow the passage of a JNA motorized brigade, sent from Mostar toward Kupres and on to Sinj and Split, with the objective of taking up strategically important positions within the scope of the JNA's preparation for aggression against Croatia. That was not the only such example. From September to the end of 1991, in line with a scenario already seen in Croatia, the Serbs in Bosnia and Herzegovina proclaimed several "Serbian Autonomous Regions." Consistent with their plan of seizing 66% of the territory of Bosnia and Herzegovina, on 9 January 1992 the Serbs proclaimed the "Sovereign Serbian Republic of Bosnia and Herzegovina" at Pale (after 12 August 1992 "Republika Srpska"), with the intention of annexing it to the Yugoslav state, that is, Serbia.

Faced with uncertainty and considering the questionable likelihood that the Bosnian-Herzegovinian authorities could protect them from the threatening Serbian aggression, part of the Croats in Bosnia and Herzegovina proclaimed the "Croatian Community of Herzeg-Bosnia" (HZ HB) in Grude on 18 November 1991. It was envisioned as a political, cultural, economic and regional entity, founded on protecting the interests of Croats in Bosnia and Herzegovina. The decision on its proclamation stressed that it did not question the sovereignty and integrity of Bosnia and Herzegovina, and that "the democratically elected government of Bosnia and Herzegovina will be respected as long as Bosnia and Herzegovina remains independent in relation to the former or any future Yugoslavia." The HZ HB was to comprise the municipalities of Jajce, Kreševo, Busovača, Vitez, Novi Travnik, Travnik, Kiseljak, Fojnica, Skender Vakuf (Dobretići), Kakanj, Vareš, Kotor Varoš, Tomislavgrad, Livno, Kupres, Bugojno, Gornji Vakuf, Prozor, Konjic, Jablanica, Posušje, Mostar, Široki Brijeg, Grude, Ljubuški, Čitluk, Čapljina, Neum, Stolac, Trebinje (Ravno), and Mostar as the capital. The region of Bosanska Posavina ("Croatian Community of Bosanska Posavina") joined the HZ HB on 24 October 1992 after a meeting at Posušje. On 28 August 1993, the decision to establish the Croatian Republic of Herzeg-Bosnia (HR HB) was passed in Grude. Of course, the interests of the Croats in Bosnia and Herzegovina living outside the territory of the proclaimed Croatian Republic of Herzeg-Bosnia were not to be neglected either.

Disorder in Bosnia and Herzegovina began immediately after the majority of its citizens, mainly Muslims and Croats (the Serbs mainly boycotted the referendum), opted at the referendum on 29 February 1992 for an independent Bosnia and Herzegovina (94.4% of the 63.7% of voters at the referendum voted for independence). Considering the close ties of the Croats in Bosnia and Herzegovina and Croatia, the referendum results confirmed that the official Croatian policy and President Franjo Tuđman supported Bosnia and Herzegovina on its way to independence. On 27 March 1992, the self-styled "Assembly of the Serbian People in Bosnia and Herzegovina" proclaimed the Constitution of the Serbian Republic of Bosnia and Herzegovina in the building of the Assembly of Bosnia and Herzegovina in Sarajevo. In spite of that, based on the referendum results, on 6 April the member states of the European Community recognized the independence of Bosnia and Herzegovina. One day later, the United States of America recognized Bosnia and

Herzegovina, and Croatia and Slovenia. On the same day, the Republic of Croatia also recognized the independence of Bosnia and Herzegovina.

The negotiations that ensued between the representatives of the three constituent peoples in Bosnia and Herzegovina (Croats-Serbs, Muslims-Serbs, Croats-Muslims) did not prevent the war. After setting barricades on transportation routes and minor Serbian attacks in March (around Čapljina and Neum, and in Bosanski Brod), the Serbs launched open aggression against Bosnia and Herzegovina. In order to defend themselves militarily from Serbian aggression, and considering the "inability of the legal Bosnian-Herzegovian authorities" to protect them, on 8 April 1992 in Grude the Croats in Bosnia and Herzegovina established the Croatian Defense Council (HVO). It was the "highest body of defense of the Croatian people in the Croatian Community of Herzeg-Bosnia responsible for the defense of the sovereignty of the territory of the HZ HB and protection of the Croatian people and other people in the community from attacks of any aggressor." On the same day, the rump Presidency of Bosnia and Herzegovina proclaimed a state of immediate war danger and founded the General Staff of the Territorial Defense of Bosnia and Herzegovina (after 4 July 1992, the Army of Bosnia and Herzegovina). In battles along the Livno front between 13 and 23 April 1992, Croatian units succeeded in stopping the breakthrough of Serbian forces and consolidating their defenses; this front was the jump-off area for liberation operations of the Croatian forces in 1994 and 1995.

On 20 June 1992, the Presidency of Bosnia and Herzegovina proclaimed a state of war, general mobilization, and compulsory work order. Serbia, Montenegro, "the former JNA and the extremist part of the Serbian Democratic Party (SDS)" were declared aggressors. At the beginning of the war, Croatian and Muslim forces (the HVO and the Army of BH) planned a joint action in the defense of Bosnia and Herzegovina. Therefore, "proceeding from the common interests of their countries in the protection of their independence and territorial integrity," the President of the Republic of Croatia Franjo Tuđman and President of the Presidency of Bosnia and Herzegovina Alija Izetbegović signed the Agreement on Friendship and Cooperation Between the Republic of Bosnia and Herzegovina and the Republic of Croatia on 21 July 1992 in Zagreb. The Agreement expressed "serious concern for the continuing aggression of the remnants of the JNA of the former SFRY, and Serbian and Montenegrin regular and irregular military forces on the territory of the Republic of Croatia and Bosnia and Herzegovina." The Presidents agreed that the "future state system of Bosnia and Herzegovina would proceed from the full equality of the three constituent peoples, Muslims, Croats and Serbs, and that the future constitutional and political system of the country would be based on constituent units in the establishment of which due account will be taken of ethnic, historical, cultural, economic, transportation and other elements." (Art. 1) The state delegation thanked Croatia for accepting and tending to the refugees from Bosnia and Herzegovina in numbers "beyond its capacities" (in mid-June 1992 Croatia tended to about 260,000 displaced persons from Croatia, about 270,000 refugees from Bosnia and Herzegovina, and about 30,000 refugees from Serbia – Vojvodina and Kosovo).

The Agreement noted that the "armed component of the Croatian Defense Council (HVO) is an integral part of the united military of the Republic of Bosnia and Herzegovina, that the HVO would have its representatives in the joint command of the military of Bosnia and Herzegovina," and that "the provisional civil authorities, established in wartime conditions within the scope of the HVO, would be made to conform, as soon as possible, to the constitutional and juridical system of Bosnia and Herzegovina, and talks would be initiated immediately in the spirit of the mentioned principles." (Art. 6). Given the "continuing aggression of the Serbian and Montenegrin military forces against the Republic of Bosnia and Herzegovina, as well as against many parts of the Republic of Croatia from contiguous areas of Bosnia and Herzegovina, the Presidents of the Republic of Croatia and Bosnia and Herzegovina urged the international community, especially the UN, EC and the U.S., to take real and effective steps in order to vigorously stop the aggression against their countries, to prevent further loss of human life, persecution and expulsion of their citizens, and the destruction of property." It was accordingly decided that both states "will carry on their previous successful cooperation and continued coordination of their defense actions in their contiguous zones... (and) ...if aggression against them is not stopped urgently (...) will take all necessary steps to establish broader cooperation in the military sphere and coordinate military operations to conclusively repel the danger threatening them." (Art. 8)

Seeing as the Serbian aggression against Bosnia and Herzegovina and the Republic of Croatia continued, on 23 September 1992 in New York, Presidents Franjo Tuđman and Alija Izetbegović signed the Annex to the Agreement on Friendship and Cooperation between the Republic of Bosnia and Herzegovina and the Republic of Croatia. "Vigorous action of the international community" (Art. 1) was again called for to protect against aggression, along with the need "for enhanced effort in the search of a political solution to end the war." (Art. 2) "In keeping with the right to self-defense and to joint defense from aggression, it was also agreed to form a joint committee to harmonize defense efforts until the aggression stops completely," (Art. 3) and that "Bosnia and Herzegovina and Croatia will jointly seek the lifting of the embargo on the import of arms into these states as prescribed by Resolution 713 of the UN Security Council" (Art. 4).

On the basis of these agreements, Croatian army units drove the Serbian and Montenegrin forces from parts of Bosnia and Herzegovina adjoining the Republic of Croatia, and remained there to defend them from new Serbian and Montenegrin attacks. However, the agreements (except for the contiguous areas), did not provide for a proper integral military cooperation between the Croats and Bosniaks (Muslims). Such a cooperation would only be agreed on 22 July 1995 in Split.

After signing the agreement in Zagreb on 21 July 1992, the President of Bosnia and Herzegovina Alija Izetbegović stated for

Croatian TV that the time was not ripe for a military agreement because "the Serbian people would certainly see it as a threat" and that "it would be better to leave a little more space for the action of international factors."

In spite of the signed agreements, conflicts broke out between the HVO and the Army of BH in Herzegovina and central Bosnia. During the conflict between the Croats and the Muslims, the former were largely expelled from areas controlled by the Army of BH (from Konjic, Jablanica, Travnik, Kakanj, Fojnica, Bugojno, Vareš, and many villages in the municipalities of Zenica, Kakanj, Travnik, Novi Travnik, Visoko, Busovača, Konjic, Kiseljak, Kreševo and Fojnica). The Muslims were mainly expelled from areas controlled by the HVO (Stolac, Prozor, Kiseljak, and western Mostar). Both sides established concentration camps in which civilians were also detained and crimes committed.

Through diplomatic initiatives, Croatia tried to stop the senseless Croato-Muslim conflict that mainly benefited the Serbian forces (at the time, the Serbs controlled about 70% of the territory of Bosnia and Herzegovina). In spite of problems encountered by the diplomacy (lack of trust between the Croatian and Bosniak-Muslim leaderships, clashes between the Army of BH and the HVO, high-handed behavior of local authorities in Bosnia and Herzegovina, and the absence of firm coordination between representatives of the Croats and Bosniaks-Muslims in Bosnia and Herzegovina), the conflict finally ended with the signing of the Washington Agreement (18 March 1994), which envisaged the renewal of military cooperation between the Croats and the Muslims, establishment of the Federation of Bosnia and Herzegovina between the Croats and the Muslims-Bosniaks in Bosnia and Herzegovina, and the establishment of the Confederation between the Federation of Bosnia and Herzegovina and the Republic of Croatia.

Proposals of the International Community for the Arrangement of BH

Under the auspices of the European Community, a proposal for the arrangement of Bosnia and Herzegovina was tabled in Lisbon on 18 March 1992 (the Cutillero Plan or Lisbon Agreement on the cantonization of Bosnia and Herzegovina). According to the plan, the Muslims were to have 52 municipalities (44% of the territory), the Serbs 32 (44% of the territory), and the Croats 20 municipalities (12% of the territory). The Croats would acquire the municipalities of Neum, Čapljina, Čitluk, Ljubuški, Grude, Široki Brijeg (Lištica), Posušje, Prozor, Tomislavgrad, Livno, Kreševo, Kiseljak, Busovača, Vitez, Travnik, Vareš, Orašje, Bosanski Šamac, Odžak and Bosanski Brod. Although according to the plan, 59% of the Croats would remain in non-Croatian cantons, the Croats in Bosnia and Herzegovina signed the plan, but it was not implemented.

The Vance-Owen Plan tabled in Geneva on 4 January 1993 envisaged the division of Bosnia into 9 provinces (cantons) with Sarajevo as a special district (the tenth province), which would not have an international legal personality. The centers of the Croatian provinces (Posavina, Mostar and Travnik-Livno) were to be in Odžak, Mostar and Travnik, with a total of 513,433 (68.27%) of Croats in Bosnia and Herzegovina living in them. The Croatian provinces would account for 25.4% of the territory of Bosnia and Herzegovina, the 3 Serbian provinces for 42.3%, the 3 Muslim provinces for 28.8%, and the Sarajevo district for 3.5%. The plan was signed by Croatian and Muslim representatives (on 25 February in New York and 25 March in Geneva), while the Serbs rejected it with impunity (3 April). The fate of the plan was sealed by the absence of a mechanism (and political will) which would force the Serbs to return 20% of the occupied territory of Bosnia and Herzegovina, and by the conflict between the (Bosniak-Muslim) Army of BH and the (Croatian) HVO.

Ethnic breakdown of the population in the planned Croatian provinces

Provinces	Posavina	Mostar	Travnik-Livno
Croats	142,384 (56.0%)	193,016 (54.3%)	178,033 (45.8%)
Serbs	41,025 (16.2%)	39,695 (11.1%)	45,498 (11.7%)
Muslims	47,260 (18.6%)	102,035 (28.7%)	145,424 (37.4%)
Others	23,465 (9.2%)	20,877 (5.9%)	19,602 (5.1%)

The Posavina province (2103 km^2) would comprise the municipalities of Bosanski Brod, Odžak, Bosanski Šamac, Derventa, Modriča and Gradačac;

The Travnik-Livno province (5735 km^2) would comprise the municipalities of Jajce, Travnik, Novi Travnik, Vitez, Busovača, Fojnica, Uskoplje, Bugojno, Donji Vakuf, Kupres, Livno and Tomislavgrad;

The Mostar province (6135 km^2) would comprise the municipalities of Prozor, Konjic, Jablanica, Mostar, Posušje, Grude, Ljubuški, Široki Brijeg, Čitluk, Stolac and Neum.

The Owen-Stoltenberg plan for Bosnia and Herzegovina, which departed from the original principles (integrity, repudiation of ethnic cleansing and military conquest), was presented on 20 August 1993. It envisioned on the basis of ethnic principles a loose three-part Union of the Republics of Bosnia and Herzegovina (three autonomous ethnic republics), in which the Serbs would retain the greater part of the occupied territory (49.1%); the Muslims would get 33.3%, and the Croats 17.6%. The plan was not accepted.

The Gradual Liberation of Occupied Parts of the Croatian State

The Croatian diplomacy sought a peaceful solution to the conflicts in the Republic of Croatia and Bosnia and Herzegovina within internationally recognized frontiers. In his speech at the 48th Session of the UN General Assembly in New York on 28 September 1993, Croatian President Franjo Tuđman deplored the fact that "the aggression of Serbia and Montenegro against Croatia and Bosnia and Herzegovina was not opposed more vigorously." He mentioned the "strange standards of the international community, which first asked of Croatia to negotiate with the aggressor, and then accused Croatia because of it." He reminded the Assembly that "the sanctions against Yugoslavia need to remain in force up until it stops its aggression against Croatia," and expressed dissatisfaction with "UNPROFOR's inefficiency." With respect to Bosnia and Herzegovina, he stressed that Croatia was among the first to recognize the country and that it had "provided more for its refugees than the whole world put together, and continues to do so in spite of Muslim aggression against the areas settled by the Croatian people in Bosnia and Herzegovina." President Tuđman welcomed the good offices of Turkey in the reconciliation of Muslims and Croats in Bosnia and Herzegovina, and noted that the "Croatian people agreed to many compromises in Bosnia and Herzegovina, but a point was reached where any new compromises become impossible."

Among his other actions, on 1 November 1993, President Tuđman – "deeply concerned about the failure of all endeavors to stop war and armed conflicts in the Republic of Croatia and Bosnia and Herzegovina" – proposed a Peace Initiative to all relevant international factors to stop the war and atrocities of war in the territory of the former Yugoslavia. In its first chapter, entitled Proposal for the Implementation of the Peace Plan in the Area under

Protection of the United Nations (UNPA) in Croatia, the Government of the Republic of Croatia expressed readiness:

- to conclude within 15 days an agreement on the cessation of all hostilities with representatives of the local Serbian population, who will be guaranteed local and cultural autonomy;
- to immediately address the normalization of the entire social and economic life in the UNPAs: the immediate opening of all road and rail communications throughout the Republic of Croatia (also in the areas controlled by the insurgent Serbs); opening of the Adriatic pipeline, and the repair and putting into regular operation of oil and power transmission facilities and water supply throughout Croatia; the immediate return of all displaced persons to their homes under the supervision and effective assistance of UNPROFOR and authorities of the Republic of Croatia; undertaking measures for the establishment of normal life in the UNPAs, including the opening of all communications, provision of supplies to the whole population including the Serbian population (no discrimination) during the imminent winter period, resumption of healthcare and welfare, normal functioning of schools, electric power and fuel supply, payment of pensions, re-appointment of all civil servants; integration of all other activities in the overall economic and legal system of the Republic of Croatia; plans and steps for integration, without any discrimination, of the UNPAs into the economic reconstruction of Croatia;
- to grant full local autonomy (self-government) within the scope of the Constitutional Act to the districts of Knin and Glina where Serbs make up the absolute majority; guarantee of rights of cultural autonomy to the Serbian ethnic community throughout Croatia, especially the right - to education in their language and script according to special curricula, and the posting of bilingual place names in areas in which the Serbs constitute the absolute majority; hold elections for local (district and municipal) self-government authorities under international supervision, establish special police departments in the districts of Knin and Glina, in which the ethnic

breakdown of employees would conform to the ethnic composition of the population according to the latest census;
- to establish a special international supervisory body and special Court for Human Rights, to which every citizen will be able to apply after having exhausted all the resources of a normal legal process, in order to ensure full civil and political equality and effective protection of civil and ethnic rights of the Serbs in Croatia;
- to establish a special OSCE supervisory mission for mediation between the minority and majority population in order to create full confidence;
- to negotiate a political resolution of all outstanding issues other than those affecting the territorial integrity and sovereignty of the Republic of Croatia.

The mentioned Peace Initiative included two more chapters – the Proposal for Ending the War and Establishing Peace in Bosnia and Herzegovina, and the Proposal of Steps for the Permanent Consolidation of Peace, which among other things proposed the following:
- within the scope of the Peace Conference and under the auspices of the UN Secretary General and Security Council, the signing of a solemn declaration on mutual recognition of independence and sovereignty of the newly-emerged states within their internationally recognized borders by all the states in the territory of the former Yugoslavia;
- within 3 months the signing of an agreement on the succession of rights and obligations of all the successor states to the former Yugoslavia – based on the decision of the Arbitration Committee;
- within the scope of the Conference, the signing of a solemn declaration on respecting the rights of national minorities and ethnic communities, pursuant to international standards and conventions, and international control provided for the implementation of such agreements.

With this Peace Initiative, which comprised realistic political and economic requests, the Croatian leadership sent the insurgent Serbs clear signals that it was prepared to deal with the problem of insurgency of the occupied areas in a peaceful way.

The Vatican diplomacy and Pope John Paul II offered strong support in the search for a peaceful solution within the internationally recognized borders of the Republic of Croatia, which he confirmed during his visit to the Catholic Church in Croatia and the Republic of Croatia in September 1994. UN resolutions also unequivocally confirmed that the territory under control of Serbian forces "was provisionally occupied, but an integral part of the Republic of Croatia." Thus, the Resolution of the UN General Assembly on conditions in the occupied parts of Croatia (of 21 October 1994), the draft of which was sponsored by 24 countries, including the United States of America, clearly diagnosed the problem and pointed out that "the territories comprising the United Nations Protected Areas" (UNPAs) are integral parts of the Republic of Croatia." The UN Assembly was "alarmed and concerned by the fact that the ongoing situation in the Serbian-controlled parts of Croatia is *de facto* allowing and promoting a state of occupation of parts of the sovereign Croatian territory, and thus seriously jeopardizing the sovereignty and territorial integrity of the Republic of Croatia." Therefore, it called upon all parties and "in particular, the Federal Republic of Yugoslavia (Serbia and Montenegro), to comply fully with all Security Council resolutions regarding the situation in Croatia, and to strictly respect its territorial integrity." In this regard, it concluded "that all activities aimed at achieving the integration of the occupied territories of Croatia into the administrative, military, educational, transportation and communication system of the Federal Republic of Yugoslavia (Serbia and Montenegro) are illegal, null and void and must cease immediately." The UN General Assembly Resolution of 9 December 1994 stressed the importance of preserving the territorial integrity of the Republic of Croatia within internationally recognized borders almost in the same terms.

Another important decision was the UN Security Council Resolution 981 of 1 April 1995, according to which UNPROFOR

(United Nations Protection Forces) in Croatia became UNCRO (United Nations Confidence Restoration Operation in Croatia), and undertook to control the internationally recognized borders of the Republic of Croatia. However, the leadership of the insurgent Serbs in Croatia, relying on support from Serbia, turned down every peace proposal involving the reincorporation of Croatian territory into the constitutional system of the Republic of Croatia. In their intent to create a new Serbian state and annex it to Serbia, the insurgent Serbs in Croatia were not prepared to accept any other political option, above all coexistence with Croats in the same state. Therefore, in order to liberate parts of its territory and prevent further attacks by insurgent Serbs, Croatia had to resort to limited military action.

On the first day in March 1992, Croatian military forces took Nos Kalik near Drniš. However, the attack by part of the Osijek Operational Area of the Croatian Army (HV) on Baranja on 3 April 1992 was not successful. Both actions were initiated by local commands. In Operation *Jaguar* on 23 May 1992, the Croatian Army liberated the Križ Hill in the hinterland of Bibinje near Zadar from which Serbian terrorists jeopardized traffic along the Adriatic Highway.

In April 1992, the Croatian Army stopped the breakthrough of Serbian units from Bosnia and Herzegovina towards the Adriatic coast, planned in order to achieve full occupation of the southernmost part of Croatia. Croatian units then lifted the blockade of Dubrovnik and by the end of October 1992, liberated the occupied territory in the south of Croatia (about 1500 km^2). On the initiative of local commanders, on 21 June 1992 the Croatian Army launched a quick attack and liberated the Miljevac Plateau (about 180 km^2) from which the insurgent Serbs kept shelling Šibenik and the surrounding villages.

In late January 1993, part of the Velebit range and Zadar hinterland, including the Novsko Ždrilo sea passage and Peruča hydropower plant near Sinj (in total about 1050 km^2) were liberated in Operation *Gusar* (22 January) (commonly known as Operation

Maslenica) and the Peruča Action (28 January). After the construction of a pontoon bridge at Maslenica, the link between northern and southern Croatia, interrupted since September 1991, was reestablished, while the liberation of the Peruča plant improved power supplies in Dalmatia. Serbian forces tried to demolish the dam by detonating explosive charges, which could have caused a massive human and ecological disaster downstream along the Cetina River. Damages were fortunately repaired thanks to quick reactions.

In a surprise action on 9 September 1993, Croatian soldiers and policemen liberated the so-called Medak Pocket consisting of three villages – Počitelj, Čitluk and Divoselo (about 225 km^2) from where the Serbian artillery shelled Gospić. In retaliation, the Serbian Army of Krajina rocketed Karlovac, Lučko (Zagreb suburbs), Samobor, Jastrebarsko, Ivanić Grad, Kutina, Popovača, Gospić, and other Croatian towns. Many civilians were killed and wounded, and substantial property was destroyed. Part of the international public and politicians accused the Croatian forces for their scorched-earth tactics and civilian victims, and the UN Security Council requested the Croatian units to withdraw to initial positions.

On 3 November 1994, in Operation *Cincar,* coordinated with the Army of BH, Croatian units liberated the geo-strategically important town of Kupres in Bosnia and Herzegovina.

After that, from 29 November to 24 December, Operation *Zima 94 [Winter]* liberated about 200 km^2 in Livanjsko Polje. With this operation, Croatian units prevented the Serbian forces from taking the geo-strategically important town of Bihać in Bosnia and Herzegovina, which was about to fall. The operation also marked the start of a series of operations and actions with which Croatian forces gained control over the mountains and zones in the Knin hinterland and created conditions for its liberation.

After operations *Skok 1 [Leap]* (about 75 km^2) on 7 April, and *Skok 2* (about 450 km^2) from 4-11 June 1995 and late July (25-30), and the taking of Bosansko Grahovo (28 July) and Glamoč (29 July) in Operation *Ljeto 95 [Summer]* (about 1600 km^2), Serbian forces in Knin found themselves in a hopeless position.

1995

Final Liberation of Occupied Parts of Croatia: Operations Bljesak [Flash] and Oluja [Storm]

In early 1995, the leadership of the insurgent Serbs turned down another proposal of the international community – the so-called Z-4 Plan on the political resolution of the crisis in Croatia. The plan envisioned an exceptionally wide-ranging autonomy for the Serbs in Croatia, almost a "state within a state," in the areas of the districts of Knin and Glina, which would comprise all the municipalities with a majority Serbian population. With their refusal, Serbian politicians clearly stipulated that they would not, under any condition, accept peaceful reintegration into the constitutional system of the Republic of Croatia, or coexistence with the Croats. Since all later attempts of the Croatian government and the international community to deal with the issue of occupied territory also failed, in early May 1995 Croatia launched *Flash,* another military-police liberation action, freeing about 600 km^2 of the remaining occupied territory of Western Slavonia. In only two days, on 1 and 2 May, the resistance of the Serbian units was crushed, liberating Okučani, Jasenovac and Stara Gradiška. The remnants of the defeated 18th Corps of the Serbian Army of Krajina surrendered at Pakrac in the afternoon hours of 4 May. The organized resistance of the special forces of the insurgent Serbs ceased the next morning at 06:00 hours at Omanovac. Croatian casualties included 42 killed and 162 wounded. Enemy losses were higher several times over. In retaliation, the Serbian leadership ordered the rocketing of Croatian towns. One of the cities attacked was Croatia's capital, Zagreb. Among the many buildings hit were the Children's Hospital, Academy of Dramatic Arts, and a secondary school; seven civilians were killed and at least 176 wounded. During and after Operation *Flash,* Croatian authorities ensured humane treatment and all civil rights to the Serbian population, and members of Serbian units were guaranteed protection under the Amnesty Act. Despite this, the majority of the Serbian population in the occupied part of Western Slavonia left the area on the eve of and during Operation *Flash.* Under great pressure of the Serbian leadership and faced with the threat of the resumed shelling of Zagreb, the UN organized Operation *Safe Passage* in which most of the remaining Serbian population left Western Slavonia.

After their defeat in *Flash*, the Serbian leadership tried to unite the remaining occupied territory of Croatia with parts of Bosnia and Herzegovina under Serbian control. The process climaxed in July 1995 with the drafting of the Constitution of the United Serbian Republic. At the same time, Serbian forces were about to enter Bihać (a town in Bosnia and Herzegovina close to the Croatian border). The conquest of Bihać would have been a strategically important victory for the Serbs and would have provoked a new humanitarian disaster and massive loss of civilian life in the area. Because of all this, military action turned out to be the only and immediate solution for the problem of occupied Croatian territory but also for the Bihać crisis.

On the political scene, the last attempt at a peaceful solution to the problem of the occupation of part of Croatian territory took place on 3 August in Genthod near Geneva at a meeting of the representatives of the Croatian government and insurgent Serbs from Knin.

The requests of the Croatian delegation were almost identical to the requests in President Franjo Tuđman's peace initiative of November 1993:

- immediate peaceful reintegration of the occupied areas;
- immediate opening of all communication lines in occupied areas, in particular the opening of the Zagreb-Split rail route via Knin; opening of the oil pipeline within 24 hours of the completion of the negotiations (providing Croatian authorities have control along the entire pipeline route);

- immediate enforcement (in the occupied areas) of the Constitution of the Republic of Croatia and provisions of the Constitutional Act on the rights of the Serbian ethnic community to which the Croatian government guarantees political, civil and ethnic rights;
- surrender of weapons to Croatian authorities, witnessed by UNCRO, within 3 to 8 days, and guarantee of civil safety and general amnesty to all persons other than the perpetrators of war crimes.

The insurgent Serbs of Croatia were also offered the holding of free elections for local self-government, and participation in civil and police authority in line with the ethnic composition of the population from 1991, and the implementation of all other provisions of the Constitutional Act. However, in a telephone conversation during a meeting, the leadership of the insurgent Serbs received a recommendation from their President Milan Martić in Knin to turn down the proposals and prolong the negotiation process. Their replies did not satisfy the Croatian side. Because of the serious situation at Bihać, which called for an immediate reaction as the town's defenses were about to collapse, there was no time to continue negotiations. This exhausted all possibilities for a peaceful solution of the occupied territory of the Croatian state, and the leaders of the insurgent Serbs in Croatia assumed responsibility for the start of the Croatian forces' final liberation operation, and for the loss of human life and destruction of property associated with operations of that kind.

The final military-police operation for the liberation of the occupied areas, called *Storm*, was launched by Croatia with the tacit support of the United States between 4 and 10 August 1995. At 04:00 hours on 4 August 1995, the Croatian Army and special police units launched an attack along a 630 kilometer-long front line from Bosansko Grahovo in the south to Jasenovac in the east. Croatian forces in Eastern Slavonia and southern Dalmatia were put on alert because of possible attacks by the Yugoslav Army and Army of Republika Srpska from Bosnia and Herzegovina.

The greatest success during the operation was achieved in the morning hours of 5 August, when the 4th and 7th Croatian Guards Brigades liberated Knin (whose members originated from Dalmatia, Bosnia and Herzegovina, Zagorje and other areas). Because of its strategic and symbolic significance, the day on which Knin was liberated is marked in Croatia as the Day of Victory and Homeland Gratitude, subsequently also named the Day of Croatian Defenders. Over the next few days, Croatian forces reached and secured the state borders and then began to clear the liberated areas of northern Dalmatia, Lika, Banovina and Kordun (about 10,500 km^2). Croatian casualties in the operation amounted to 196 soldiers killed, over 1100 wounded, and 15 reported as missing. Enemy losses were several times higher.

In the first hour of *Storm,* the President of the Republic of Croatia Franjo Tuđman called on members of hostile units to surrender their weapons, and guaranteed amnesty to all those who had not perpetrated war crimes under Croatian laws. Citizens of Serbian nationality in the formerly occupied areas were invited to remain at home and await Croatian authorities without fear. In spite of that, on the eve of *Storm* and afterwards, tens of thousands of citizens of Serbian nationality left their homes in the occupied parts of the Republic of Croatia before the arrival of Croatian forces. Their final and mass departure was ordered and implemented by the military and political leadership of the RSK in the afternoon of the first day of *Storm* (4 August). That was the final act of the tragedy of the Serbian people in Croatia caused by the intransigent policy of the insurgent Serbs since 1990.

At the same time, by launching Operation *Storm,* Croatian forces enabled the Army of Bosnia and Herzegovina to crush the Serbian siege of Bihać. This prevented a new humanitarian disaster in Bosnia and Herzegovina and a crime such as the massacre at Srebrenica, where members of Serbian units under the command of General Ratko Mladić killed several thousands of Bosniaks-Muslims in July 1995 (the number of about 8,000 is being reported).

The victory of Croatian forces in *Storm* is one of the most important events in Croatian history because it ensured the territorial integrity and development of the Republic of Croatia, freedom of its citizens, and survival within internationally recognized borders. Credit for the success of Operation *Storm* must be given to the unity of the majority of Croatian citizens who opposed the Serbian aggression, and the successful state policy led by President Franjo Tuđman. This was achieved with the assistance of the Croatian Army and police led by the Chief of the General Staff of the Croatian Army, General Zvonimir Červenko, Chief of the Intelligence Directorate of the General Staff, Rear-Admiral Davor Domazet, Commanders of Corps Districts (Generals Miljenko Crnjac, Luka Džanko, Ante Gotovina, Mirko Norac, Petar Stipetić), Police Forces (General Mladen Markač), and other military and intelligence officers.

Foreign statesmen, in particular U.S. officials, for the most part displayed an understanding for the operation. Among other things, they stated that "Croatia had given the international community sufficient time to resolve the conflict through negotiation, but which failed because of the intransigent position of the Krajina Serbs," that "*Storm* re-established balance in Bosnia and Herzegovina, and opened up possibilities for negotiating a peace settlement," and that "Croatia lawfully chose the offensive, and cannot be compared with the unruly armies of Radovan Karadžić (Serbian army in Bosnia and Herzegovina)."

After *Storm*, the only areas still under Serbian occupation were the Croatian Danubian area, namely Baranja and part of Eastern Slavonia, and Western Srijem – the so-called UN Sector East (4.6% of the total land territory of the Republic of Croatia). Under the Erdut Agreement (signed on 12 November 1995), the area was finally reincorporated into the Republic of Croatia on 15 January 1998 during the process of peaceful reintegration. With this, the Croatian authorities established full control over the internationally recognized borders of Croatia, if we omit the disputes with neighboring countries over certain border points. Because of a number of concessions to the insurgent Serbs, the Erdut Agreement provoked the dissatisfaction of most Croats expelled from the area. At the same time, however, it confirmed the consistency of the Croatian policy in its attempts, in spite of certain painful compromises and in moments of victorious euphoria and military superiority, to resolve problems with the insurgent Serbs through peaceful negotiation.

The victor who does not know how to forgive plants the seeds of discord and future ills. And the Croatian people do not want this. They did not want what they had suffered here in Vukovar and throughout Croatia. Everything we are doing now is not solely focused on parochial local interests but on the overall interests of Croatia and Europe, the interest of peace, the future of this region, and of Europe. Long live the coexistence of the Croatian and Serbian peoples and other ethnic communities in this region! Long live our only and eternal Croatia!

(From the address of the President of the Republic of Croatia Franjo Tuđman in Vukovar, 8 June 1997.)

The End of the War and Partition of Bosnia and Herzegovina

In addition to liberating its own territory, Croatia also contributed considerably to the liberation of the occupied territory of Bosnia and Herzegovina. In coordination with the Army of BH, and based on the agreement between the Presidents of the Republic of Croatia and Bosnia and Herzegovina of 22 July 1995, the Croatian Army and Croatian Defense Council liberated about 5000 km^2 of territory in southwestern and western parts of Bosnia and Herzegovina formerly occupied by Serbian units. About 1600 km^2 in Operation *Ljeto '95 [Summer '95]* (25-30 July 1995), 2500 km^2 (including the towns of Jajce and Drvar, and the Oštrelj Pass) in Operation *Maestral* (8-15 September 1995), and 800 km^2 (including Mrkonjić Grad) in Operation *Južni Potez [Southern Move]* (9-11 October 1995). The attempt of the Croatian Army to cross the Una River and enter Bosanska Krajina in mid-September 1995 failed with extensive casualties.

The success of the Croatian but also of the Bosniak military in Bosnia and Herzegovina enabled the realization of the Dayton (Ohio, USA) Peace Agreement concluded on 21 November 1995 and its signing in Paris on 14 December 1995. The war and open aggression against Croatia begun in the summer of 1991 by Serbia, the JNA, and Serbian-Montenegrin forces was finally over. According to the Dayton Agreement, Bosnia and Herzegovina was structured, or better yet – divided – as a state with 2 entities and 3 constituent peoples. The Serbian entity (Republika Srpska) acquired 49% of the territory, and the Federation of Bosnia and Herzegovina 51% in spite of the fact that the Serbian leaders (S. Milošević and R. Karadžić) and Serbian politics were declared the main culprits for the bloodshed in the former Yugoslavia.

According to the 1991 census, the Serbs accounted for 31.1% of the population of Bosnia and Herzegovina (1,369,258) and owned 32% of the land; the Muslims accounted for 43.7% (1,905,829), Croats 17.3% (755,895), Yugoslavs 5.5%, and others 2.4%. The Dayton Agreement achieved peace, but what was not achieved was the right to return to their homes as guaranteed to all refugees and displaced persons, particularly in Republika Srpska.

According to research carried out by UN experts for the ICTY, between 1992 and 1995, during the war in Bosnia and Herzegovina, 104,732 persons were killed: 68,101 Bosniaks/Muslims, 22,779 Serbs, 8858 Croats, and 4995 others. War had a disastrous demographic effect on the Croats in Bosnia and Herzegovina. According to a Croatian source, about 9900 Croats were killed or went missing in Bosnia and Herzegovina between 1992 and the end of 1995, and more than 400,000 were forced to abandon their ancestral homes before the attacks of Serbian forces or Army of Bosnia and Herzegovina. (It is estimated that more than a half of that number never returned to Bosnia and Herzegovina after the war.) Prior to the war, the number of Croats in Bosnia and Herzegovina amounted to 755,895 (17.3%).

The Dayton Peace Accords did stop the war but did not achieve a just peace because the establishment of Republika Srpska as a special entity encompassing 49% of the territory of Bosnia and Herzegovina actually "accepted" the results of the Serbian aggression. The Serbian entity in Bosnia and Herzegovina acquired regions from which practically all the non-Serbian population was banished (the greater part of Bosnian Posavina etc.), and even the region in which Serbian forces committed genocide (Srebrenica).

The Dayton Accords envisioned the second entity in Bosnia and Herzegovina (the Federation of Bosnia and Herzegovina) as a federation of Bosniaks/Muslims and Croats (a confederation between the mentioned Federation of Bosnia and Herzegovina and the Republic of Croatia, envisioned according to the Washington Agreement of March 1994, never came into being and is not mentioned any longer). However, coexistence in the Federation of Bosnia and Herzegovina, i.e., relations between the Croats and the Bosniaks/Muslims, were heavily strained by a period of armed conflict between the two communities, as well as the Croats' fear of the predominance of the majority Bosniak/Muslim population and the Bosniaks/Muslims' distrust of the Croats. Armed conflict between the Croatian Defense Council (HVO) and the Army of Bosnia and Herzegovina lasted with occasional truces from October 1992 until March 1994. The Croats saw the conflict as an attempt of the Bosniaks/Muslims to drive them off the areas they had inhabited for centuries and thus make up for the loss of territory conquered by Serbian forces, and as the betrayal of a people they had defended and cared for. (Before and during the conflict between the Croats and Bosniaks/Muslims in Bosnia and Herzegovina, Croatia provided refuge to many Bosniaks/Muslims from Bosnia and Herzegovina, supplied weapons to the Army of Bosnia and Herzegovina, etc.) The Bosniaks/Muslims saw the conflict as a betrayal of their wartime ally and an endeavor to create a "Greater Croatia," i.e., the annexation of part of Bosnia and Herzegovina to Croatia. In line with such thinking, anti-Croatian propaganda claimed that Croatia had attacked Bosnia and Herzegovina based on an agreement between Croatian President Franjo Tuđman and Serbian President Slobodan Milošević on the partition of Bosnia and Herzegovina, concluded in Karađorđevo in March 1991, which is not true. Official records and the statesmanlike moves of Croatian President F. Tuđman with respect to Bosnia and Herzegovina, and the course of the Serbian aggression against the Republic of Croatia and Bosnia and Herzegovina lead us to conclude that such an agreement did not exist. At the same time, talks between the Bosniaks/Muslims and the Serbs, and plans of the Serbian and Bosniak/Muslim leaderships are ignored.

Of course, some time still has to pass, primarily because of the degree of organization and availability of official records held in archives, for a comprehensive and objective presentation of the role of the Croats and Croatia and Croatian President Franjo Tuđman in the war in Bosnia and Herzegovina. Nevertheless, a chronology of the events and certain key facts cannot be disregarded.

- Voting of the Croats at the referendum for the independence of Bosnia and Herzegovina (29 February 1992) as recommended by Croatian President F. Tuđman was crucial for its success.

- Croatia recognized Bosnia and Herzegovina as an independent state on 7 April 1992, that is, immediately following the member countries of the European Community and on the same day as the United States of America – which Serbia did not do until the end of the war.

- Croatian units together with the Army of Bosnia and Herzegovina took part in the defense and liberation of Bosnia and Herzegovina. In 1992, Croatian units prevented Serbian forces from capturing strategically extremely important points in Bosnia and Herzegovina – Mostar and the Neretva Valley, Bosnian Posavina, Livno, Tomislavgrad, Rama – and occupying an even larger part of that country. In 1995, Croatian units liberated over 5000 square kilometers of Bosnia and Herzegovina, saved Bihać from Serbian occupation, and prevented another Serbian genocide over Bosniaks/Muslims.

- An analysis of the strength and number of volunteers and units from Croatia involved in the conflict with the Army of Bosnia and Herzegovina shows that their task was primarily a defensive one (to ensure the survival of the Croatian people in their native areas), and that they could have been used only to "patch up the line of confrontation" and certainly not for aggression. (The number of Croatian Army troops never exceeded the complement of a light JNA brigade – 1400 to 1800 – and they were never concentrated along a single tactical line or point!) Croatian Army forces in Bosnia and Herzegovina were mainly engaged against Serbian forces on the basis of the agreement between Croatian and Bosniak/Muslim leaderships in order to prevent Serbian attacks of the latter from

Bosnia and Herzegovina on Croatia and protection of Croats from Serbian aggression.

- The Croatian leadership accepted all proposals of the international community regarding a resolution of the conflict and internal arrangement of Bosnia and Herzegovina.

- The Croatian Community of Herzeg-Bosnia and its military and administrative organization were created on 18 November 1991 in response to the decisions of the Serbs in Bosnia and Herzegovina, and in a period of uncertainty and questionability as to whether Bosnian-Herzegovinian authorities could protect the Croats from the threatening Serbian aggression. (The Croatian Republic of Herzeg-Bosnia was proclaimed on 28 August 1993, after the start of the conflict between the Croats and Bosniaks/Muslims in Bosnia and Herzegovina, and in accordance with the political framework of the internal arrangement of BH as proposed by the international community).

- Croatia helped arm and train the Army of Bosnia and Herzegovina.

- During the war in Bosnia and Herzegovina, Croatia cared for refugees and displaced persons from that country regardless of their ethnicity or religion. From the start of the war until mid-October 1994 – that is, even during the conflict between the Croats and Bosniaks/Muslims – the Office of the Government of the Republic of Croatia for Refugees and Displaced Persons provided care for more than 600,000 refugees and displaced persons from Bosnia and Herzegovina. (About 425,000 Bosniaks/Muslims, about 170,000 Croats and about 5000 others.) At the same time, hospitals in Croatia also treated wounded members of the Army of Bosnia and Herzegovina and Bosniak/Muslim civilians from Bosnia and Herzegovina along with HVO members.

One cannot ignore either the fact that the territory of Bosnia and Herzegovina was the springboard for the Serbian aggression against Croatia in 1991, and that Croatia was also directly threatened from the same territory after 1991 as well. Furthermore, during one stage in the war in Bosnia and Herzegovina, a tragic conflict occurred between the Croats and the Bosniaks/Muslims, with crimes committed on both sides, and whose perpetrators need to be brought to justice and punished. There were unacceptable moves by Croatian and Muslim extremists in Bosnia and Herzegovina and cases of unlawful conduct at local levels. However, one needs to first take into account the cause of the war, that is, the responsibility of the Serbian leadership, the leadership of the Bosnian Serbs, and of the JNA for the onset of war in Bosnia and Herzegovina. The war in Bosnia and Herzegovina is actually a continuation of the war in Croatia and the second stage of Serbian aggression which began with the attack on Croatia in the summer of 1991, focused on achieving the goal of "all Serbs in one state." All other events, including the war between the Croats and Bosniaks/Muslims, and the significantly reduced number of Croats in Bosnia and Herzegovina, are all consequences of that aggression.

Summary

The goal of Serbian policy since the mid-19th century was to secure Serbia access to the sea and its western border deep in the territory of Croatia, so that all Serbs could live within one state (the so-called Greater Serbia). This goal had mainly been achieved with the creation of (the first and the second) Yugoslavia. However, aspirations of part of the Serbian political elite focused on the total domination of Serbia over the other Yugoslav republics publicly expressed in the mid-1980s ultimately caused the disintegration of Yugoslavia. Specifically, the process of democratization in the countries of Southeastern Europe, symbolically linked with the fall of the Berlin Wall in November 1989, facilitated the introduction of a multi-party system in the Yugoslav republics, but also ushered in the issue of the rearrangement of Yugoslavia. After the multi-party elections, the leaderships of Yugoslavia's (pro)Western republics – Slovenia and Croatia – committed themselves to a greater decentralization of the state. Conversely, the ultimatum of the Serbian leadership called for a strictly centralized state (greater power of federal authorities, reduced prerogatives of the republics), with the dominance of the most numerous (Serbian) people in it (after the principle of "one man one vote"). The top JNA echelons also opted for the preservation of Yugoslavia as a centralized state without hiding their intent, if required, to impose their commitment through armed force as well.

For the Greater Serbian ideologues, the alternative to a Serbian-dominated Yugoslavia was the creation of a single Serbian state (Greater Serbia) comprising the territory of the former Yugoslavia, roughly east of the Virovitica – Pakrac – Karlovac – Ogulin – and part of Gorski Kotar – Karlobag line. That goal could only be achieved through military means, by conquering a considerable part of Croatia and Bosnia and Herzegovina. Having secured an alliance with the JNA by May 1991, the Serbian political leadership led by

Slobodan Milošević was ready for a military option, even more so as one year earlier, through the cooperation of the Serbian leadership and JNA, the weapons of the Croatian Territorial Defense were placed under the control of the JNA. Thus, the almost entirely disarmed Croatia seemed to be an easy prey. At the same time, thanks to an aggressive media campaign and support of part of the Serbian Orthodox clergy, the new "leader of all Serbs" Slobodan Milošević secured the support of most Serbs in the former Yugoslavia for the implementation of his aggressive, imperialist policy.

The relief of the leaderships in the autonomous provinces of Kosovo, Vojvodina, and Republic of Montenegro (1988/1989), and the appointment of cadres ready to obey the policy of the new Serbian "leader" Slobodan Milošević, show that even before the Croatian Democratic Union came to power in Croatia (late May 1990), the Serbian leadership had already prepared a project for a redesigned Yugoslavia. The disarmament of Croatia in May 1990 and the promulgation of the new Serbian Constitution in September 1990, which de facto abrogated the autonomy of Vojvodina and Kosovo, contrary to the provisions of the Yugoslav Constitution in force at the time, are proof that the project's implementation had already begun without the agreement of Croatia or other Yugoslav republics.

When the events of late June 1991 in Slovenia finally confirmed that Yugoslavia could not be sustained within its borders, the Republic of Croatia suffered the launch of open aggression by Serbia and Montenegro, that is, the armed forces of the SFRY comprised of the JNA, Territorial Defense (TO) units of Serbia and Montenegro, parts of TO units from Bosnia and Herzegovina (mainly from areas settled by Serbs), and Serbian paramilitary (volunteer, mainly chetnik and prochetnik) units. The open aggression was preceded by terrorist actions waged by Serbian extremists and anti-constitutional policies of the leadership of part of the Serbs in Croatia – and, after August 1990, by the armed rebellion of part of the Serbs, supported operatively by

Serbian services with the help of JNA "officers". During the aggression against the Republic of Croatia, the SFR of Yugoslavia, whose disintegration began on 25 June 1991 with the proclamation of independence from Croatia and Slovenia, was formally run by the rump Presidency consisting of Serbian and pro-Serbian members. It was obviously subservient to the policy and decisions of the "leader of all Serbs," Slobodan Milošević. By late June 1991, the JNA already openly operated as the Serbian army. The first step in the transformation of the JNA from the Yugoslav into the Serbian army was its restructuring, carried out in the second half of the 1980s, which excluded the republics from the chain of command and adjusted the territory of the newly formed army commands to the envisioned borders of Greater Serbia.

A considerable number of Serbs endorsed the rebellion as a way to resolve the issue of their "self-determination," and then supported the JNA and took part in the aggression against Croatia. By committing at the time numerous crimes against Croats and other non-Serbs, but also against their compatriots, the Serbian extremists set in motion a spiral of evil, which is uncontrollable in any war. This had a direct bearing both on the internal and overall relations between Croats and Serbs, and triggered unacceptable actions of certain groups or individuals on the Croatian side as well against individual ethnic Serbs and their property. Nevertheless, even in wartime circumstances, almost all major decisions of the Croatian Parliament and Government included special enactments or charters on the rights of Serbs and other ethnic minorities, which bears witness to the readiness of the Croatian leadership to ensure the Serbs in Croatia their required civil and ethnic rights. Admittedly, the extent to which these decisions were implemented in certain areas and in wartime conditions is open to argument, while also taking due account of the security conditions at the time, and the fact that Croatian police could not exercise control throughout the entire territory of the Republic of Croatia.

Conversely, the leadership of the rebel Serbs in Croatia was not ready, at any moment, for a political solution, nor did it accept the possibility of living in an independent Croatia. The proposals of the leading Serbian politicians in the Republic of Croatia regarding the political and cultural autonomy of the Serbs within the boundaries of the Republic of Croatia as mentioned in 1990 were only a negotiating maneuver. Because of the military superiority of the JNA, by the end of 1991 Serbian forces occupied almost one-third of the territory of the Republic of Croatia. By mid-1991, the leadership of the rebel Serbs in Croatia started negotiations with Serb representatives in Bosnia and Herzegovina on the establishment of a Serbian state on the territory of Croatia and Bosnia and Herzegovina. Subsequent negotiations, intensified up to the end of 1992, show that such a state, to be called the "United Serbian Republic," would have been proclaimed in August 1995 had it not been for the defeat of the Serbian forces in the military-police Operation *Storm [Oluja]*. To be sure, negotiations on the establishment of the United Serbian Republic did not interrupt the process of unification of Serbs in Croatia and Bosnia and Herzegovina with Serbia, i.e., the plan on the unification of all Serbs in one state. Due to international circumstances in 1991 and later, S. Milošević and Serbia did not recognize the Republic of Serbian Krajina nor did they approach an open process of unification, but helped it in every way to the extent that this occupied part of the Republic of Croatia actually appeared to be a part of Yugoslavia or a Serbian province.

The contents of numerous Serbian documents showing the reasons for the failure of all peace negotiations in 1990-1991 can be summarized in the statement of the Prime Minister of SAO [Serbian Autonomous Region] of Krajina Milan Martić in 1991. *I assure you that we in Krajina will rather die or emigrate from Krajina to Europe before agreeing to any kind of life in any Croatian state. My position is endorsed by the plebiscitary, one-hundred percent will of the Serbian people in Krajina.*

Analogously, the contents of numerous Serbian documents showing the reasons for the failure of all attempts at a peaceful reintegration of occupied Croatian territory into the constitutional and legal order of the Republic of Croatia can be summarized in the following statements of the Prime Minister of the Republic of Serbian Krajina Milan Martić of February 1995:

- *How can we accept the concept of the so-called peaceful reintegration of Krajina into Croatia? Can we spit on all the victims of this war? Are we supposed to agree to our own death? Life in Croatia would be worse than any war. Life in Croatia – would that be life?* (8 February 1995)

- *The war between the Republic of Croatia and RSK [Republic of Serbian Krajina] must end with the victory of one and defeat of the other side. Until that happens, the war will not and cannot end.* (10 February 1995)

Thus, because of the intransigent decision of the Serbian leadership to turn down living in the Republic of Croatia and live only in a Serbian state, a military option imposed itself as the only way for Croatia to secure its territorial integrity. This was endorsed by international recognition in January 1992, and especially by the admittance to the United Nations in May of the same year, along with a series of UN resolutions (815/1993; 847/1993; 871/1993; 908/1994; 947/1994; 958/1994; 981/1995; 994/1995 etc.).

Already in late 1991, in a series of small-scale military operations, Croatian military and police forces succeeded in liberating over 2200 km^2 of occupied territory in Western Slavonia *(Operations Orkan 91, Otkos 10 and Papuk).*

In 1992, the area of Nos Kalik between Šibenik and Drniš was liberated in early March and the Križ Hill near Zadar in May. About 1500 km^2 were liberated between April and late October in southern Croatia ("Southern Front") and the blockade of Dubrovnik lifted. In June, about 150 km^2 were liberated on the Miljevac Plateau in the Šibenik hinterland.

In January 1993, 1050 km^2 were liberated in the Zadar hinterland (Novsko Ždrilo and Maslenica, Rovanjska, Zemunik airport, parts of the Velebit mountain range), including the Peruča hydropower plant. In September, about 225 km^2 were liberated in Lika – namely the villages of Počitelj, Čitluk and Divoselo (the so-called Medak Pocket near Gospić).

The small but strategically important town of Kupres in Bosnia and Herzegovina was liberated during Operation *Cincar* in early November 1994.

Between December 1994 and mid-August 1995, Croatian forces liberated the Dinara mountain range and parts of Bosnia and Herzegovina (Operations *Zima '94 [Winter]* in November-December 1994; *Skok 1 [Leap] in* April 1995; *Skok 2* in June 1995; and *Ljeto '95 [Summer]* in July 1995. The liberation of the remaining occupied territories followed: 600 km^2 in Western Slavonia (Operation *Bljesak [Flash]* 1 to 4 May 1995), and 10,500 km^2 in Dalmatia, Lika, Banovina and Kordun (Operation *Oluja [Storm],* 4 to 10 August 1995).

In September 1995, (after *Storm*) Croatian forces liberated about 2500 km^2 of territory in Bosnia and Herzegovina (Operation *Maestral,* 8-15 September 1995) (including the towns of Jajce, Drvar, and the Oštrelj Pass) and about 800 km^2 in Operation *Južni potez* (9-11 October 1995) including the town of Mrkonjić Grad.

Croatia's decision regarding the military option *Storm* was not rash, and it could not and was not in a position to lose time in useless negotiations with representatives of rebel Serbs. This conclusion is borne out by the following facts:

Because of the intransigent leadership of the rebel Serbs in Croatia since 1990 (refusal of all peace initiatives – both by the Government of the Republic of Croatia and the international community, and even of the Z-4 Plan which offered the Serbs in Croatia an exceptionally broad autonomy, almost a "state within the state"), a military option was the only solution for the reintegration of the occupied territory of the Republic of Croatia into its constitutional and legal order.

Dramatic conditions in the defense of the strategically extremely important town of Bihać in late July 1995 ("The Second Bihać Crisis"), an area which had been proclaimed a "safe haven" by the UN Security Council in mid-1993, was also a reason why military action, i.e., *Storm,* could no longer be postponed in August 1995. (The fall of Bihać would have improved the position of Serbian forces in an almost decisive way.)

Continuous activities (since 1991) of the Serbs in Croatia and Bosnia and Herzegovina focused on the creation of a single Serbian state in the occupied areas of the Republic of Croatia and Bosnia and Herzegovina – the "United Serbian Republic" – had entered into its final stage with the enactment of the draft constitution just before Operation *Storm.*

War actions in Croatia came to an end with the liberating tactics of Operation *Storm* and the victory of Croatian forces. Military defeats finally forced the "leader of all Serbs," Slobodan Milošević, and leadership of the rebel Serbs in Croatia to sign an agreement on the peaceful reintegration of the remaining occupied territory of Eastern Slavonia, Baranja and Western Srijem (Croatian Danubian Area) into the constitutional and legal order of the Republic of Croatia. With the end of the process of peaceful reintegration on 15 January 1998, Croatian authorities established almost complete control (save for a few border points) over the internationally recognized borders of the Republic of Croatia.

Therefore, the crisis and disintegration of the SFRY, and the war in Croatia and Bosnia and Herzegovina, were caused by the Serbian (Greater Serbian) policy, i.e., by the attempt to realize the project of "all Serbs in one state" which a part of the Serbian political elite began to promote in the mid-1980s. The threatening restructure of Yugoslavia from a federation into a centralized state in which Serbia and the Serbs would predominate influenced the political circumstances in Croatia. The homogenization of the Croats followed. Instances of rather extreme conduct by individuals on the Croatian side were mainly isolated reactions to the actions (terrorist actions in particular) of Serbian extremists.

In order to justify their armed revolt, the leadership of the rebel Serbs in Croatia and Serbian politicians claimed in the media that the liquidation of Serbs in Croatia had already begun in 1990, which is not true. There is no concrete piece of information indicating any liquidation of Serbs or murder of ethnic Serbs, (Croatian citizens) before the breakout of the high intensity armed conflict (in late June 1991). The two ethnic Serbs (Croatian citizens) killed in 1990 – a civilian killed in Kordun (August 1990) and a policeman killed near Obrovac (November 1990) were murdered by Serbian extremists. Similarly, it is not true that the Serbs were "excluded from the new Constitution of the Republic of Croatia," claimed by the leadership of the rebel Serbs in Croatia to have been the reason for the armed rebellion.

In the attacks on Croatia and during the occupation of one-third of its territory, Serbian extremists committed many crimes against Croats but also against citizens of other nationalities who did not support the Greater Serbian policy. At least 149 uncovered mass graves and about 1200 individual graves of victims of the Serbian aggression bear witness to this fact. Almost the entire non-Serbian population was killed or banished from areas under the control of Serbian forces. Serbian extremists torched and demolished many homes owned by Croats and almost all the Catholic churches and religious buildings. The Croatian national heritage was also plundered and destroyed. During the war in the Republic of Croatia, the following property was destroyed or damaged: 195,000 to 217,009 housing units (depending on the census; mainly during the attacks of Serbian forces in 1991), about 120 industrial buildings and 2423 cultural monuments (of which 495 were religious buildings, mainly Catholic, in areas occupied by the Serbs). The total direct war damage in the Republic of Croatia was assessed at US $ 37.1 billion (Government of the Republic of Croatia, State Commission for the Census and Assessment of War Damage; *War Damage*, final report, Zagreb, September 1999.) In the first year of the war, 590 settlements in 57 Croatian municipalities were affected by the war – 35 were totally destroyed, and 34 sustained major damage (including larger towns).

The aggressive and extremist conduct of part of the Serbs in Croatia and Serbian politicians towards the democratically elected Croatian authorities, followed by the crimes committed by Serbian units against Croats and other Croatian citizens, forced the Croats to a determined and sometimes uncompromising resistance. The cruel and bloody Serbian aggression against Croatia and crimes committed by Serbian forces facilitated inappropriate and unacceptable reactions of individuals on the Croatian side, with resulted in an adverse effect on the condition of public security and growth of crime and violence even in areas under control of Croatian authorities. There are records of murders of Serbian civilians and destruction of the property of Croatian citizens of Serbian nationality, among other things.

The Croatian judiciary has largely instituted criminal proceedings against perpetrators of crimes in the Homeland War. However, just as in any war, the perpetrators of all the murder cases were not prosecuted. Nevertheless, the sentences so far pronounced in Croatia, public debate, history textbooks and other facts show that Croatian society has to a considerable extent faced up to the negative events in the Homeland War (much more so than many democratic and especially victorious countries immediately after the end of other bloody wars worldwide). Naturally, this is also a process that requires a specific time period to pass, as well as the satisfaction of justice. As history has shown, a precondition for that is the clear-cut definition of the aggressor.

History has also shown that crimes are committed in all defensive wars, and that revenge as a reaction to crime is always vicious. Of course, this cannot be used to compare crimes committed by individuals on the Croatian side, but on the other hand, one cannot ignore the chronology of such events and the fact that such cases involved incidents typical of wartime conditions and not any planned action by Croatian authorities. The dishonorable actions of individuals on the Croatian side are in sharp contrast to the honorable conduct of Croatian officers, soldiers and policemen in the Homeland War. However, crimes committed by the Serbian forces in Croatia after 1991 (killing and banishment of Croats and other non-Serb citizens, the destruction of villages and towns, and cultural and religious monuments), were within the scope of the planned policy focused on the creation of an "ethnically clean" Serbian state.

Every crime must be condemned and its perpetrators punished regardless of who committed it or in what or whose name. This is a precondition for retaining an unblemished idea and purity of the event; otherwise, the victor becomes a moral loser. Therefore, the memory of the days of pride and glory in the Homeland War cannot be complete unless we pay particular reverence to the Croatian defenders who lost their lives in the war, but also to all the innocent victims of the war regardless of their ethnic or religious background.

The Homeland War is the Brightest Period in Croatian History

The constitution of the democratically elected Croatian Parliament (Sabor) on 30 May 1990, promulgation of the new democratic Constitution on 22 December 1990, proclamation of the Independent Republic of Croatia on 25 June/8 October 1991, and the defense from Serbian aggression and liberation of occupied parts of Croatia between 1991 and 1995 make up the brightest period in Croatian history.

The Homeland War – the name usually given to this period – was a legitimate and defensive war of liberation because the Republic of Croatia was attacked and forced to defend its independence and territorial integrity. Thanks to the courage, humaneness, solidarity and skillfulness of the Croatian defenders, as well as the unity of the political leadership and majority of its citizens, Croatia emerged as the victor in the war. Formally, the state of war ended on 23 August 1996 with the signing of the Agreement on Full Normalization and Establishment of Diplomatic Relations between the Republic of Croatia and the Federal Republic of Yugoslavia (actually Serbia and Montenegro). With that document, Serbia finally recognized the existence of the Croatian state within its internationally recognized borders!

As compared with other wars in the area of the former Yugoslavia and beyond, especially considering final military operations and actions of the victorious armed forces (Croatian in this case), the Homeland War in Croatia and major operations for the liberation of the country, *Flash* and *Storm,* are distinguished by the lowest number of collateral (civilian) casualties. With due respect to every casualty and victim, and every person that suffered pain during the war, this should always be borne in mind if the course of the Homeland War and its aftermath are to be represented comprehensively and objectively.

PHOTOGRAPHS

Antonov An-2 corn crop duster. The aircraft in the picture belonged to the First Independent Air Force Platoon from Osijek. The crew - Osijek – Marko Živković, Mirko Vukušić, Ante Plazibat and Rade Griva flew combat missions in this aircraft. They were shot down and killed on the night of December 1-2 1991 in Slavonia. The aircraft was not equipped with navigational instruments. Photograph by Marko Perić

CROATS DO NOT FEAR ANYONE / EXHIBITION OF WAR PHOTOGRAPHY AND INSIGNIA OF THE UNITS OF THE ZAGREB CORPS DISTRICT 1991-1995 / Author: Ivo Vrtarić, Zagreb, 1995, photograph by Željko Gašparović, published by: Ministry of Defense of the Republic of Croatia, General HV Staff, Zagreb Corps District

Dubrovnik, December 6 1991; the author of this photograph, Pavo Urban, was killed near Orlando's Column by a mortar bomb shortly after taking this picture. Orlando's Column is a symbol of Dubrovnik's history and its independence. The Libertas flag was often raised on the column. The flag is also a symbol of the city's enduring spirit of independence

Croatian police and a column of JNA vehicles, Pakrac, March 2 1991. Photograph by Toni Hnojčik

Review of ZNG (National Guard Corps) units, Zagreb, May 28 1991. Photograph by Marko Perić

Rocketing of the Viceroy' Palace, Zagreb's Upper Town, October 7 1991. Photograph by Hrvoje Knez

Đakovo, eastern Slavonia, December 15 1991. Photograph by Pero Šola

Novi Varoš, western Slavonia, second half of September 1991; The soldiers in the photograph returned to retrieve the body of a fallen comrade from enemy controlled area. During the war some of the soldiers in the photograph become high-raking officers of the Croatian army (from left to right): Ante Gotovina – then commander of a reconnaissance company, Mihajlo Matokanović, Damir, Šimun Đolan, Mato Modrić, Damir Tomljanović-Gavran and Ante Kikić (with a hand-grenade in his hand). Photograph by Mario Filipi

Croatian Medical Corps in action; doctor Miroslav Kinčl – "Needle"; Prekopakra, November 1991. Photograph by Toni Hnojčik

According to the records of the Croatian Ministry of Families, Veteran Affairs and Intergenerational Solidarity, 23080 women aged 14 to 72 took active part in the Homeland War (14194 on combat duties); 127 killed women have been granted veteran status posthumously, and 1115 disabled women have been granted war veteran status; 5334 women are on record as widows of veterans. Photograph by Mario Filipi

A destroyed JNA tank in the middle of Nuštar, October 1991. Photograph by Mario Filipi

Improvised armored vehicles of the Croatian Armed Forces in 1991. Photographs by Toni Hnojčik

Prekopakra, western Slavonia, 1992. Photograph by Toni Hnojčik

Pakrac, western Slavonia, summer 1992. Photograph by Toni Hnojčik

“Blue helmets” in western Slavonia, 1992. Photograph by Željko Gašparović

Maslenica, January 22 1993

Croatian Army and BH Army soldiers on the state border at Tržačka Raštela, August 6 1995

Croatian Army forces cross the river Sava near the village of Krapje on the early morning of August 4 1995. Photograph by Željko Gašparović

Croatian President Franjo Tuđman and Minister of Defense Gojko Šušak review the honor guard comprising soldiers belonging to the 4th and 7th Guards Brigades, Knin, August 6 1995. Photograph by Gordan Laušić

Vukovar, June 8 1997: the "Freedom and Return Train" symbolically brought Croatia back to Vukovar. Photograph by Božo Biškupić

The Croatian President Franjo Tuđman and the President of the BH Presidency Alija Izetbegović sign the Split Declaration with the President of the BH Federation Krešimir Zubak and BH Prime Minister Haris Silajdžić (July 22 1995); the Agreement on Military Cooperation was particularly significant. Photograph by Gordan Laušić

Burial of the Croats killed by Bosnian Muslims at Uzdol, September 14 1993

Burial of the Croats killed by Bosnian Muslims at Uzdol, September 14 1993

Monument to the Croats killed by Bosnian Muslims at Trusina, April 16 1993

Monument to the Bosnian Muslims killed by Croatian units at Ahmići, April 16 1993

Memorial cemetery of Croatian victims killed during the Homeland War in Vukovar (938 white crosses)

Croatian soldiers in liberated Lipik, December 6 1991. Photograph by Toni Hnojčik

Hospital in Pakrac, damaged by the JNA and Serb paramilitaries, autumn-winter 1991. Photograph by Toni Hnojčik

Serbian soldiers in Vukovar singing:

"Hey Slobo dear comrade, send us some greens

The meat won't go bad, we'll slaughter Croats for fresh proteins."

Dead bodies of the citizens of Vukovar killed by Serb artillery and air force during the siege of the city. The bodies were brought to the courtyard of the Vukovar Harbormaster's Office in November 1991 because the shelling was too intense for proper burial. This photograph was taken in November 1991 and was seen throughout the world. Ironically enough, the photograph was first presented by Serbian propaganda as a crime committed by Croatian forces in the battle of Vukovar in 1991, and later on as evidence of a crime committed by Croatian troops in Operation Storm in 1995 (!): in the collected papers on "Serbian refugees and displaced persons in the late 20th century" (Belgrade, 2000), published by the Centre for Strategic Studies of the University of Belgrade, the photograph is presented with the caption "After Operation Storm the Serbs were not even buried". The publication also contains other photographs showing the ruins of Vukovar and Croatian refugees leaving the ruined city, also presented as examples of "Serbian suffering". Photograph by Ante Arić

Destroyed JNA tanks on Trpinjska Road mid-September 1991. Photograph by Franjo Živković and Andrija Marić; courtesy of Marko Babić, Ivan Leutar

Vukovar hospital; the result of the Serbian aggression, autumn 1991. Courtesy of Damir Radnić

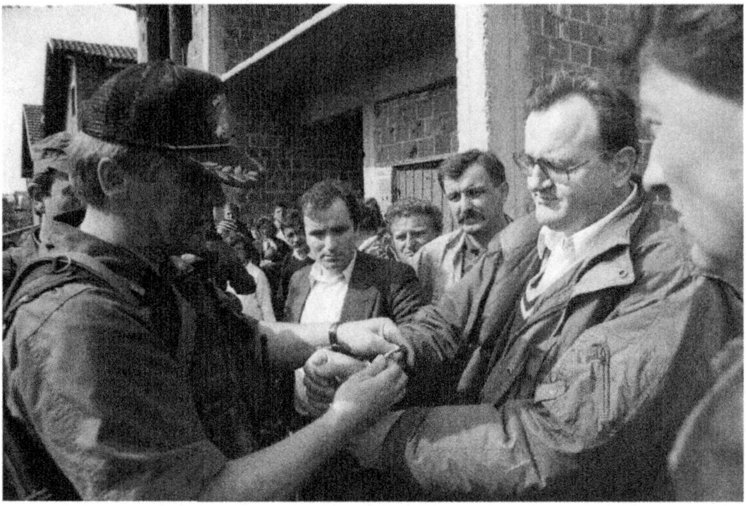

Surrender of the commander of the 51st (Pakrac) Infantry Brigade of the 18th "SVK" corps, Lieutenant Colonel Stevo Harambašić, and Veljko Džakula, one of the leaders of the Serbian rebellion against the democratically elected authorities of the Republic of Croatia in Western Slavonia, to the commander of the Croatian police forces Nikola Ivkanec, on the afternoon of May 4 1991, at Gavrinica (above Pakrac). Photograph by Toni Hnojčik

Special Forces of the "Serbian Army of Krajina", Slunj training ground, June 28 1995. (Taken from *Vojska Krajine* – list Srpske vojske Krajine, br. 11, Juli 1995. – *Army of Krajina* – magazine of the Serbian Army of Krajina, No. 11, July 1995)

Special Forces of the "Serbian Army of Krajina", Slunj training ground, June 28 1995. (Taken from Vojska Krajine – list Srpske vojske Krajine, br. 11, Juli 1995. – Army of Krajina – magazine of the Serbian Army of Krajina, No. 11, July 1995)

Review of the Special Forces of the "Serbian Army of Krajina", Slunj training ground, June 28 1995. (Taken from Vojska Krajine – list Srpske vojske Krajine, br. 11, Juli 1995. – Army of Krajina – magazine of the Serbian Army of Krajina, No. 11, July 1995)

Review of the Special Forces of the "Serbian Army of Krajina", Slunj training ground, June 28 1995. (Taken from Vojska Krajine – list Srpske vojske Krajine, br. 11, Juli 1995. – Army of Krajina – magazine of the Serbian Army of Krajina, No. 11, July 1995)

JNA tank destroyed at Stari Grabovac in Western Slavonia, October 1991; the defeat of the JNA in Croatia in 1991. Photograph by Željko Gašparović

Undamaged Orthodox church of the Protection of the Virgin (Temple of Protection of the Holy Virgin) in Knin. Photograph by Stanko Ferić, August 20 1995

Interior of the Catholic parish church of St. Anthony in Knin destroyed by the rebel Serbs. Photograph by Stanko Ferić, August 20 1995

Meeting of allies: Croatian Army general Marijan Mareković and BH Army general Atif Dudaković near Tržačka Raštela, August 6 1995; Miroslav Tuđman, Director of the Croatian Intelligence Service, in the background

President Franjo Tuđman and the Croatian delegation in the "Father Dr Mato Nikolić" Franciscan hospital at Nova Bila during their visit to the Croats in the Lašva valley, June 14 1994. Photograph by Ante Čakić; courtesy of Slobodan Lang

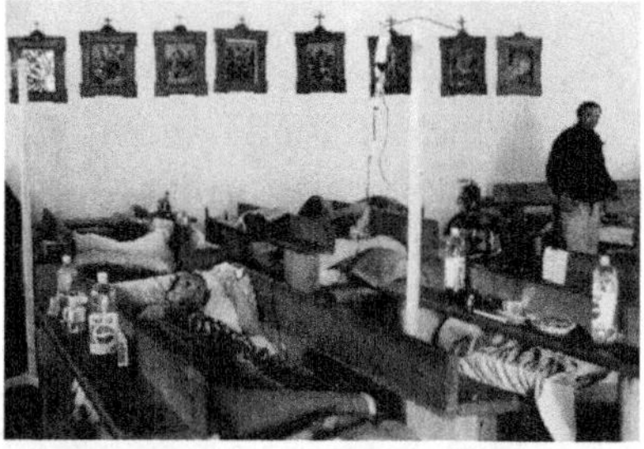

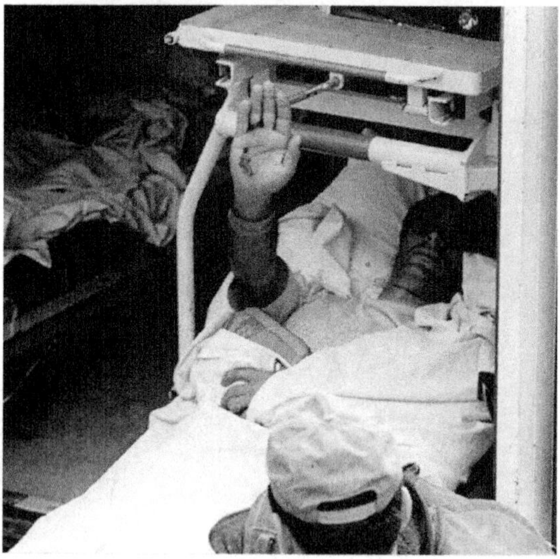

Improvised Franciscan hospital "Father Dr Mato Nikolic" in Nova Bila (BH); the parish premises of the Church of the Holy Spirit were adapted to receive about 80,000 Croats under siege in the Lašva Valley

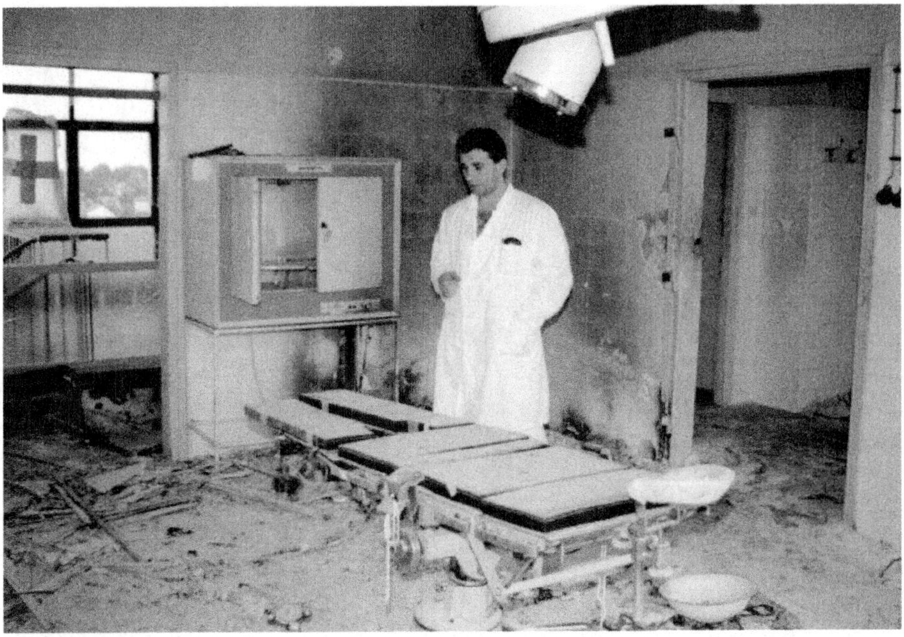

Vinkovci hospital, maternity ward; the result of Serbian attacks, autumn 1991.
Photograph by Mario Filipi

Burned cross on the charred remnants of a Catholic church in western Slavonia, and a preserved Orthodox church in the background; after the liberation operations Flash and Storm such scenes could be seen in the liberated area of the Republic of Croatia. Photograph by Toni Hnojčik

APPENDICES

The President of the Republic of Croatia Franjo Tuđman (1922-1999)

(The data presented in this book have mainly been taken over from Nikica Barić, The first Croatian President Dr. Franjo Tuđman on the Yugoslav President Josip Broz Tito, in Dr. Franjo Tuđman in Croatian Historiography, Collected Papers, Zagreb, 2011, 313-341; John Sadkovich, Tuđman, The First Political Biography, Zagreb, 2010).

In the evaluation of the significance and role of President Franjo Tuđman in Croatian history, one cannot sidestep the fact that it was under his leadership, in the challenging political and military circumstances prevailing in 1990 and 1991, that the modern Republic of Croatia was created and defended from ruthless Serbian aggression, that it won international recognition and freed the occupied parts of its territory, and that after a long time, during this period, Croats did not wage war against one another.

It is true of course that the greatest credit for the defense and victory of Croatia in the Homeland War is owed to the Croatian people and citizens who accepted "Our Beautiful Homeland," to quote the initial words of Croatia's national anthem, as their own state, and first and foremost to its defenders who directly opposed the enemy with weapons in their hands. At the same time, due mention must be made of the role of Franjo Tuđman and the fact that he was President of the Republic of Croatia in a dramatic period of Croatian history. It was indeed a dramatic period, primarily because of Croatia's struggle for survival in the war which Serbia thrust upon it in its attempt to conquer territory. The war resulted in massive economic devastation and social upsets caused by the Serbian aggression and occupation of parts of Croatian territory, as well as the influx of hundreds of thousands of displaced persons and refugees, first from the occupied parts of Croatia and then from Bosnia and Herzegovina.

One cannot neglect either the fact that Tuđman retained the trust of the Croatian people in wartime conditions. His winning the democratic presidential elections in 1992 and 1997 supports this claim. Moreover, his authority and charisma contributed significantly to the victory of the Croatian Democratic Union at the Croatian parliamentary elections in 1992 and 1995.

In addition to the consequences of war and occupation, in the 1990s Croatia also faced typical transition problems, including economic and financial disarrangements caused by the disintegration of Yugoslavia and privatization of the economy. Along with the aggressive Serbian nationalism supported by the JNA, the Croats also faced negative perception from the greater part of the international community that was opposed to the collapse of Yugoslavia. They also had to face an arms embargo imposed by the international community (25 September 1991, Resolution 713), an exceptionally unjust step considering the aggression of a vastly superior enemy against Croatia, which also gave individuals the opportunity to engage in disgraceful actions for personal gain. President Tuđman had to achieve his diplomatic goals with an embryonic diplomatic corps, as well as ensure the country's territorial integrity and satisfaction of its citizens with freshly formed armed forces and an economy devastated by war and occupation. Despite all that, during his presidential terms, Croatia was created as a modern democratic state with all the formal mechanisms of Western democracy. In reply to the justified question of whether these mechanisms operated properly at all times, due account ought to be taken of the context of the period we are considering.

President Tuđman promised he would respect the "civil and national rights" of Croatian citizens of Serbian nationality, and expected Serbian authorities to respect the rights of Croats living in Serbia. Even during the most difficult period of the war, November 1991, only a few days before the fall and occupation of Vukovar, in a despondent and agonizing time the end of which was not in sight, when conditions in Croatia – owing to the daily Serbian destruction of towns and villages, and Serbian crimes – definitely "favored" revenge, banishment and other crimes against Serbs, President Tuđman requested from Croatian authorities the full respect of the rights of citizens of Serbian nationality (minutes of the meeting in the President's Office on 14 November 1991). He consistently sought to cooperate with political leaders in neighboring countries and the international community. He wanted to avoid war, and after it started, searched for solutions to put an end to the conflicts in Croatia and Bosnia and Herzegovina. He favored political and diplomatic solutions, and was reluctant to resort to military action.

President Tuđman's main goals were the creation of a sovereign Croatia and its reintegration in Europe. For President Tuđman, Croatia's reintegration in Europe held many meanings: he saw Croatia as a Mediterranean and Central European country, and a link with Southeastern Europe. He believed that membership in the European Community would guarantee the political stability and economic prosperity of Croatia. He also hoped that it would reverse the demographic decline suffered by Croatia under communist rule, and bring back the Croatian expatriate community from which he sought help in reviving the country's economy by embracing the market economy. That was, in his belief, a precondition for demographic revival.

In President Tuđman's mind, one of the preconditions for the establishment of the independent Croatian state was the reconciliation of the Croatian people ("the reconciliation of all Croathood"), with which he sought to overcome the ideological opposition rooted in the events of the Second World War. He believed that condemnation of all crimes and rejection of all fallacies of the past such as fascism and bolshevism, and the acceptance of all positive past developments, would permit at least human reconciliation if not political unity of the "Croatian ustashe who wanted the Croatian state" and the "Croatian partisans who fought for Istria." In line with his refusal to accept extremism, he warned that Croatia must not be jeopardized by the "frantic and insane right" and the "no more clever left".

His critics have accused him of having actually revived "ustashedom" with his "policy of reconciliation of the ustashe and partisans," and opened the door to historical revisionism. However, they forget the context of the time at hand, the possibility that the aggressive and pro-chetnik behavior of some Serbian politicians and "rally-goers," as well as the traumatic aftermath of the bloody war thrust upon Croatia, might have favored the radical reactions of individuals or smaller groups in Croatian society that found their models in the ustashe movement. But the scale of their appearance in the Croatian public (and, particularly significant, in the Serbian media) was much greater than the result of their actions. They did not radicalize the policies of the new Croatian government, and their impact on developments in Croatian society was so negligible (and often conditioned by Serbian aggression!) that any discussion of the "revival of ustashedom" in Croatia is not appropriate.

When President Tuđman is censured for having glorified the Independent State of Croatia (NDH), along with criticism for renaming some street and squares, in most cases reference is made to a sentence in his address at the First HDZ Convention held in Zagreb in late February 1990. He said that the NDH "was not just a mere 'quisling' creation or 'fascist crime' but the expression of both the historical aspirations of the Croatian people for their independent state, and the perception of international factors, in this case of the government of Hitler's Germany (...), of Croatia's aspirations and of its borders," that the "NDH was the consequence of very specific international factors."

At the same time, what is passed over in silence are his words in the same address that "the Croatian people, with the Federal Republic of Croatia established by decision of the ZAVNOH [National Anti-Fascist Council of the People's Liberation of Croatia], found itself at the end of World War II on the side of the victorious democratic forces," and that this decision was "of far-reaching historical importance." He did not forget the "historical merits of ZAVNOH's Croatia," or of the "Croatian communists and partisans, with whom Istria and other areas along the Adriatic, from Lastovo to Zadar and Rijeka, and Međimurje, found themselves within Croatia's borders," which does not mean that it would not have happened in some other circumstances. At the same time, he claimed that the Croats did not join the antifascist movement because of communism but because they aspired to freedom and equality.

Tuđman did not find the NDH acceptable because of its "genocidal program and genocidal crimes." He did not hesitate to state that even before Croatian emigrants (for instance, in Sweden in September 1989), in an environment to which some "high" Croatian officials (who presented themselves as "great" antifascists) succumbed to saying what the emigration wanted to hear. He believed that people who glorified the NDH by flaunting ustashe and Nazi insignia "discredited Croatia and disgraced the Croatian people." His message to such people was that "they should, if they truly cared for Croatia, desist from such 'provocative stupidities' that are opposed to 'normal democratic development,' " so that Croats would "never again suffer another Bleiburg" or the misery after the end of World War II. He also pointed out that the "genocidal program for the destruction of the Croatian people" implemented by the chetnik movement of Draža Mihailović was even more radical.

He believed that the existence of the Socialist Republic of Croatia, in spite of all Croatian dissatisfactions, was the "foundation of Croatian viability and the starting point for the achievement of the full state sovereignty of the Croatian people." He found confirmation for such thinking in Serbian attacks on Josip Broz Tito as the "greatest culprit for all the problems of Serbhood," especially because of his establishment of federalism "to which the predominant part of the Serbian political elite had never resigned itself." For him, Tito was a statesman of "European and even global scale," who would "be appraised severely as a communist leader who brought evil" (mass executions and terrorizing of political opponents) by objective historical judgment. At the same time, he believed, "due account ought to also be taken of Tito's merits."

Given that Serbian anti-Croatian politics blamed the entire Croatian people for crimes committed by the ustashe regime during World War II, and denied Croatia's outstanding contribution to the antifascist struggle, President Tuđman knew that the assertive Serbian diplomacy would use every international opportunity to present the new Croatian state as an extension of the NDH. That is why he particularly stressed the fact that Croatia also based its democracy on the contribution of the Croatian people to the antifascism underlying modern European and global democracy. In so doing, he did not neglect to highlight modern Croatia as a multi-party democracy and a state of equal citizens, as necessarily and in principle distinguished from the NDH as well as from the Croatia as it was under communist rule in Yugoslavia. Moreover, he drew attention to the fact that – after international recognition and victory in the Homeland War, which ensured the territorial integrity of the Republic of Croatia within its internationally recognized borders – the return of any new regional communities or of a restored Yugoslavia, or the so-called "Western Balkans," would be disastrous for the Croats.

Following the activity of the renewed Greater Serbian politics, Tuđman was aware, in the early 1990s, that the issue of Croatia's status could not be resolved within the framework of Yugoslavia. However, because of international circumstances and the balance of forces he had to use finesse and patience. Because of that, his critics accused him of being indecisive, especially with respect to the JNA. It is questionable, however, whether his optimistic statements that the JNA would have to adjust to the reality of democratic changes in Yugoslavia were intended to delay the conflict and gain time for the structuring of Croatia's armed forces, or whether they were an expression of his conviction. In the early 1990s, Croatia was inferior both militarily and politically. Considering the strong anti-Croatian propaganda, and circumstances in which Croatian diplomacy had to build an international image of the country practically from scratch, President Tuđman had to show restraint with regard to the military option even when it was obvious that it was inevitable. He also tried to avoid war and the military option because of his responsibility for human lives, which was an important guideline in his policies, and so he kept negotiating as long as there was even the slightest hope of a peaceful settlement. In accordance with the aforementioned, and with respect to the objection that the process of restoring the territorial integrity of the Republic of Croatia took too long, one might say that perhaps the occupied territories could have been liberated faster, but with a considerably higher casualty rate – which also needs to be taken into account. In any case, open discussion of such and similar issues is one of the characteristics of democratic society, and all arguments must be subservient to scientific methodology and not to political goals.

Any discussion of the 1990s war in the former Yugoslavia that fails to point out who was the most responsible for "sowing the seed of evil" and who set in motion the spiral of crime, which is then so difficult to control, omits the difference between the cause and the consequence of war. Such an approach relativizes the responsibility of the Serbian policy of the time and ignores the fact that the cause of the recent war in the former Yugoslavia was not a conglomerate of bad policies (suggesting that the policies of Slobodan Milošević and Franjo Tuđman were equally responsible for the war), but the continuity of the Greater Serbian policy. At the same time, the aim is to hold Croatia responsible for the partition of Bosnia and Herzegovina, and even for aggression against it, which is not true. Criticisms that President Tuđman pursued a double policy with respect to the Serbs in Croatia and that he wanted to effect the partition of Bosnia and Herzegovina with Serbian leader Slobodan Milošević are based on a lack of understanding of Tuđman's policy and the realities of the 1990s. They are also based on the ignorance of the differences between his views expressed as a historian and decisions made as a President. Of course, they are also based on considerable amounts of misinformation launched into the public, most frequently the lie about his having agreed the partition of Bosnia and Herzegovina with Slobodan Milošević in Karađorđevo in March 1991.

President Tuđman insisted on cooperation with the Croatian Serbs, but did not want to relinquish part of Croatia's state territory to the rebels. He also wanted to protect the Croats outside Croatia. His ideal was a Croatia that would accommodate as many Croats as possible, but at the same time, he shaped his policies in accordance with the demands of the international community by accepting the inter-republican borders as state borders! The suspicion that Bosnia and Herzegovina would not survive the collapse of Yugoslavia because it suffered from the same problems enhanced his concern for the destiny of the Croats in Bosnia and Herzegovina. He supported their organizational efforts as a response to Serbian policy actions in Bosnia and Herzegovina, but only within the boundaries of that state as long as it existed. The survival of Croats in the area of the former Banovina Hrvatska (part of the territory of the historical Turkish Croatia with a considerable Croatian population even before the 1990s) was for him a vital Croatian interest.

The fact that the world failed to find an appropriate solution to the problem of Bosnia and Herzegovina was to a considerable extent the consequence of the stalemate caused by the intransigence of the Muslim and Serbian leaderships. President Tuđman did not turn down any solution for Bosnia and Herzegovina proposed by the international community. He emphasized that Croatia got involved in the BH crisis because the Croats in that country were attacked and because the "future of the Croatian state" depended on the establishment of a "stable order" in the Balkans. As a solution, he offered the restructuring of Bosnia and Herzegovina into a confederation, which was in line with the proposals of the international community. At the same time, while supporting the

Croats in Bosnia and Herzegovina diplomatically and militarily, he offered the Bosniak/Muslim government a military alliance, allowing it to acquire weapons and other equipment through Croatia, and cared for many Muslim refugees. Eventually, the Croato-Muslim alliance made possible the end of the war and breaking of the Serbian siege of the Muslim enclave in Bihać, and prevented a new tragedy in which if the Serbian forces managed to overrun the town thousands of Bosniaks/Muslims would have been killed.

Of course, no leader and no policy are immune to mistakes. The seriousness of certain mistakes can be debated, but President Tuđman cannot be held responsible for the war tragedy which he first tried to avoid and then to end as soon as possible. It is a fact that the start of the revival of the Greater Serbian project preceded the rise of President Tuđman to power in Croatia. It is a fact that the war and Serbia's aggression against Croatia could have been prevented in two ways only: by acceptance of a strictly centralized Yugoslavia, meaning the predominance of Serbia and the Serbs in such a state, or by acceptance of the Greater Serbian plan according to which all Serbs are to live in one country." The western border would run along the Virovitica – Pakrac – Karlovac, Karlobag line, including part of Gorski Kotar. Luckily, the Croatian people were determined to prevent this and elected a president with whom they could achieve their dream of an independent state.

President Tuđman could not influence the break out of war, nor could he influence the way it would end. Croatia had the right and obligation to liberate its own occupied territory, and in the process, the Croatian political and military leadership neither planned not implemented any "criminal enterprise." The leadership of the rebel Serbs in Croatia and Greater Serbian strategists in Belgrade are exclusively responsible for the departure of the Serbs from occupied parts of the Republic of Croatia during Operation *Storm.* As compared with other 20th century wars and final operations (in terms of proportional ratio of forces, area, and population of the war-affected territory, and the intensity of the war and civilian suffering on the victorious Croatian side prior to the final victorious operations), it can be claimed that the Croatian Homeland War, as far as the victorious Croatian armed forces are concerned, was a war with a very low civilian collateral casualty rate. (Especially if due account is taken of the suffering of civilians in the attacks by the JNA and Serbian unit on Croatia in 1991.) There is no doubt that along with the commanding officers who planned and implemented the Croatian military-police operation, credit is also due to President Franjo Tuđman. A history of wars has shown that in final military operations the reactions of the liberators who were formerly attacked, banished and humiliated, have always been fierce, and that should be kept in mind before any discussion of the aftermath of such operations and Homeland War casualties!

Accordingly, in spite of the war and problems typically encountered by countries who have emerged from a single-party to a multi-party system, or from a totalitarian system to democracy, and which had a particular bearing on the economic situation and social stratification in the period of Tuđman's rule, it may be concluded that the independent and free, internationally recognized and democratic Republic of Croatia and its victory in the imposed war is a result that makes President Tuđman one of the most meritorious persons in Croatian history.

The Liberation of the Occupied Parts of Western Slavonia in 1991

The Serbian aggression against Croatia, which had become quite overt after the summer of 1991, focused first on splitting Croatian territory, and then on occupying Croatia or at least the parts of Croatian territory to be annexed to the planned Greater Serbian state. The greater part of Baranja was already occupied in August 1991 after the drive of the 12th JNA (Novi Sad) Corps from Vojvodina, while Slavonia was to be occupied by the concerted concurrent action of JNA forces from Serbia and Bosnia and Herzegovina in the fall of 1991. Also occupied in September were parts of Slavonia, Dalmatia, Lika, Banovina and Kordun.

In late September and early October 1991, the JNA and Serbian and Montenegrin units launched decisive attacks on all battlefields in Croatia. By embarking on such an offensive strategy, the JNA command planned – by means of a synchronized thrust of strong forces from Serbia and Bosnia and Herzegovina – to break within 20 days the blockade of JNA barracks in Croatia, and then use these forces to crush Croatian defenses. The successful defense of Pokuplje prevented the JNA plan to break through to Karlovac and Sisak, and on to Zagreb, and break the blockade of the barracks in the Croatian capital, including Jastrebarsko and Dugo Selo. The JNA also planned to extricate the 13th (Rijeka) Corps and parts of the 10th (Zagreb) Corps from the blockaded barracks.

Breaking through from the east, the JNA Novi Sad Corps and the First Guards mechanized a JNA brigade from Belgrade, assisted by units of the Serbian territorial defense. They were to neutralize the defense of eastern Slavonian towns and follow through to western Slavonia, where they were expected to link up with units of the 5th (Banja Luka) JNA Corps (approximately along the Suhopolje – Okučani route). At the same time, the 5th BH Corps, reinforced with

JNA units from Serbia and Macedonia, territorial defense units from Bosnia and Herzegovina pushing from the south, and rebel Serb units from western Slavonia, were supposed to break the blockade of the 10th and 32nd (Varaždin) Corps in JNA barracks in the greater Zagreb area, Varaždin, Koprivnica, Križevci, Bjelovar and Daruvar. They were to then push on to the Croatian border with Hungary, and cut off eastern Slavonia from the rest of Croatia. The main thrust of the 5th JNA Corps' attack on Croatia followed the line Okučani – Lipik – Pakrac – Daruvar – Bjelovar – Virovitica – Varaždin, with secondary drives towards Novska – Kutina – Zagreb, and Nova Gradiška – Slavonski Brod. By occupying (western and eastern) Slavonia, the JNA hoped to achieve operational depth and favorable conditions to advance further to Zagreb and the overall completion of the Greater Serbian strategic goals.

In evaluating the results achieved by the JNA in the war against Croatia, the Yugoslav Defense Minister General Kadijević, stated in his book *My View of the Collapse* (*Moje viđenje raspada*, Belgrade, 1993, p. 137) that the bulk of the JNA ground forces – mainly armored and mechanized units in eastern Slavonia – had two main missions. The first was to free Serbian lands in eastern Slavonia, and the second to be the main maneuvering force of the High Command for the push towards Zagreb and Varaždin.

However, already in August and September, the JNA was stuck at Vukovar. Because of that, it deployed exceptionally large forces in the battle. They were divided into two operational groups (north and south), which failed to achieve the planned objectives even by the end of October. With their tenacious defense sustained until 18 November 1991 (or even 20 November in some city districts), the defenders of Vukovar held back substantial hostile forces, including elite JNA units. Their effort contributed to the organization of the Croatian Armed Forces and successful defense of other parts of Croatia. The JNA, exhausted and demoralized by its losses in the battle for Vukovar, was no longer capable of a decisive strike.

The capture of the JNA barracks and weapons depot (the "battle for the barracks" or "battle for weapons") was of particular and strategic significance for the defense of Croatia. Not counting weapons and ammunition (2000 automatic rifles and 125 tons of ammunition) captured by the Croatian defenders in the port of Ploče in the second half of July 1991 (*Zbrojovka* Action), the capture of barracks and seizure of large quantities of weapons started on 14/15 September with the *Zelena Tabla – Male Bare* Action in Ploče. The port of Ploče became (by order of 20 September 1991) the first naval port of the Croatian Navy. The war booty was of crucial importance for organizing the units of the Croatian Armed Forces (vast quantities of light and heavy weapons, and rounds of ammunition, including weapons of the Territorial Defense that the JNA had placed under its control in 1990). Croatian defenders captured the weapons and equipment of almost the entire 32nd Corps, parts of the 10th and 13th JNA Corps in Gorski Kotar (Delnice) and Lika, and parts of the Yugoslav air force and navy (34 vessels were captured in Šibenik). The weapons of the 9th (Knin) Corps remained beyond reach of the Croatian forces because the Corps units had already deployed in their operation areas and taken northern Dalmatia and Lika. The advance of the Corps was stopped at Šibenik (defended in the "September War" between 16 and 23 September 1991), at Pakovo Selo, where a JNA column advancing to Šibenik was destroyed on 20 September, and at Zadar (early October 1991) and the Zadar environs (early January 1992). The successful defense of Šibenik prevented the splitting of Dalmatia, and was the first major victory scored by the Croatian defenders in the Homeland War. In the same period, other important victories were also scored and parts of occupied territory freed, for example in Banovina during the battle for Farkašić (18 October 1991), the Lika battlefront (Gacka, Otočac and Gospić), and other fronts especially in western Slavonia.

A survey of developments on Croatian battlefronts after the Sarajevo ceasefire agreement came into force on 3 January 1992, illustrates that the JNA and Serbian and Montenegrin forces, in spite of their considerable military superiority, failed to achieve their main two objectives. One was defeating the Croatian armed forces and the other establishing control over the entire territory envisioned in Greater Serbian plans. Because of the tenacious and determined defense of the Croatian defenders, the JNA fell short of achieving full success of its plans in eastern Slavonia (it did not capture Osijek and Vinkovci); similarly, it did not capture strategically important towns on other Croatian fronts (Šibenik, Zadar, Gospić, Otočac, Karlovac). It failed to take Dubrovnik, the importance of which could not be measured only in terms of its geographical position. The JNA also scored no strategic success in trying to capture western Slavonia, and pushing on to the border with Hungary, thereby splitting Croatia. In spite of their initial success, hostile forces were stopped after fierce fighting at Lipik, Pakrac, Grubišno Polje, Daruvar, Novska, and Nova Gradiška. Therefore, after the occupation of Vukovar, the JNA did not manage to capture any other town in Croatia (other than Lipik briefly, which fortunately was freed soon on 6 December 1991).

Nevertheless, contrasting the situation on other fronts, the Croatian defenders not only stopped the advance of the JNA Banja Luka Corps, but also managed to free a substantial part of the area by 3 January 1992. The liberation of Bilogora, Papuk and Psunj in western Slavonia, already in the autumn and winter of 1991, in several distinct yet linked operations *(Otkos-10*, the first successful liberation operation of occupied parts of the Republic of Croatia, *Orkan-91* and *Papuk-91)* was extremely important for the defense of Croatia. That is, if the Banja Luka Corps had managed to link up with rebel Serb and chetnik forces on Mount Bilogora, and push on to Virovitica and the border with Hungary, Croatia would have been split, and the defense of eastern Slavonia jeopardized. The foregoing military-police operations, carried out in extremely difficult conditions (the Croatian armed forces were just becoming organized, with scanty equipment, lack of artillery ammunition, adverse freezing weather, etc.), freed more than 2000 km^2 of territory. They prevented the splitting of

Croatia, opened up important communication links, and militarily relieved the towns of Pakrac and Lipik. They also considerably reduced the front line so that units in this area could be deployed to other fronts in Croatia. Substantial quantities of weapons, ammunition and material were captured, and conditions created for the ultimate liberation of the whole of western Slavonia in Operation *Flash* in early May 1995.

The Battle of Vukovar

The first armed conflict in eastern Slavonia took place on 2 May 1991, when Serbian extremists in Borovo Selo near Vukovar ambushed and killed 12 Croatian policemen. A large-scale rebellion ensued in settlements with a predominantly Serbian population in the municipalities of Vukovar and Vinkovci. The JNA used these villages to bring in men, equipment and material, and gradually create a circular launch pad for the attack on Vukovar. The attacks of Serbian terrorists, which had been going on in the Vukovar area since April and especially after May 1991 (the murder of Croatian policemen at Borovo Selo), intensified in July with JNA air and artillery attacks on Vukovar and Borovo Naselje in particular. The overt and continuous attack of the JNA ensued on 25 August after Croatian defender Luka Andrijanić shot down a day earlier two JNA fighter jets that had attacked the positions of Croatian guardsmen in Vukovar (they were the first JNA planes to be shot down in the Homeland War). Considering the strength of the deployed and mechanized JNA units, the occupation of Vukovar seemed to be an easy task. However, Croatian defenders repulsed that attack as well as the following ones, and their organized defense inflicted considerable losses in the aggressor's men and material. A turning point in the battle of Vukovar occurred on 1 October, when the JNA deployed massive force and captured Marinci, thus cutting the only remaining communication with Vukovar (Vinkovci – Nuštar – Marinici – Bogdanovci – the "corn route" – Vukovar). Although it succeeded in totally encircling Bogdanovci and Vukovar, it took the JNA another month and a half to crush the tenacious Croatian defenses. All the attempts of the Croatian armed forces to recapture Marinci and break the blockade of Vukovar, a necessary condition for its defense, proved to be unsuccessful. Still at the organization stage, with weapons and equipment hardly comparable to the strength of the JNA forces deployed at Vukovar, the Croatian forces could not wage successful attack operations. That is why the three-month defense of Vukovar is a phenomenon rarely seen in the history of modern warfare. The organized defense of Vukovar ceased on 18 November 1991, and the defenders of Borovo Naselje (part of Vukovar) surrendered on 20 November.

According to some figures, which include the overall logistics manpower and medical staff of the Vukovar Hospital, about 4020 defenders defended the city (and the village of Bogdanovci) during the Serbian siege. However, the number of armed defenders in the city itself never exceeded the figure of 1800 to 2000 which included policemen, members of the National Guard, HOS (Croatian defense forces) and volunteers from all parts of Croatia, organized in the 204th (124th) HV brigade, which covered a front line exceeding 10 km.

Along with Croats, members of other ethnic groups in Croatia, including Serbs, also defended the town. Of course, the defense was organized with the overall support and contribution of all civil structures in the town – the Vukovar Medical Center, Water Company, Borovo Company, Voluntary Fire Brigade, Public Utility Company, Croatian Power Utility, Municipal Services Company, and Croatian Post. The activities of all these organizations were coordinated by the Crisis Management Committee led by Marin Vidić Bili, the Commissioner of the Croatian Government for Vukovar. They cooperated continuously, day in day out, with the command of the city defenses under Mile Dedaković, nicknamed "Jastreb" *(Hawk)* (after 1 September) and Branko Borković, nicknamed "Mladi Jastreb," *(Young Hawk)* (after 16 October) as well as the police department and its chief, Stipe Pole.

At the same time, the GS HV (General Staff of the Croatian Army) and the HV Operational Zone in Osijek planned actions to break the blockade of the town, and some units, artillery in particular, were deployed in its surroundings in order to provide military assistance to Vukovar. On 16 October, Operational HV

Groups from Vinkovci, Vukovar and Županja were established for the same purpose. Under the assessment of its commander Mile Dedaković, the city of Vukovar had about 6800 soldiers, 15 tanks, 11 armored personnel carriers, 52 20-100 mm guns, 32 guns above 100 mm caliber, one multiple rocket launcher, and 68 mortars at its disposal during the final battle for the city. As it turned out, these forces could not defend the town from an attack by the numerically greater and better-armed aggressor.

According to incomplete data, the Serbian aggressor deployed over 1000 armored combat vehicles, aircraft and naval vessels, several hundred artillery pieces, and rocket launchers in the battle of Vukovar, which indiscriminately fired hundreds of thousands of shells and other projectiles on the city.

According to a JNA source *(Survey of the Manpower and Equipment of the First Military District Units Deployed in Action in Eastern Slavonia;* 16 November 1991; First Military District Command; strictly conf. No. 1614-162), in mid-November 1991, the strength of the JNA (First Military District) in Eastern Slavonia was the following: 37,613 troops, 676 tanks, 505 armored personnel carriers, 428 support artillery units, 158 anti-armor artillery, 380 anti-aircraft artillery; while the "military personnel" in the Serbian territorial defense units numbered 9582.

In the most critical moments during the defense of Vukovar, logistic assistance, especially drugs and medical supplies for the hospital, were delivered on several occasions by air with smaller Cessna-172 and UTVA-75 aircraft, and larger, An-2 agricultural biplanes. They were piloted by the incredibly brave Croatian pilots of the Independent Air Force Platoon, established in early October 1991 in the Osijek Operational Zone. Of course, that was merely a drop in the ocean in terms of the requirements of the defenders and hospital staff, but the night flights of the four-man crews of the Croatian planes morally meant so much more than the help itself. Their courage, ingenuity, capacity to improvise, flying skills and determination, in spite of fierce hostile AA fire to help the Vukovar defenders with obsolete, slow and definitely unfit aircraft, deserves the same admiration as the superhuman efforts of the defenders themselves, hospital staff, firemen, and other services that endeavored to sustain at least minimal living conditions in the surrounded and devastated city.

According to records of the Ministry of Health, on 19 November 1991 there were about 14,000 civilians in Vukovar: about 10,000 in Vukovar itself, 4000 in Borovo Naselje and 100 in the village of Lužac. The number of Croatian defenders was about 900: 450 in Vukovar and 450 in Borovo Naselje. On the day Vukovar was occupied there were 420 wounded and sick people in the Vukovar Hospital, and about 250 wounded people in the Borovo Commerce warehouse/in-patient hospital.

According to records of the Administration for Detained and Missing Persons of the Ministry of the Family, Veterans' Affairs and Inter-Generational Solidarity of the Republic of Croatia from November 2007, during the Serbian siege of Vukovar in 1991 at least 1739 persons were killed, mainly civilians, and 2500 wounded (records of the Croatian Medical HQ). The civilians killed in the Vukovar-Srijem County included at least 51 children (of which 25 in Vukovar). About 22,000 Vukovar citizens were displaced, and more than 4000 persons from the Croatian Danubian area were forcibly taken away to Yugoslavia (Serbia), from where they were deported to the then free parts of the Republic of Croatia. At least 2796 persons were taken prisoner in Vukovar in 1991, and tortured and maltreated in camps and prisons in Serbia and Yugoslavia: the youngest detainee was 15, and the oldest 81 years old.

Serbian forces committed the first major massacre in Vukovar in mid-September after capturing part of the Sajmište District, and immediately set up a concentration camp for Croats and non-Serbs in the warehouses of the Velepromet Company, which functioned until March 1992.

On 20 November 1991, at least 266 persons (wounded civilians, defenders, and medical staff) were taken from the Vukovar Hospital and executed at a number of locations. Of these, 200 persons, including 20 members of the hospital staff, were executed at the Ovčara farm and dumped into a trench. Two hundred bodies of the executed persons between the ages of 16 and 72 were exhumed from the mass grave in September and October 1996.

Along with Ovčara, which has become a symbol of martyrdom for the freedom and independence of the Republic of Croatia, many other execution sites of Croatian defenders and civilians have been discovered in the greater Vukovar area., E.g., Antin, Berak, Bogdanovci, Borovo Selo, Bršadin, Ćelije, Čakovci, Dalj, Daljski Atar – Globovac, Ilok, Lovas, Marinci, Mikluševci, Mohovo. Negoslavci, Novi Jankovci, Petrovci, Slakovci, Stari Jankovci, Svinjarevci, Sotin, Tordinci, Tovarnik, Vukovar – Novo Groblje, Nova Ulica, Velepromet warehouse, etc. In the Vukovar-Srijem County, the Administration for Detained and Missing Persons discovered 52 mass graves and hundreds of individual graves where JNA troops and Serbian units buried their victims. By December 2009, the mortal remains of 2036 victims were exhumed, of which the remains of 1761 Croatian defenders and civilians were identified. Furthermore, according to records of the Administration for Detained and Missing Persons of January 2009, of 1030 persons still reported missing in the aggression against Croatia in 1991/1992, 456 disappeared in the Vukovar-Srijem County, 340 of which were forcibly taken from the Municipality of Vukovar (including Sotin, Grabovo and Lipovača).

Vukovar was occupied, but the persistent and tenacious defense waged over several months by its defenders stopped the initial momentum and slowed down the offensive operations of the enemy. By sacrificing their own lives, they bought precious time for mobilization in other parts of Croatia, formation of new units, and acquisition of weapons and military equipment, as well as intensifying diplomatic efforts of the Croatian leadership focused on international recognition. Moreover, by tying down the main body of the hostile forces, which were considerably routed and demoralized in the battle of Vukovar, the defense of Vukovar prevented the link-up of JNA forces in eastern and western Slavonia, which was strategically important for the JNA plans to conquer Croatia. At the same time, the murdering of civilians and scale of Vukovar's destruction exposed the true picture of Serbian aggression to the international public, and the defenders of Vukovar showed that one can be successful in fighting against a vastly superior aggressor. In the process, they contributed to the understanding of the developments in Croatia and accelerated the international recognition of Croatia, and their patriotism and courage won them an honorable place in Croatian history.

With their outstanding role in preventing hostile forces from occupying all of eastern Slavonia, and thereby achieving the required operational depth and favorable conditions for further advancement towards Zagreb and the attainment of its ultimate goal – the creation of the so-called Greater Serbia – the defense of Vukovar was an important strategic development for the overall defense of Croatia. This is why it can be claimed that the Vukovar defenders opened the door for the establishment of a free and independent Croatia, and for Croatian victory in the Homeland War.

DUBROVNIK, ONCE A FORTRESS OF TREASURE AND BEAUTY, NOW A FORTRESS OF DESTRUCTION, FEAR AND DEATH – IN 1991

From Poster No. 9 from the HELP! STOP WAR IN CROATIA series

Večernji List photographic records

Text by: Varina Jurica Turk and Mišo Đuraš

The JNA (Užice and Titograd Corps, Boka Naval Sector, and territorial defense forces from Montenegro and eastern Herzegovina) attacked Dubrovnik on 1 October 1991 from Popovo Polje and Montenegro. On 5 October, tanks forced their way into Slano. Cavtat was captured on 15 October, and Župa Dubrovačka on 24 October, whereby the enemy emerged to the very threshold of Dubrovnik. The aggressor demanded the disarmament and surrender of the small number of defenders, and called on the population to abandon the city. When the attack on the completely surrounded city began (at the time there were 60,000 inhabitants and refugees in the town), hostile forces cut off the water and power supply, and thwarted the delivery of food and drugs through a naval blockade. In addition to all this, they shelled the city and its historical center, which has been protected by the UNESCO Charter since 1979. All the monuments within the town walls suffered damage to a varying degree (9 palaces burned to the ground, over 70% of the roofs were moderately or severely damaged, several dozen shells hit the main street, Stradun, and the monastery of the Franciscan Brothers Minor, the Cathedral and other churches were also hit). Dubrovnik suffered particularly fierce attacks between 9 and 13 November and 6 December 1991, when it sustained the greatest damage in its history since the 1667 earthquake. More than one thousand shells hit the city and its surroundings between dawn and the evening hours. Nineteen Croatian defenders and civilians were killed, and over sixty wounded. As the city was successfully defended on 6 December 1991, the aggressor suffered a decisive military and political defeat, and the further advance of hostile forces was halted.

Casualties in the Serbian-Montenegrin aggression against Dubrovnik included 184 Dubrovnik defenders, over 250 Croatian defenders from other parts of the Republic of Croatia, and 92 civilians (including 15 children). In December 1991, 33,000 people were displaced from Dubrovnik who fled the area as refugees. About 13,900 housing units (over 50% of the total stock) were damaged, 2071 apartments or homes burnt down or were totally destroyed, and more than 80% of the town's hotel facilities were destroyed. In its conquering and plundering raids, the aggressor troops devastated and plundered the occupied area: the equipment at Dubrovnik's Ćilipi Airport was dismantled and carted off to Montenegro and Serbia, along with electrical substations, telephone exchanges, public transit buses, printing works machines, complete hotel laundries, etc.

GOVERNMENT OF THE REPUBLIC OF SERBIA
PRESIDENT
Belgrade, 5 October 1991

TO: THE GOVERNMENT OF THE REPUBLIC OF CROATIA
Zagreb

At its meeting on 4 October 1991, the Government of the Republic of Serbia has been briefed on the dangers threatening the civil population and city of Dubrovnik, which is part of the history of the Serbian and Croatian peoples, and a magnificent monument of global cultural heritage.
Your decision to deploy your paramilitary units, black legions and numerous foreign mercenaries to a city of inestimable historical and cultural value, and to launch armed attacks from that area on settlements in Herzegovina and Boka Kotorska, is an extremely uncivilized, inhuman and disgraceful act.
We hope you have also become aware of this and that you will take the necessary efforts in order to prevent your armed formations from destroying Dubrovnik as they have done with many other towns.
In sending you this appeal to prevent the destruction of Dubrovnik, the Government of the Republic of Serbia expresses its firm conviction that all members of the JNA and TO units will make a maximum effort to preserve this historic town.

President
Dragutin Zelenović

(Copy of letter in: Hrvoje Kačić, *In the Service of the Homeland – Croatia Rediviva;* U službi domovine – Croatia rediviva, Zagreb, 2006, 454)

The letter from the Government of the Republic of Serbia sent to the Government of the Republic of Croatia on 5 October 1991 during the vicious attacks of the JNA and Serbian-Montenegrin forces on Dubrovnik and Croatia epitomizes the cynicism and action of Serbian policies in the 1990s. They did not shrink from launching "information" into the world that was completely different from what was actually taking place. In particular, the number of Serbian victims was exaggerated to extreme proportions. Reports mentioned thousands of Serbs killed in Croatia, e.g., "6000 Serbs killed in the woods around Pakrac, and 2000 to 5000 Serbs killed in Pakrac during Operation *Flash";* or "3000 civilians and 10,000 poorly armed Serbian troops killed during the Croatian aggression against Western Slavonia." Or "about 4000 elderly people, women and children killed only in the first four days of Operation *Storm*, the fate of 12,000 Serbs still unknown" (Jelena Guskova, *History of the Yugoslav Crisis 1990-2000;* Istorija jugoslovenske krize 1990.-2000., Vol. II, Belgrade, 2003, 236-238, 245). Fabricated evidence includes figures where "up to 1994, 87 mass graves with bodies of 14,000 Serbs shot with their families," and "1250,000 Serbs killed by Croatian fascists during World War II." Or that there were "30% of Serbs in Croatia in 1990, as opposed to the 11 or 12% as claimed by the Croatian government," and other lies with which the Serbian diplomacy fed the world (Slobodan Jarčević, *Republic of Serbian Krajina – State Records;* Republika Srpska Krajina – državna dokumenta; Belgrade, 2005, 420, 435, 440). In sending this letter, the Government of the Republic of Serbia tried to conceal from the domestic and international public its involvement in the destruction of Croatian towns and convince the world that the JNA, which by the summer of 1991 had become the Serbian Army, was not destroying Dubrovnik. In keeping with the subject of the letter, Serbian media reports claimed that "the smoke rising above Dubrovnik was not due to shelling but from car tires set on fire by the ustashe Croats," and that the destruction of the town and suffering of civilians were "the consequence of clashes between Croatian fighters and foreign mercenaries." Such lies only additionally confirm the responsibility of Serbia for the aggression against Croatia.

At the same time, it was precisely the attack on Dubrovnik by JNA and Serbian-Montenegrin "reservists" that fully revealed the true reason for the Serbian aggression against Croatia. It confirmed that Croatian towns were not attacked in order to "break the blockade of the JNA barracks," as the JNA leadership claimed, but in order to conquer territory, because there were no JNA barracks in Dubrovnik or in its immediate surroundings. In spite of everything, in 1991, Croatian defenders succeeded in defending Dubrovnik. With the help of forces transferred from other parts of Croatia, they managed to lift the siege by late October 1992 and free almost the entire state territory in the southernmost part of the Republic of Croatia.

The Course of the Military-Police Operation Flash

Operation *Flash* was planned as a continuation of the plan to liberate western Slavonia in late 1991 and early 1992. Detailed planning began in early December 1994 after it had become clear that the leadership of the rebel Serbs would not agree to a peaceful reintegration in the constitutional and legal system of the Republic of Croatia. According to the original idea, the operation was to be carried out as an ultimate surprise within two or three days, with several strong and quick strikes against vital targets, and concurrent thrusts from several directions in order to break up and rout hostile forces. The mission of the operation included the liberation of the remaining part of western Slavonia and opening up of the Zagreb – Lipovac highway, pushing to the Sava River (internationally recognized border of the Republic of Croatia), and crushing potential remaining hostile units. The plan of the operation also involved the infiltration of stronger police units in the enemy rear in order to cut off hostile units north of the Novska – Nova Gradiška road and thereby create conditions for a breakthrough towards Novska – Okučani. The signal for the start of the operation was received at 05:21 hours on 1 May 1995, when 7200 Croatian army troops and policemen attacked with no artillery support in order to surprise the enemy and avoid civilian casualties.

On the first day of the operation (May 1), HV (Croatian Army) units linked up with special police units (SJP) in the village of Benkovac (south of the village of Bijele Stijene). The occupied part of Slavonia was thereby cut in half. The units of the 18th (Western Slavonian) SVK Corps were split in two. Armored and mechanized HV units advanced from Novska to the village of Vrbovljani and established control over that part of the highway, and the town of Okučani was semi-encircled. At the time, HV units cut off and established control over the Stara Gradiška – Okučani road. In the morning hours of the same day, Jasenovac was also liberated, which prevented the enemy from putting up a pontoon bridge and bringing in reinforcements from occupied parts of Kordun, Banovina, and Bosnia and Herzegovina.

On the second day (2 May), the concerted strike of HV and special police units was focused on hostile units at Okučani, which were overpowered by 13:20 hours. That marked the end of the local units of the 18th SVK Corps. By the end of the day, HV units advanced to the Sava River and established control over the state border. The encircled parts of the 18th SVK Corps were forced to surrender north of Trnakovac. The mission was thus accomplished, but the units were still engaged in clearing, blockading and destroying any residual enemy forces in the area.

On the third day (3 May), HV units set up defense positions all along the Sava River, with special focus on the villages of Mačkovac and Davor, in order to prevent possible intervention from Bosnia and Herzegovina across the river. HV and special police units continued their clearing and mopping up missions in order to detect possible remaining hostile forces and block the remaining 18th Corps troops in the area of Šumetlica – Brusnik – Omanovac.

On the fourth day of the operation (4 May), a reinforced company of the 81st Guards Battalion with support units was flown by helicopters for an assault at the village of Bjelajci. Because the remaining units of the 18th SVK Corps refused to surrender, Croatian artillery engaged with concentrated fire targets at Šumetlica, Brusnik, Kraguj, Japaga, Čaglić and Omanovac. An infantry attack followed. Between 17:00 and 19:00 hours, the troops of the 18th SVK Corps (about 1500 men) surrendered unconditionally. Their surrender marked the defeat of the Greater Serbian plans and aggression in western Slavonia. Early on 5 May at 06:00 hours, special police units established full control of the fortifications at Omanovac.

Chronology of Important Developments on the Eve of Operation Storm

3 November 1994: In Operation *Cincar* (1-4 November) Croatian units, acting in concert with the Army of Bosnia and Herzegovina (ABH), liberated the town of Kupres. The liberation of Kupres was of extraordinary strategic and psychological importance, and a precondition for advancing on to Glamoč and Bosansko Grahovo.

29 November – 24 December 1994: Offensive Operation *Zima '94* (Winter)

Mission of the Croatian units:

- weaken the Serbian offensive on Bihać
- ensure a favorable strategic space for the liberation of the occupied parts of Croatia and Bosnia and Herzegovina

The Croatian Army (HV) and the Croatian Defense Council (HVO) established control over the greater part of Livanjsko Polje and liberated an area 10 km wide by 20 km deep (200 km^2). However, hostile artillery on mounts Dinara and Staretina could still engage targets in Livanjsko Polje and jeopardize the liberated territory by attacking its flanks.

December 1994: More intensive Serbian attacks on western Bosnia and Bihać, defended by the 5th ABH Corps and the 101st HVO Battalion.

Early 1995: The international community (USA, Russian Federation, European Union and International UN Conference on the Former Yugoslavia in Geneva) proposed the Z-4 Plan for the political settlement of the crisis in Croatia. The Plan highlighted the sovereignty and integrity of the Republic of Croatia, but also provided for very broad autonomy of the Serbs in UNPA Sectors North and South (own legislation and government, special police, currency, coat of arms, flag and other emblems, judiciary, tax collection, etc.). The Croatian side had serious objections to the Plan, and the Serbs in Knin did not even want to consider it. At the time, about 20% of Croatian land territory was under occupation.

1 April 1995: By decision of the UN Security Council (Resolution No. 981), the UNPROFOR (United Nations Protection Forces) in Croatia became UNCRO (United Nations Confidence Restoration Operation in Croatia), and overtook the obligation of supervising the internationally recognized borders of the Republic of Croatia.

7 April 1995: Offensive action *Skok 1* (Leap)

Mission:
- occupy more favorable positions on Mount Dinara in the Crvene Grede and Zeleno Brdo areas
- get closer to the villages of Uništa and Cetina
- prevent hostile counterattacks from the village of Uništa

Croatian units captured an area 15 km deep by 5 km deep (75 km^2) on Mount Dinara (above Knin), and put the Knin hinterland under control ("firing control"), especially the hostile strongholds in the villages of Uništa and Cetina. The enemy broke the "Zagreb Agreement" with their artillery fire from the village of Cetina (occupied territory of the Republic of Croatia), and aimed at forcibly regaining lost positions by counterattacks, which were met with failure. After this action, the Serbs reinforced their defenses around Bosansko Grahovo.

Early May 1995: Military-police Operation *Bljesak* (Flash)

4-11 June 1995: Offensive Action *Skok 2* (Leap)

Mission:

- free the eastern and western side of Livanjsko Polje
- move towards Bosansko Grahovo and create conditions for engaging military targets in the area by artillery
- stabilize the battlefront from Mount Dinara to Kupres

Croatian units pressed back hostile forces towards Bosansko Grahovo and Glamoč, overpowered a major Serbian stronghold at Crni Lug (4 June) and surrounding villages, including Mali Šator (7 June) and Veliki Šator (11 June). This opened up the entire Livanjsko Polje as a maneuvering space for Croatian units, which linked up from Mount Dinara, Mount Šator and Staretina all the way to Kupreška Vrata. Glamoč was semi-encircled (from the south, west and north), and the pressure of the Serbian units on Bihać abated. Croatian artillery gained control over the important communication line Glamoč – Bosansko Grahovo in Bosnia and Herzegovina, and Cetinska Dolina and Vrličko Polje in Croatia. The liberated area was 30 km wide and 14-15 km deep (about 420-450 km^2). After this action, the international community sought to deploy a rapid action force in the area of Mount Dinara, but the Croatian leadership did not go along with the idea.

11 July 1995: Serbian troops captured Srebrenica and then Žepa (25 July), UN "safe havens," killing thousands of Muslims at Srebrenica (the number of around 8000 is being reported) and banishing the rest.

19 July 1995: Serbian units, including rebel Serb units from Croatia, launched a strong offensive on the "protected" Bihać, (by UN resolution). The capture of Bihać would have been an important strategic success for the Serbian side. Moreover, it would have been another major humanitarian disaster because there were many refugees in the town along with the local population.

21 July: The Command of the 5th ABH Corps in Bihać informed the HV General Staff that "the Corps had sustained large losses of

'manpower and territory' .... The supply of ammunition and material had dropped below the critical level and the Corps could not hold out against the aggressor for a longer period.... At such a rate of Serbian attack, the Corps could only put up an organized defense for the next two or three days."

The dramatic conditions in Bihać are also described in a letter which Adnan Alagić, mayor of Bihać, sent to Croatian President Franjo Tuđman: *Because of intense shelling, the population in the outlying areas is fleeing and moving towards the town of Bihać. Our position is getting more complex every hour, because the humanitarian situation has already been disastrous for several days. You probably know that we have already had the first deaths from starvation. The hope that the situation would improve at least a little after the harvesting of the wheat in the areas around the town is now gone. The aggressor is attacking these very areas with incendiary shells. Conditions are especially grave at the Bihać Hospital, which is short of drugs, medical supplies, and due to a food shortage, the patients are receiving only one meal a day. The fate of the 180,000 inhabitants of the Una-Sana Canton is uncertain. We can only promise to fight regardless of the cost and indecision of the international community. Our only hope are our brave fighters and the friendly Croatian people because the fate our enemy has in store for us is the same. Therefore, we beg you to do all you can to save this heroic town and its long-suffering population."*

22 July 1995: "Split Declaration"

The President of the Republic of Croatia (Franjo Tuđman), President of the Presidency of Bosnia and Herzegovina (Alija Izetbegović), President of the Federation of BH (Krešimir Zubak), and Prime Minister of BH (Haris Silajdžić) signed the Declaration on the Renewal of the Washington Agreement, Joint Defense from Serbian Aggression and Realization of a Political Solution with the Aid of the International Community.

23 July 1995: The Command of the 5th ABH Corps informed the HV General Staff that conditions had worsened and the situation was getting out of control. It added that the Bihać area could be cut in half by the evening, and the "5th Corps routed."

24 July 1995: The Command of the 5th Corps, General Staff of the Bihać HVO, and Municipal HDZ Committee in Bihać appealed to the political and military bodies in Zagreb for help. "Please pay the utmost seriousness to the situation and take immediate and radical steps in order to save the population and territory of the Una-Sana Canton."

25-30 July 1995: Operation *Ljeto '95* (Summer)

Mission:
- free Bosansko Grahovo and Glamoč
- cut the Knin – Drvar communication line
- increase security in Livno and Kupres
- halt the Serbian offensive on Bihać
- create preconditions for taking Knin and freeing the remaining occupied parts of Croatia

With the liberation of Bosansko Grahovo on 28 July, and the Derala Pass and Glamoč on 29 July, Croatian forces semi-encircled the rebel Serbs in northern Dalmatia and created preconditions for advancing to Banja Luka. The communication of Serbian units was limited along the Knin – Otrić – Srb and Obrovac – Gračac routes. Croatian units liberated about 1600 km^2 of territory in Bosnia and Herzegovina.

3 August 1995: Negotiations between Croatian authorities and rebel Serbs at Genthod near Geneva ran into a deadlock; the leadership of the rebel Serbs turned down the proposals of the Croatian side.

In the evening hours of the same day, Serbian artillery attacked the greater Dubrovnik area: three civilians were killed, and three wounded.

Structure and Numerical Strength of the Armed Forces of the SFRY (JNA + TO) in peacetime and wartime conditions, on the eve of the war in SFRY (from Slobodan Praljak, *Aggression of BH on the Republic of Croatia*; Agresija BiH na RH; 6)

JNA Manpower: peacetime complement 180,000 (15%); wartime complement + 1,200,000 (85%)

Territorial defense (TO): peacetime manpower 1000 (2%, only command structures); wartime manpower + about 1,200,000 (98%): Slovenian TO 110,000; Croatian TO 230,000; BH TO 270,000; Montenegrin TO 40,000; Macedonian TO 60,000; Serbian TO 300,000; Vojvodina TO 60,000; Kosovo 130,000. (Only on paper, because it was disarmed after the Albanian demonstrations in spring 1981, and weapons removed to Serbia; Kosovo Serbs and Montenegrins – about 12% of the region's population – kept their weapons or were later armed through parallel, extra-institutional channels).

Armed Forces of the SFRY, total war complement (with 8% strain on population) 2,400,000, of which 500,000 in industry and logistics, the remainder in combat units.

Land Forces

Composition: 17 corps + 1st Guards Brigade (Belgrade), and the 63rd Paratroop Brigade (Niš) as independent General Staff units; heavy weapons: 2100 tanks, 1000 APCs, 8000 artillery, and 1300 anti-armor rocket systems.

Yugoslav Navy

1 torpedo boat brigade (14), 1 rocket boat and rocket gunboat brigade (16), 1 patrol boat brigade (4), 1 minesweeper battalion (9), 1 submarine brigade (11), 1 marine commando detachment, and 3 marine infantry brigades.

Air Force and Air Defense

The 5th Air Force and Air Defense Corps (Zagreb), 1st Air Force and Air Defense Corps (Belgrade), 3rd Air Force and Air Defense Corps (Skopje).

512 combat aircraft, 104 transport aircraft, 152 helicopters, and 118 other aircraft; 5100 AA guns and 2800 AA missiles.

According to records of the Headquarters of the RSK Territorial Defense from June 1992, the JNA left the following weapons in the RSK: 262 tanks, 56 combat vehicles, 1360 artillery pieces of various caliber, 2573 motor vehicles and about 65,000 infantry weapons. In mid-1994, the SVK had 300 tanks, 295 combat armored vehicles, 360 artillery units of 100 mm caliber (and higher). (Davor Marijan, *Storm*, 38). By Operation *Storm,* the number apparently increased.

The JNA left the Serbs in Bosnia and Herzegovina about 300 tanks, 231 large caliber artillery units, 24 combat-training planes, 20 helicopters, 4 air defense missile battalions, and large quantities of infantry weapons and ammunition.

According to official records of the Federal Republic of Yugoslavia of June 1996, the Yugoslav Army had 230 planes (16 MIG-29s, 98 MIG-21s, and 67 Supergalebs), 56 combat helicopters, 1512 tanks (239 M-84s, 64 T-72s, 783 T-55s and 426 T-34s), 4919 105 to 155 mm artillery pieces, 99 VLR Plamens, 65 VLR Oganjs, 1396 120 mm mortars and 1792 82 mm mortars. (Davor Marijan, *The Collapse of Tito's Army*, 400)

The Course of the Military-Police Operation Storm

Mission:

- free occupied Croatian territory
- return of refugees
- help the Army of Bosnia and Herzegovina (ABH) to break the blockade of Bihać and prevent a humanitarian disaster
- advance to the internationally recognized borders of the Republic of Croatia

Basic strategic plan:

- break through hostile defenses by concurrent action from several directions (31) and free the occupied areas of the Republic of Croatia
- switch to offensive action in the central part of Croatia and free the towns of Knin, Gračac, Korenica, Slunj, Glina, Petrinja, Hrvatska Kostajnica and Hrvatska Dubica
- organize a determined defense in the eastern and southern parts of the country the attack will be spearheaded by guards brigades
- reserve units and special units of the Ministry of the Interior of the Republic of Croatia (MUP HR) will be used to exploit success and sustain the rate of combat action

4 August (Friday) 1995:

The military-police Operation *Storm* commenced at 05:00 hours.

At the start of the Operation, the Croatian Air Force knocked out the enemy radio-relay node Ćelavac and communication centers on mounts Petrova Gora and Zrinska Gora. On the same day, Croatian forces freed Sveti Rok, Čista Mala, Čista Velika, Uništa, Gornji Baljci, Davar, Novoselija, Sibić, Gora, Strašnik, Graberje, Višnjica, Predore, Uštica, Tanac, the Mali Alan Pass and the Dulibe – Tulove Grede area on Mount Velebit.

In the morning hours of the same day, Serbian forces shelled Dubrovnik, Biograd na Moru, Gospić, Otočac, Sisak and Sunja (Karlovac, Nuštar and other Croatian towns were targeted next); the attacks resulted in loss of civilian life and destruction of civilian facilities.

5 August (Saturday) 1995:

Croatian forces freed Knin (the "Royal Croatian Town") and its surroundings, Ljubovo, Žitnić, Lovinac, Gračac, Novi Lički Osik, Ostrovica, Primišlje, Plaški, Dubica, Vrlika, Kijevo, Drniš and its surroundings, Obrovac, Benkovac, Zemunik Gornji, Biljane Gornje, Biljane Donje, Škabrnja, Nadin, Smilčić, Karin, Saborsko, Lička Jesenica, Vaganac, Ličko Petrovo Selo, Rakovica, Drežnik Grad, Željava, Medak, Petrinić Polje, Trnavec, Lički Ribnik, Gornji Poloj, Glinsko Novo Selo, Župić, Župić brdo, Šanja, Vilusi, Pecki, Luščani, Križ, Cepeliš, Strmen, etc.

6 August (Sunday) 1995

Freed towns and villages: Petrinja, Kistanje, Muškovac, Kaštel Žegarski, Vrhovine, Kostajnica, Udbina, Krbava, Korenica, Bunić, Slunj, Broćanac, Plitvice, Glina, Otrić, Bruvno, Malovan, Rudopolje, Stražbenica, Blinja, Umetić, Slabinje, Čaire, Utolica, Rausovac, Gornja i Donja Bačuga, Jabukovac, Banski Grabovac, Šaš, Veliki Šušnjar, Majski Trtnik, Barlete, Vrebac, Mogorić, Ploča, etc. On the same day, at Tržačka Raštela on the Korana River right along the border, Croatian Army units (Major General Marijan Mareković) linked up with the 5th Corps of the Army of Bosnia and Herzegovina (general Atif Dudaković).

7 August (Monday) 1995:

Freed towns and villages: Gornji Lapac and Donji Lapac, Mazin, Dobroselo, Boričevac, Kulen Vakuf, Cetingrad, Veljun, Krnjak, Vojnić, Gornje Mekušje, Kamensko, Tušilović, Turanj, Šanac, Jelaši etc. In a statement, Croatian Defense Minister Gojko Šušak confirmed that the operation was over by 18:00 hours of the same day, and that the victory of the Croatian forces was undisputable. Of course, some resistance pockets still had to be dealt with.

8 August (Tuesday) 1995:

The surrender of Colonel Čedomir Bulat, commander of the 21st SVK Corps in Topusko at 14:00 hours marked the end of the operational part of *Storm* and the cessation of hostilities in the territory of the Republic of Croatia, although certain military actions were still underway, e.g., crushing the remaining hostile units and mopping up. Thus, Croatian forces entered Srb on 8 August, and Vrginmost and Dvor na Uni on 9 August. Having defeated the enemy, Croatian units reached the internationally recognized border between Croatia and Bosnia and Herzegovina.

	Serbian Forces	Croatian Army	Force Ratio
Tanks	385-450	350	1.1:1
APCs	195-210	150	1.35:1
Aircraft	20-25	7	3.18:1
Helicopters	10-13	13	1:1
Motor vehicles	1100-1500	2500	1:1.9
Artillery	515-570	200	2.5:1
AA guns	295-340	200	1.55:1
Troops, NCOs, officers, policemen	37,000-50,000	127,000-200,000	1:2.5 – 1:5.4

During *Storm* the Serbian Army of Krajina (SVK) could get no overt help from Bosnia and Herzegovina or Serbia because the situation on the Bosnian fronts could not afford the Army of Republika Srpska (VRS) any military help, and an overhasty military intervention in Croatia was not acceptable to the Serbian leadership in Belgrade for political and military reasons. Moreover, because of the rate of advance of Croatian forces, even the involvement of the Yugoslav Army would not have saved the SVK from defeat. Nevertheless, Yugoslavia promised to provide the Krajina leadership with military help and put diplomatic pressure on Croatia. After an emergency session of the Yugoslav Supreme Defense Council, held at the command post at Dobanovci, on 4 August 1995 at 17:00 hours, a telegram of encouragement was sent to SVK Commander General Mrkšić, advising him to sustain stiff resistance for at least two days, after which Yugoslavia would be able to help him with all available means. (M. Bulatović, *Pravila ćutanja: istiniti politički triler s poznatim završetkom* [Silence Rules: A Genuine Political Thriller with a Known Ending]; Belgrade, 2004, 181-182)

It has been reported that on the first day of *Storm,* Milošević also phoned Martić and urged him that Krajina hold out for five to six days in order to give Belgrade room for action (Milisav Sekulić, *Knin je pao u Begradu* [Knin Fell in Belgrade], Bad Vilbel, 2001, 178). After *Storm,* Goran Hadžić, former Prime Minister of the Republic of Serbian Krajina, also supported this in a statement. Along with expressing his belief in the survival of the RSK in Slavonia and Srijem, and the message that he would never accept the possibility that Krajina was no more, he answered a question on the possible attack by the Croatian Army. *I am certain that Serbia will help this part of Krajina and I have positive indicators of that, although they cannot be divulged to the media at this point. Serbia would certainly have helped that part of Krajina if they had only put up some resistance.* (*Srbija će pomoći* [Serbia Will Help], Nin, 2329, 18 Aug. 1995, 17-19). Milan Milanović, then Assistant Defense Minister of the RSK, also referred to the degree of organization and readiness of the remaining RSK to defend Krajina, noting that Yugoslav help could be anticipated in a greater emergency and that no plan or action was being considered without agreement from

Belgrade. (*Svi se boje Srbije* [Everybody is Afraid of Serbia], *Intervju*, 22 Sept. 1995, 6-7).

After *Storm,* Croatia was determined to launch a new military operation and ready to free the last square inch of its occupied state territory in the east. However, in spite of the readiness of Croatian soldiers and exceptional superiority of the Croatian armed forces over the armed forces of the rebel Serbs, and despite great pressure from the Croatian public (especially of displaced persons) to restore the occupied part of eastern Slavonia through military means, the President of the Republic of Croatia Franjo Tuđman again negotiated with the rebel Serbs and sought a way for a peaceful settlement of the remaining occupied territory. The negotiations resulted in the Basic Agreement on the Peaceful Reintegration of Eastern Slavonia, Baranja and Western Srijem in the Constitutional System of the Republic of Croatia, which the representatives of the rebel Serbs signed in Erdut on 12 November 1995 (The Erdut Agreement).

Because of a number of concessions to the rebel Serbs in a situation when Croatia was militarily capable of freeing the remaining occupied part in eastern Croatia, the Erdut Agreement provoked great discontent among the Croats banished from the area in 1991, but it confirmed the consistency of Croatian policies in its endeavors to resolve the issue of its occupied areas by peaceful means in spite of painful compromises. In order to implement the decisions of the Erdut Agreement, the UN Security Council (Resolution No. 1037 of 15 January 1996) established a special UN Transitional Authority in Eastern Slavonia (UNTAES). On that occasion, the Security Council once again reaffirmed its commitment to the independence, sovereignty and territorial integrity of the Republic of Croatia, and emphasized that "eastern Slavonia, Baranja and western Srijem (Sector East) were integral parts of the Republic of Croatia".

The UNTAES mandate expired on 15 January 1998, when the region was finally reintegrated in the constitutional and legal system of the Republic of Croatia.

"Let's Save Lives"

The great majority of Croatian soldiers and policemen respected strict orders regarding the protection of civilians and civilian buildings – especially religious (Orthodox). Unfortunately, certain individuals did not, and there were reported cases of murdered Serbian civilians and the destruction of their property, which was condemned by the Croatian leadership, just as it condemned the shelling of Croatian towns by Serbian artillery during *Storm*, causing new destruction and loss of human life. During the Operation, the media continuously repeated the call of the President of the Republic of Croatia, Franjo Tuđman, to Croatian citizens of Serbian nationality, urging them to remain in Croatia as the Constitution and Constitutional Law on Minorities guaranteed all their civil rights. However, after the leadership of the rebel Serbs passed a decision on evacuation on 4 August 1995, most of the Serbs in the self-proclaimed Krajina left Croatia. UN representatives and US ambassador to Croatia, Peter Galbraith, confirmed that Serbian civilians largely left the area before the arrival of the Croatian forces; their number is estimated at about 90,000 (Croatian sources), or 150,000 (UN sources) or even 200,000-300,000 (Serbian sources).

In mid-September 1995, the population of Croatian areas freed in Operations *Flash* and *Storm* (former Sectors West, North and South) amounted to 38,594: of which 14,613 persons were present at the time of liberation, 10,772 displaced persons returned, and 13,209 arrived after they were banished from Bosnia and Herzegovina and Serbia (mainly Vojvodina). About 10,500 mainly elderly persons of Serbian nationality (about 70%), remained in the former Sectors North and South (freed in *Storm*), scattered in about 600 settlements, with no security, family or health protection, often with no electricity, water or heating. Immediately after the end of *Storm,* Croatian authorities began providing humanitarian assistance and took a number of steps to protect the population in the areas under consideration. By 18 August, 1203 persons (in 826 households) in the freed areas received financial assistance. It was provided on three occasions, and by December 1995 it was received by 7456 households with a total of 13,185 persons. In December 1995, they were all included in the regular welfare system. All the inhabitants who had remained in the free areas and required medical assistance became entitled to healthcare irrespectively of whether or not they were covered by social insurance. In order to protect old and infirm persons who had remained in their homes in the freed areas, welfare centers were immediately founded in Knin, Drniš, Benkovac, Glina and Petrinja. Because of the situation on the field, new welfare centers were established in Hrvatska Kostajnica, Slunj and Topusko, with outlying facilities in Vojnić, Gvozd (Vrginmost), Dvor, Korenica, Obrovac, Gračac and Donji Lapac. Serbian civilians on their way to Serbia were provided assistance in centers at Glina, Sisak, Lipovljani, Lužani and Lipovac. The Croats who were at the same time banished from Serbia (Vojvodina) and Bosnia and Herzegovina in retaliation for *Storm* were accommodated in provisional reception centers in Bjelovar, Slatina, Orahovica and Virovitica.

Because of the advanced age of the majority of the population remaining in the area, current living conditions and the imminence of winter, Croatian institutions, ministries, and Croatian and international NGOs (Red Cross, Red Crescent, UNHCR, UNICEF, and others) prepared a special organized care project during the winter, entitled "Let's Save Lives." The project was launched in early October 1995, and supported by Croatian President Franjo Tuđman, who urged that it must be given top priority.

In a period of two months, the project provided care for 10,594 persons in 604 settlements over an area of 10,497 km^2 (6380 women and 4214 men; 70.4% Serbs, 27.6% Croats, and 2% others). Among the derelict persons, 76% were above the age of 60, and about 20% between 26 and 59 years of age.

Only one person decided to remain living in a total of 73 settlements, 2-5 persons in 155 settlements, 6-10 persons in 104 settlements, 11-20 in 73 settlements, more than 21 in 119 settlements, while 80 settlements were completely abandoned.

Over 80% of the remaining inhabitants had no source of income, and 80% of them suffered from health ailments. After November 1995, and with the help of the International Committee of the Red Cross, eight mobile welfare teams, two medical teams, and two technical teams of the Croatian Red Cross were engaged continuously in the liberated area. By the end of the year, 379 derelict persons accepted accommodation in nursing homes throughout Croatia.

In order to normalize Croato-Serbian relations, and create conditions for the return of Serbian refugees to Croatia, the House of Representatives of the Croatian Parliament passed the General Amnesty Act at its session on 20 September 1996. This Act granted "general amnesty from criminal prosecution and proceedings against perpetrators of criminal acts committed during aggression, armed rebellion or armed conflict, and with respect to the aggression, armed rebellion or armed conflicts in the Republic of Croatia" in the period between 17 August 1990 and 23 August 1996. The amnesty was also related to the execution of a final verdict passed against perpetrators of the foregoing criminal acts. Such an Amnesty Act for criminal acts committed in the war against the Republic of Croatia had already been passed by the Croatian Parliament on 2 September 1992, and after the military-police Operation *Flash* in May 1995.

By the end of 1997, 118,000 refugees and displaced persons returned to their homes in the Republic of Croatia, including about 30,000 Serbs. In order to speed up the return process, in 1998 the Croatian Government enacted the Return and Care Program for Refugees and Displaced Persons. An organized return was only possible after the provision of minimal conditions, including basic infrastructure.

"Storm" is a Legitimate Liberation Operation of the Armed Forces of the Republic of Croatia, During Which Croatian Officers Honorably Commanded Their Units

Note: This book and its chapters were written in December 2011, after which on 15 April 2011 in the first instance verdict of the International Tribunal for the former Yugoslavia in The Hague, Croatian Generals Ante Gotovina and Mladen Markač were sentenced to prison terms of 24 and 18 years respectively for events in Operation *Storm.* However, following appeals, and based on sources that are in part published in this book, the second instance verdict of the ICTY on 16 November 2012 dismissed charges that *Storm* was "a joint criminal venture with the aim of ethnic cleansing," and Generals Ante Gotovina and Mladen Markač were acquitted of all counts and immediately released. With this final judgment, the ICTY confirmed that *Storm* was a legitimate operation, that Croatia was not built on crimes, and the highest military and political leadership of Croatia was freed of all charges in the Homeland War.

In order to punish the war crimes committed in the former SFRY during and after its collapse, the UN Security Council decided in 1993 to establish the International Tribunal for War Crimes Committed in the Former Yugoslavia with its seat in The Hague (Netherlands). The Republic of Croatia supported its establishment in the hopes that the perpetrators of war crimes committed in the former Yugoslavia would be brought to justice and tried by a neutral and fair court. Most of the indicted and sentenced persons tried by the ICTY are Serbian politicians, commanders, and members of Serbian units. However, this element is less important than the fact that the Tribunal only deals with the effects and not the causes of the war. Its mission, which needs to be supported, is to prosecute crimes committed by all parties in the war, but that is not enough to dissuade a future aggressor from waging a new war of conquest. When a war starts, crimes cannot be avoided, and there is certainly no war in history in which even the attacked side has not committed crimes. In line with this, along with the controversial wording debated by jurists that "there is no war crime in defense," one could also say, "there is no defense without violence and crime." This implies that any debate (legal debates included) about the effects of war must not ignore the cause of the war and difference between the attacker and defender, that is, between the aggressor and the victim. Of course, this does not exclude the necessity of punishing all perpetrators of crimes including "war crimes" and "crimes in war." But first, everything must be done to prevent wars in general, and to unanimously censure and drastically punish all aggressors and culprits in war. Only by doing so can a clear message be sent out that conquest policies and wars will no longer be tolerated. Unfortunately, the ICTY does not have such a mandate, and considering the world in which we live and the different interests of global powers and leading UN members, it is questionable whether conditions for objective condemnation and punishment of aggression exist at all.

In spite of all shortcomings, the establishment of such tribunals is a civilizational breakthrough because of the endeavor to prevent the recurrence of war crimes by means of impartial and just punishment. Just verdicts ought to confront the populations of all warring sides with the negative pages of their own past in order to reinforce awareness on the need to punish each and every crime, and the need to pity the victims of war regardless of what side, ethnicity or religion they belong to. However, because of uneven criteria in the choice of suspects and cases, part of the public has begun to doubt the impartiality and equity of the ICTY. This doubt was expressed publicly after the verdicts in cases relating to Serbian crimes in Srebrenica and Vukovar, and especially after 15 April 2011, when Croatian Generals Ante Gotovina and Mladen Markač were handed first-instance verdicts of 24 and 18 years imprisonment respectively for their participation in the "joint criminal enterprise the objective of which was the permanent removal of Serbs from Croatia."

Of course, court verdicts, whatever their tenor or momentary political weight, should not significantly affect the writing of history or the historiography of the Homeland War. History is not written based on verdicts related to specific events, but on the basis of historical sources, and the historian must take into account the overall process and chronological sequence of events in it. Even the mere thought that a court verdict is a primary historical source demonstrates ignorance and non-comprehension of the methodology of historical science. But even if we take into account the fact that court verdicts determine only the legal aspects of complex historical events, and that they are limited in determining criminal accountability and do not explain the historical context of an event or process, one cannot say that the Hague Prosecutors have proven the existence of a joint criminal enterprise or responsibility of Croatian Generals Ante Gotovina and Mladen Markač for civilian casualties and the departure of Croatian citizens of Serbian nationality during Operation *Storm.* According to the same criteria, there was hardly a final liberation operation in the second half of the 20th century (including the Second World War, which ended some time before) that could not be qualified as a criminal enterprise, or a military commander or politician that could not be held accountable for war crimes.

Every nation also has to face the dark sides of its past if it wants to present its history impartially. But that is also a process – when wars are concerned – which is conditioned by determining the causes of the war and clear-cut naming of the aggressor. Texts on the Second World War and Homeland War in history books used in Croatian schools, which also mention dishonorable acts on the Croatian side, attitude of the Croatian authorities and large majority of the public regarding war crimes, including other examples such as verdicts for crimes committed against Serbian civilians in Croatia, show that Croatian society is to a great extent aware of negative conduct in its ranks. Especially when due account is taken of the scale and effects of Serbian aggression against Croatia in the Homeland War, and the relatively short period that had elapsed since the end of the bloody war in Croatia. The reaction of most Croatian politicians and vast majority of Croatian citizens to the mentioned verdicts handed down on Croatian Generals Ante Gotovina and Mladen Markač do not demonstrate Croatia's unwillingness to face the past, but outrage due to the unjust sentences. The sentenced Croatian generals did not execute any criminal enterprise nor are they responsible for the murder of civilians. Therefore, accepting the pronounced sentence does not imply facing the past but a resignation to injustice.

Justice is not satisfied by convicting innocent people, and neither can the victims obtain appropriate satisfaction, which ought to be the objectives of the Tribunal. Analogously, reconciliation of the parties in conflict cannot be achieved based on unjust verdicts. Most Croats and citizens of the Republic of Croatia are of the opinion that these verdicts are unjust. For many this is no longer a legal or political issue, but first and foremost an issue of morality, conscience, and self-respect. All these are lacking in persons indifferent to crimes, as well as to the unjust sentences handed down to those who are among the most meritorious for the defense and liberation of their homeland!

It is a fact that during and after *Storm* there were incidents of crimes committed against the Serbian population and in which Serbian property was damaged or destroyed, but it is also a fact that such crimes are not the consequence of a joint criminal enterprise and that the people responsible for them are not the indicted Croatian generals. The incidents that happened after *Storm* are a problem related to the efficiency of the authorities and security in the liberated area, and cannot be related to the Generals who were in command during the Operation. It is precisely because of the professional and honorable conduct of the Croatian commanders that the number of victims on the Serbian side during *Storm* was minimal. Especially when it is known that part of the Serbian leadership was prepared to sacrifice their own civilians and fellow citizens in order to be able to accuse the Croatian forces of war crimes. This fact has also been raised by commanders and members of the Serbian forces vanquished in *Storm;*

Could one even raise a question that might read: Why would anyone on the "Serbian side" need the encirclement of the population in Kordun? Doesn't that mean an expectation that the Croatian army would "pose" before the world and its sponsors while it carries out mass murders of children, women, old people, and encircled soldiers? Was the expected massacre supposed to serve as crown proof that the Croats were a genocidal people, and their army the same as in the times of Ante Pavelić and World War II? And finally, would the massacre in Kordun be a welcome excuse for the decision to lead the people into exodus and on the road to no return? Wouldn't that massacre eventually and forever cover up all the lies with which the Serbs in Krajina were misled not only since 1991 but even earlier? Although unfortunately encirclement did occur, luckily the conduct of the ***Croatian army was rational and quite controlled****. Croatia knew what it wanted and firmly controlled the situation. One could say it did not fall into a trap.* (From *Knin je pao u Beogradu* [Knin Fell in Belgrade] by Milisav Sekulić, Major General of the "Serbian Army of Krajina"; Bad Vilbel, 2000, p. 221)

"... *The 'hold out' could have been translated only one way: keep fighting, and something will come of it. All the people sitting in that office knew that it was a battle we could not win, it was obvious that we were sacrificed (...) that Belgrade wanted to score some cheap points by surrendering twenty or twenty-five thousand people* (5000 troops and 20,000 civilians). *I never believed that the Croats would come and kill them all. And neither did, I believe, Tošo Pajić* [Officer of the State Security Office in Belgrade and then Minister of the Interior of the Republic of Serbian Krajina]. *They* [the Serbian leadership in Belgrade] ***wanted to turn Topusko into a Srebrenica.*** *In that case, they would accuse the Croatian side. The idea was to present matters to the world in this way, by saying that nobody was an angel, that they were the same, just as bad as we were, and that they just killed a group of civilians at Topusko.* (Testimony of S.L., Intelligence and SVK Officer, at the Hague Tribunal, after a question by General Gotovina's defense team on the meaning of the message *"hold out"* sent during *Storm* by representatives of the Yugoslav military, police, and political authorities to the command of the 21st SVK Corps; record on file at the HMDCDR).

Let jurists discuss the legal aspects of the ICTY verdicts. Through a historian's prism, however, the main objection to the verdict handed down on Croatian Generals Ante Gotovina and Mlade Markač refers to the fact that the Trial Chamber did not take into consideration the documents of the defense or the historical context of the events. The contents of the historical sources and obligation to appreciate the historical process comprehensively suggest the conclusion that the verdict, according to which Generals Ante Gotovina and Mladen Markač are responsible for the excessive, non-selective shelling of Knin and "ethnic cleansing," i.e., elimination of the Serbian population from Croatia, does not match facts. Especially when it is known that not a single civilian was killed during *Storm* by Croatian artillery attacks on military targets in Knin. (Even the prosecution, during the proceedings, admitted that the Trial Chamber did not find a single case of any civilian being wounded or killed by shelling, and the evidence submitted by the prosecution during the hearing only left the possibility of one civilian in Knin killed by shelling.) The same goes for the towns of Gračac, Obrovac, and Benkovac in terms of no civilians killed by shelling. Therefore, the fact that it could not reliably be proven that at least one civilian was killed by shelling denies the conclusion of the Trial Chamber about the "unlawful" (!) shelling of civilians during *Storm,* on which such a severe verdict is based. Moreover, it is not known that any Serbian civilian when testifying on the reason of his/her departure from Krajina, indicated "unlawful" shelling.

The conclusion in the foregoing verdict on the non-selective shelling of the listed towns is also refuted by the fact that only 5% of the 1205 shells fired on military targets in the towns involved fell outside the imaginary (and arbitrarily determined!) circle and 200 m radius from the military target. (Of these, no more than 13 shells hit places that cannot be considered as jeopardizing a civilian target!). Because the verdict did not consider the possible reasons why a shell may have fallen away from the target (existence of mobile targets, equipment failure, higher tolerable error range for used weapons systems, etc.), and because it was not unequivocally established where the shells were fired from or who fired them, the mentioned percentage is probably even lower than the stated one. (Witnesses also mentioned mortar shells fired on 4 August, but they could not have been fired from Croatian positions at that time.)

The claim about the excessive/non-selective shelling of Knin is also denied by records of the Serbian army of Krajina, which list the number of shells fired on Knin in the first five hours of *Storm* (200 to 300 projectiles, mainly on military targets), as well as by the fact that Croatian armed forces launched *Storm* despite the fact that the available stocks of artillery munitions were below the level used by modern armies when embarking on such decisive, strategic ("final") offensive operations.

All these data favor the conclusion that the Serbs did not leave the occupied parts of the Republic of Croatia during *Storm* because of shelling, as claimed in the verdict but for other reasons. Historical sources show that the cause of their exodus needs to be sought first and foremost in the decision of the RSK leadership not to live in Croatia under any conditions.

As a key piece of evidence for the charge that the Croatian leadership had planned a "joint criminal enterprise to expel the Serbs from Croatia," the prosecution and the Trial Chamber indicated the so-called Brioni Transcript and referred to specific selectively chosen sentences stated at the meeting of the political and military leadership of the Republic of Croatia on the Brioni Islands on the eve of *Storm*. However, comprehensive insight into the transcript shows that these sentences were misinterpreted in the verdict, and that the transcript of the Brioni meeting contains no evidence of the intention of the Croatian leadership to cause the physical destruction of the Serbian civil population in Krajina. The meeting deliberated on the implementation of a military operation against Serbian military forces in the occupied parts of the Republic of Croatia, and not against civilians, and the use of lawful means in the re-establishment of Croatian authorities in the area. It is indubitable that at the Brioni meeting no "official decision" was made to drive the Serbs out of Croatia, or any order given to target civilians by artillery, as suggested in the verdict.

Analogously, the provision of a route ("corridor") for the pullout of Serbian forces during *Storm* is no proof of an intention to destroy the Serbs in Krajina, as suggested in the verdict, but rather the opposite. The Croatian leadership intended to avoid a situation in which Serbian troops and civilians would be totally encircled, because in that case they would have been forced to resort to a determined defense and fight "to the end," which would have increased the casualty rate among soldiers and civilians many times over. The decision of the Croatian authorities was completely justified in military and humanitarian terms, as borne out by many examples from military history. Books on the art of warfare have been suggesting such conduct for over 2500 years. Here is one example from *The Art of War* by Sun Tzu, the ancient Chinese general, strategist and philosopher (about 500 or 300 BC): *When you surround the enemy, leave him a free passage for retreating. This does not at all mean that you have let the enemy escape. The objective is to leave him the possibility to withdraw in safety and prevent his fighting with desperate courage*.

As opposed to the so-called Brioni Transcript, the documents of the rebel Serbs clearly show that they had made their choice very early on. In May 1991, in part of the territory they would later on proclaim as their own state, 99.80% of the Serbs (of the 79.48% voters at the referendum) decided that the so-called Krajina would be part of Serbia. Based on that, the leadership of the rebel Serbs in Croatia decided in 1991 that the "**Serbs would rather die or move out of Croatia than live in any Croatian State**". In line with this decision was the June 1993 decision on unification with the Serbs of Bosnia and Herzegovina in a single state, supported almost one-hundred-percent by Serbs in the occupied part of the Republic of Croatia. Also included was the draft constitution of such a state, the "United Serbian Republic" of July 1995, and many other records, especially the refusal to accept in early 1995 the Z-4 Plan with which the international community actually offered the Serbs in Croatia a state within a state. Ultimately, during Operation *Storm,* the leadership of the rebel Serbs implemented the mentioned decision from May 1991 that the "Serbs would rather die or move out of Croatia than live in any Croatian State."

Of course, one should not generalize and say that all Serbs were extremists, or ignore the context of the time period in question. This means that due account also needs to be taken of the fact that the underlying cause of the almost 100% support of Serbs in the RSK for their extremist leadership, followed by their similarly 100% departure from occupied parts (Sectors North and South) during *Storm,* could have been the media blockade and strong Croatian propaganda, but also fear of revenge of the displaced Croats and terror of their fellow countrymen. But that does not refute the fact that the past aggressive policies of the Serbian leadership are the reason for the departure of the Serbs on the first day of *Storm* and the overall tragedy of the Serbs in the Republic of Croatia during the 1990s.

Along with RSK records, the reports published in the Serbian and Montenegrin media immediately after *Storm* also confirm that the political and military leadership of the rebel Serbs in Croatia was responsible for the departure and suffering of the Serbian population in Croatia during *Storm*. Such a conclusion is suggested by many questions and comments in Serbian newspapers: *Why didn't the Krajina leadership accept peace on time, if it could not hold out in the war? Indeed, who issued the order on the retreat of the people and the army?* These were only some of the questions raised by Serbian journalists. The Serbian public wanted a "Krajina leadership that did not run to the back of the column," to answer the question: *Why, and per whose advice, did it decide to move hundreds of thousands of people towards Serbia?* (Zoran Jevđović, *Bežanje na čelu kolone* [Flight at the Head of the Column]; Večernje Novosti, 16 August 1995).

Actually, the Yugoslav press already deplored the conduct of the RSK leadership on the first day of *Storm: They are spinning a yarn about unifying all Serbian lands, and then the going gets tough and they call to Serbia for help. Serbia gave them weapons, sent them a commander to organize them. They were told to negotiate with Croatia and thus pacify the situation. No! They just wanted a big show, a celestial drama. But the Croats are now deep inside, they cut them off; now they are also losing their diplomatic positions and their stakes are much lower.* (*Pakao na Drini* [Hell on the Drina], Monitor, independent Montenegrin weekly, 250, 4 August 1995, 8-9).

Along with comments that the Z-4 Plan was a "last ditch" plan permitting the Serbs to achieve their maximum given the fact that "the West would never recognize the RSK," Serbian media reported that the refusal of the plan and "fuelling unrealistic RSK ambitions" was also sponsored by many political factors in Belgrade. Thus, Milošević's close associate, Borisav Jović, was reported as saying that "Krajina was militarily strong enough to withstand a possible attack by the Croatian army. The chetnik *vojvoda* and president of the Serbian radicals Vojislav Šešelj stated that the Z-4 Plan was totally unacceptable." Newspapers also published the viewpoint of one of the best-known Serbian opposition leaders, Zoran Đinđić, showing that Serbian political parties were fairly united with regards to the issue of Serbs outside Serbia and the "right to Serbian territories." *The fact that the Serbian people in the RSK do not accept the plan suggests that we should not accept it either* (Miljenko Pešić, *Da li je propuštena istorijska šansa?* [Was a Historical Opportunity Missed?], Politika, 8 August 1995).

By referring to the narrow-minded position of the Serbs in implementing the decision of all Serbs necessarily living in a single state, Vuk Drašković also sought culprits in "his own yard." Drašković was then leader of the Serbian Renewal Movement opposition party and one of the more vehement champions of Greater Serbian policies in the early 1990s. His reply to the reporter's question on "who was to blame for the fall of Krajina and fate of the Serbian population in the area," unambiguously shows why the Serbian people in Croatia suffered a tragedy and who was responsible for it. *For years, people have been shouting all over Serbia that Krajina will never even think of living anywhere but in Greater Serbia. This unrealistic position was so strong that it entered the conscious and unconscious mind of a great number of people. All those who have been feeding the nation with such a dangerous illusion are to be blamed. On the other hand, it turns out that those of us who did not think so were not able to explain to the nation that it was being grossly misled. We are also guilty because we were not able to tell the people on time what lay in store.* (*Gurat ću na svaka vrata* [I'll Push Any Door], Vreme, 21 August 1995).

Addressing the media, RSK officials accused one another or justified their decisions, and thereby admitted their responsibility. Thus, the last RSK Prime Minister, Milan Babić, expressed his shock at the fact that "the SVK General Staff and President Milan Martić ordered the general evacuation of the population and retreat of the army," (*Povlačenje umesto borbe* [Withdrawal Instead of Fight], Večernje Novosti, 9 August 1995). The censured Milan Martić denied the allegations and claimed that he had only ordered that the population be moved and accommodated in surrounding villages, and that "no mention was made of any withdrawal" (*Nisam naredio povlačenje vojske* [I Didn't Order any Army Withdrawal], Politika, 13 August 1995).

But his statement on moving the population only to the "surrounding villages" was denied in a letter by RSK Foreign Minister Milivoj Vojnović from 5 August 1995 sent to UNPROFOR spokesman Yury Miyakotnik, informing him that the "RSK Government and SVK General Staff had decided to proceed with the immediate evacuation of children, women and elderly persons from the RSK territory to Yugoslavia, and sought UNPROFOR assistance." (Radovan Kovačević, *Tko je doneo odluku o evakuaciji RSK* [Who Decided to Evacuate the RSK], Politika, 27 August 1995.) Vojnović's statement, published in the Serbian daily press (Politika, 23 August 1995), that the *objective of the evacuation was also to draw Serbia and Yugoslavia into the war* is particularly significant.

Any doubts on who and when ordered the evacuation of the Serbs and who was responsible for their departure from occupied parts of the Republic of Croatia on the first day of *Storm*, were eliminated in Belgrade on 22 August 1995 at a press conference at which for the first time after the fall of the RSK members of the RSK Government and Assembly appeared and spoke in public. On the occasion, Serbian reporters were presented with the Decision of the Supreme RSK Defense Council on the Planned Evacuation of the Population from the Municipalities of Knin, Benkovac, Obrovac, Drniš and Gračac (No. 2-3113-1/95), prepared at 16:45 hours on 4 August 1995 and signed by Milan Martić. Subsequently, at 17:20 hours, it was "endorsed by the SVK General Staff" (M. Bošnjak, D. Dimitrovska, *Bežaniju naredio Martić* [Martić Ordered the Flight], Večernje Novosti, 23 August 1995; *Odluku o evakuaciji doneo Martić* [Martić Decided to Evacuate], Politika, 23 August, 1995, 7).

The subsequent comment of the Serbian press was relentless. The Krajina getaway has a clear identification code.... It is obvious that by accepting the policy set at Pale [political center of the Serbs in BH during the 1990s], **the entire RSK leadership, from the President of the Republic to the Government and the top**

military echelons, failed their history test, and that they are **exclusively responsible** for the fate of the 200,000 Serbs from western Krajina. (Radovan Kovačević, Tko je doneo odluku o evakuaciji RSK [Who Decided to Evacuate the RSK], Politika, 27 August 1995).

According to Serbian documents, the RSK leadership began to plan evacuation as the latest by 1993, while specific preparations of the RSK Civil Defense Headquarters for the evacuation of the RSK population began on 29 July 1995. The Supreme RSK Defense Council proclaimed the state of war on 30 July, that is, five days before the start of Storm. Given that Serbian forces in northern Dalmatia found themselves in a very difficult position after the fall of Grahovo and Glamoč, such decisions were understandable. In the afternoon hours of the first day of Storm, the RSK Supreme Defense Council only put into force that which the population had been prepared and trained for in case the Serbian Army of Krajina would not be able to hold the defense line. All this additionally confirms the fact that the "main and direct cause" of the departure of Serbian civilians from the RSK during Storm was not "excessive, non-selective, or unlawful" Croatian artillery attacks, as suggested by the ICTY verdict, but the evacuation order of the RSK leadership! Especially considering the fact that evacuation had to be carried out, and that Serbs refusing to join the fleeing columns faced death threats from their fellow countrymen, as shown below.

Our leadership informed the people that they had to flee. People were made afraid of the Croatian army, so we had to run away. Those of us who did not run had to hide very carefully in order to avoid detection... we had to run or the Serbs would kill us... They went from home to home and checked whether people were leaving... (Statement by a Serbian refugee from Croatia, N. Drače, 23 July 1998; Military Operation Storm and its Aftermath, Croatian Helsinki Committee, Zagreb, 2001, 14). These were not mere threats, and this foregoing was not the only statement of its kind, as shown by the following experiences of Serbian refugees. M.P. from

Biskupija near Knin: Martić's men killed my son in bed because he did not want to join the column. M.J., Gračac: One of my neighbors was killed because she refused to join the column. M.K., Knin: I was in the basement of the building in which the dentist Milan Babić had an apartment, and then the militia came and forced us into the column. (Copies of Protocol No. 1269 of 1 Sept. 1995 and No. 1396 of 18 Sept. 1995, on file at the HMDCDR.)

To corroborate the reason why the Serbs left Croatia during Storm as their decision not to live in Croatia, is also supported by a Serbian source (Serbian Refugees and Displaced Persons in the Late Twentieth Century, Center for Strategic Studies of the University of Belgrade, Belgrade, 2000). According to the source, 77,317 persons of Serbian nationality of the total population in the area, 128,316 (meaning more than 60% of the Serbs in the area), left the Croatian Danubian region during peaceful reintegration, that is, after the cessation of hostilities.

For the same reason – that is, refusal of any government other than a Serbian one – Serbs also massively left the districts of Sarajevo that became part of the Federation of BH and were not part of the Serbian entity in Bosnia and Herzegovina. Faced with the decision of the international community that Ilidža would be under the administration of the Federation of BH as of mid-March 1996, three months after signing a peace agreement in Paris (14 December 1995), most Serbs left Ilidža with visible endeavors to have the "Serbian martyrdom" recorded by international TV cameras. Along with their property, they also took church bells, crosses and other relics, and even the dead from their graves. TV cameras recorded statements such as "we must leave because the Muslims will slaughter us" or "this is the ethnic cleansing of Serbs from Ilidža." Upon their departure, the Serbs torched factories, their own homes, and other buildings. Unfortunately, just as in the freed parts of the Republic of Croatia, the few Serbs that did remain in Ilidža became targets for the vengeance of the enraged (until then displaced) Muslims and "plundering mobs." They could not be protected by the police of the BH Federation or by the international community (NATO, IFOR, UN Police), which had previously guaranteed their security and had three months to prepare for the task (one can only wonder what would have happened if Ilidža had been freed by military action). A similar situation developed in Kosovo after the UN took over control in 1999.

Therefore, Serbian sources clearly show that the leadership of the rebel Serbs in Croatia is exclusively responsible for the departure of Serbs from occupied parts of Croatia. In line with instructions from the Greater Serbian strategists in Belgrade, the leaders of the Croatian Serbs who were focused on the creation of a unified Serbian state first incited an armed rebellion of part of the Serbs in Croatia, followed by participation in the Serbian aggression against Croatia, and led them eventually into exile. Of course, the Serbian leadership in Belgrade was also responsible for the tragedy of the Serbs in Croatia in the 1990s. And no verdict can refute these facts!

It is also a fact that in early August 1995, due to Serbian attacks on the strategically extremely important town of Bihać and the dramatic condition of its defense, a Croatian military operation could no longer be postponed. Along with the above mentioned, and considering the historical sources and need for a comprehensive appreciation of the process, it would be hypocritical to accuse the Croatian Government of a "joint criminal enterprise for the elimination of the Serbian population" when it is known that on 3 August 1995 only two options were available. The first was that the Serbian Army of Krajina would have won, and the so-called Krajina – the occupied part of the Republic of Croatia, would have become part of a new, unified Serbian state (Greater Serbia). The other is that the area would have been abandoned by all those refusing to recognize the Croatian Government – and that, according to Serbian sources, meant the majority of the Serbian population in the area. Unfortunately, a third option was not possible at the time due to the intransigent policy of the Serbian leadership, which can be summarized in a message by RSK President Milan Martić to SVK

Officers in February 1995. The war between the Republic of Croatia and the RSK must end with the victory of one and defeat of the other side. Until that happens, the war will not and cannot end.

The SVK Officers supported the position of their President, as confirmed in an interview by SVK Commander, Lieutenant General Mile Mrkšić, on St. Vitus' Day, 28 June 1995, in which he wished that all SVK members celebrate the next St. Vitus's Day united – in a single Serbian state (Vojska Krajine, 11, July 1995, 24).

From the order of the RSK Civil Defense Headquarters to regional civil defense offices concerning the implementation of evacuation and relief plans (Knin, 29 July 1995)

REPUBLIC OF SERBIAN KRAJINA
REPUBLICAN CIVIL DEFENSE HEADQUARTERS
DEFENSE
No. Nov. 01-78/95
OFFICIAL SECRET
Knin, 29 July 1995

REGIONAL CIVIL DEFENSE OFFICES

To Whom It May Concern:

Pursuant to the Decision on the Proclamation of the State of War, and in accordance with the latest situation, the Republic Civil Defense Headquarters hereby issues the following

ORDER

1. Immediately activate Regional Civil Defense Offices, establish a continuous tour of duty, and as required, have some staff members continuously available on call.
2. Municipal civil defense offices shall be ordered to:
– organize a continuous tour of duty and staff member activity related to evacuation and relief
– update evacuation and relief plans, putting on standby personnel responsible for specific assignments

* * *

From the Decision of the Supreme Defense Council of the Republic of Serbian Krajina on the Proclamation of the State of War (Knin, 30 July 1995)

Decision of the RSK Supreme Defense Council

STATE OF WAR PROCLAIMED THROUGHOUT THE RSK

Knin, 30 July
At its meeting held on Friday evening, the RSK Supreme Defense Council has decided, considering the latest developments after the occupation of Grahovo and possible Croatian aggression against RSK, to proclaim the state of war throughout the entire RSK territory in accordance with Article 102 of the Constitution.

* * *

Decision of the RSK Supreme Defense Council on the evacuation of the population from the municipalities of Benkovac, Obrovac, Drniš, Gračac and Knin to Srb and Lapac (Knin, 4 August 1995)

REPUBLIC OF SERBIAN KRAJINA
SUPREME DEFENSE COUNCIL
Knin, 4 August 1995
16:45 hours
No. 2-3113-1/95

Due to the latest situation caused by the open general aggression of the Republic of Croatia on the Republic of Serbian Krajina, and after the first initial defense success, a large part of the territory of Northern Dalmatia and part of Lika have become threatened. Accordingly,

WE HAVE DECIDED

1. To proceed with the planned evacuation of all persons unfit for combat from the municipalities of Knin, Benkovac, Obrovac, Drniš and Gračac.
2. To implement evacuation according to prepared plans and routes from Knin via Otrić towards Srb and Lapac.
3. Request assistance from the UNPROFOR Command, Sector South, with headquarters in Knin.

Knin, 4 August 1995

PRESIDENT OF THE REPUBLIC
Mile Martić
(round seal: RSK, General Staff of the Serbian Army)

CERTIFIED IN THE SVK GENERAL STAFF at 17:20 hours and filed under the above number.

***

Serbian Document on the Shelling of Knin
SVK General Staff
Intelligence Department
Str. Conf. No. 2/3110-1
4 August 1995

Intelligence Report

The attack of the Croatian Army on the RSK began on 4 August 1995 at 05:00 hours with the shelling of the towns of Knin, Drniš, Benkovac, Karin, Obrovac, Gračac, Korenica, Udbina Airstrip, Vojnić, Vrginmost and Petrinja. The artillery preparation lasted until 05:30 hours, followed by the engagement of single weapons of 130, 152 and 155 mm caliber and multiple rocket launchers.
The ustashe infantry attack began at about 06:00 from Sunja towards Kostajnica, with the engagement of tanks, but units of the 39th Corps successfully repelled the attack.
Another infantry attack was mounted from the village of Brlog (Otočac) – Drenov Klanac – village of Glavace, but it was also successfully beaten back.
Knin was shelled from several directions on Livanjsko Polje, and by the time this report was written, **200 to 300 projectiles of different type and caliber have hit the town**. **The target of the first strike was the building of the General Staff of the Serbian Army of Krajina**, which sustained considerable damage and the almost complete loss of its motor pool. Afterwards, the fire was focused on the **'1300 Corporals' barracks, TVIK plant, railway junction,**

and housing below the Knin fortress [area of the residence of RSK President, Mile Martić – author's note] **and other targets.**
At 10:00 hours, as this report is being written, hostile forces continue to attack Knin alternately with guns and multiple rocket launchers, unremittingly shelling the Udbina Airstrip and sporadically opening fire on other settlements in the RSK.
By monitoring the radio links and mobile telephones of the Croatian Army, we have been able to establish that the ustashe are sustaining considerable losses at Dubrovnik, Biograd na Moru, Gospić, Otočac, Sisak and Sunja.
You will be duly informed of all the latest information.
Head of Department
Lieutenant Colonel Mihajlo Knežević

Deliver to:

7th, 11th, 15th, 21st, 39th Corps, Special Unit Corps
General Staff of the Yugoslav Army – Second Directorate
General Staff of the Army of Republika Srpska in Bosnia and Herzegovina – Intelligence Directorate
Command of the 1st and 2nd Krajina Corps of the Army of Republika Srpska in Bosnia and Herzegovina

***

From the diary of an officer of the Army of Serbian Krajina on the shelling of Knin

Marko Vrcelj, then Artillery Chief of the SVK General Staff was present in Knin when *Storm* began.

Drumfire barrage started all over Krajina. Everything had been planned to the smallest detail. Every shell and every artillery attack. Several days ago, observers and gunners were infiltrated in order to direct fire. **The most important targets in the town included the**

General Staff building, residence of the President of the state, the northern barracks, Senjak barracks, and the main intersection in Knin... I jumped over the fence of the northern barracks and entered the building in which I had worked four months ago... Shells were hitting the barracks, but we were lucky and avoided shells falling on our heads... We got into a Golf and set off towards the General Staff. Shells were still falling, this time less frequently. We arrived at the Dešlić intersection. The area round the General Staff is being hit more heavily. I stop the driver and tell him to return to the barracks, and proceeded on foot... Seeking shelter behind trees, I reached the General Staff. I entered the building: what a sight. Two shells had hit the parking space between the buildings and the explosion destroyed the entire motor pool. That must have been quite a gunner, to land them right there (Marko Vrcelj, Rat za Srpsku Krajinu, 1991-1995/War for the Serbian Krajina, 1991-1995/; Belgrade, 2002, pp. 212-213).

***

During *Storm,* Croatian troops did not destroy or torch any religious (Orthodox) building. However, during and after the Operation, some houses and property belonging to Croatian citizens of Serbian nationality were torched. According to reports on some incidents, Serbs who did not leave the area were killed. These dishonorable acts were largely committed out of revenge or for gain, but any figures according to which Croatian forces were responsible for the death of about 600 civilians and the torching of over 22,000 Serbian homes, persistently reported in the media for ten years now, are exaggerated many times over. In addition to being inaccurate, such reports are also incomplete if they omit the fact that that over 6000 Croats (troops and civilians) were killed already in 1991 during the Serbian aggression (with the participation of many Serbs from occupied parts of the Republic of Croatia), that the number of people killed doubled by the launch of *Storm*, and that over 200,000 housing units were destroyed largely already in 1991 in the attacks of Serbian forces on Croatia before the start of *Storm*.

Victims are an extremely delicate issue, primarily because of the emotions arising after the suffering of innocent people. Every innocent person killed deserves respect, and everything must be done to ensure that an awareness prevails in people minds that there is no justification for crimes. At the same time, one must be cautious when publicly presenting the number of victims in order to prevent manipulations such as those concerning the victims of World War II in the former Yugoslavia. Such manipulations are only aimed at stirring up hate. In that process, particular responsibility lies with historians who are obliged, along with exploring the numbers of people killed, to explain based on historical sources the underlying causes of the crimes and circumstances in which they were committed. Historical sources have unequivocally shown that the 1990s war in the former Yugoslavia was caused by Greater Serbian politics and that the countless victims in that war are primarily the consequence of an attempt to implement the political goal of "all Serbs in one state" [an ethnically clean state, as examples on the ground have shown]. Analogously, along with the fact that the perpetrators of some murders are not known and neither are the circumstances surrounding them, sources have confirmed that Croatian forces were not responsible for all the tribulations of the civilians of Serbian nationality in *Storm*. Serbian sources on events after *Storm* report murders and suicides committed among Serbs during their retreat, and the suffering of Serbian civilians due to so-called "friendly fire." (For example, at the meeting of Serbian military commanders on 9 October 1995, it was reported that during *Storm* one of their own planes attacked a Serbian column by mistake, killing more than 20 and wounding over 60 persons; audio file: HMDCDR, 18, Inv. No. 2913). The distress of Serbian civilians in *Storm* mentioned in these examples (especially those regarding victims whose bodies were not buried immediately) may be attributed to the action of Croatian forces. Some testimonies are listed below.

... Considering the climate of fear sustained over the previous four years and the tactics of intimidation applied after the start of the Croatian offensive, few Serbs were willing to remain in Topusko. All the people there panicked, and in some cases, Serbs even shot at one another when quarrelling over vehicles or property as they prepared to flee. In one very unpleasant episode, someone shot an elderly man, who was killed and buried on the spot.
(From the testimony of S.L. Intelligence and SVK Officer, at The Hague in early 2009; transcript on file at the HMDCDR.)

From a story (in the Serbian press) of a Serb who fled Croatia and the "many suicides on the road":
An old man, seventy-three, just got off the road into a cornfield and killed himself with a hand grenade ... The bridge on the Nova Grada river was destroyed, and a woman killed herself there. When we got to the bridge, she just grabbed the fence and jumped into the water, poor soul.
(Progoni istočno od raja [Persecutions East of Eden], Intervju, 367, 25 Aug. 1995, 5).

Here is a part of a moving story by Radmila D. (34):
Five babies died in our column, and many old people; we left them by the road because they told us that ambulances would collect them.
Miloš B. (39): A man who had no more fuel in his tractor, probably deranged, took out a gun and killed his wife, their two children and then himself. They tried to stop him, but failed.
(Ljudi s traktora [The People on the Tractor], Nin, 2329, 18 Aug. 1995, 29).

An old refugee also described the chaos in the Serbian refugee columns leaving Croatia:
In the Topusko Pocket, we heard that the Muslims were slaughtering everybody at Glina. Chaos ensued, people cried and moaned, armed

and drunken soldiers threatened, two men killed themselves. Then the police from Kordun restored order. They beat people with long wooden sticks. (Milena Marković, Kroz psovke i batine [Through Curses and Beating], Večernje Novosti, 15 Aug. 1995).

Testimony of Višnja (32):
We were in the column from 5 to 10 August 1995. We just stood on the spot, or moved slowly. We had food, what we had taken along, but I could hardly eat. I lost my appetite because of everything that had happened to us. We heard that there had been some negotiations and that we should move on. They formed us into ranks, set the column in order (Croatian militia) and ordered everyone to leave their weapons because you could not cross the border with weapons. They let people take the fuel from the remaining tanks, but no weapons. Some people could not bear being separated from their weapons, so they committed suicide.
(Žene Krajine – rat, egzodus i izbeglištvo [The Women of Krajina – War, Exodus and Exile]; Belgrade, 1996, 287).

Some Serbs in the refugee columns were crushed by tanks; for example, an SVK tank ran over a man in a militia car before the arrival of Croatian troops... *On the right side of a small narrow road (leading to the administration of the diesel fuel depot), I found a militia car, a Zastava 101. Tracks showed that it had been run over by a tank. It was completely flattened, and a human leg protruded from it... I went on to the corps command... I saw a Russian Lada with two dead men in camouflage RSK army uniforms, 25-30 years old... The car was riddled with bullet holes at chest level. Croatian troops had not yet entered the town, and I don't know how they died. They must have been killed by gunfire.*

(The Croatian Helsinki Committee, Military Operation *Storm* and its Aftermath, p, 27).

There is a well-known story about retreating Serbian tanks running over a column of Serbian refugee vehicles in the region of Banovina, of which there exist official records and eyewitness accounts. Milenko Predragović of the Serbian *Večernje Novosti* reported that *according to eyewitnesses, a sad column of 32,000 displaced persons was overrun by tanks under the command of Serbian General Mile Novaković retreating from Petrova Gora.* He then went on to conclude that *most probably the column was indeed overrun by Serbian, but captured tanks* (!), which is not true (N. Predragović, *Kolona izgažena tenkovima* [Column Overrun by Tanks], Večernje Novosti, 14 August 1995, 4).

The ICTY verdict handed down against Croatian Generals Ante Gotovina and Mladen Markač listed 44 proved murders of civilians during and immediately after *Storm*, for which Croatian forces could possibly be blamed on grounds of command responsibility, and which indicate a "low level of collateral victims" due to the action of such forces during the Operation. Even the incorrect figure of "600 murdered civilians" (which ignores the fact that not all of the mentioned persons were civilians, and that Croatian forces were not responsible for the deaths of most of them), cannot deny the foregoing fact, especially if the following is taken into consideration:

- area of the territory on which the liberation operation *Storm* was carried out (over 10,000 km^2), and the number of people involved (troops on both sides and civilians – over 200,000);
- the four-year agony of several hundred thousands of Croatian displaced persons (in December 1992 there were 663,493 displaced persons and refugees in Croatia; on the eve of *Storm*, the number was 384,664, of which more than a half were people banished from occupied parts of the Republic of Croatia; since 1991 over 40,000 Croats were banished or forced to leave Vojvodina alone (autonomous province within Serbia, where there was no war);
- the continuous threat of artillery – actually terrorist attacks by Serbian units from the occupied parts of Croatia on towns and

villages in the free parts of the Republic ("real threat strategy"), with which the rebel Serbs in Croatia intended to force the Croats to desist from liberating the occupied territory and returning to their homes;

- the comparison with similar final military operations worldwide and in the former Yugoslavia, especially the Serbian force operations in Croatia and Bosnia and Herzegovina between 1991 and 1995, in which numerous crimes were committed on the non-Serbian population.

Equally so, the number of houses torched in *Storm* as reported in the media was also considerably overstated, as shown by a report of UN observers according to which the mentioned figure of 22,000 refers to the number of **observed** and not **torched** houses. A detailed analysis of the report shows that the number of torched houses probably amounted to ten times less! Moreover, Serbian sources show that some (private and public) buildings were torched by Serbs themselves as they pulled out, and that a number of buildings were torched before Croatian forces captured the formerly occupied parts of Croatia.

As reported by Politika, *a soldier from Kninsko Polje who had been given leave (as shown in his pass), just prior to the attack to go home and clean up, "packed" all the people in his hamlet (40 of them) into a large trailer truck and drove them to Belgrade. Only the driver's father, 63, stayed behind; the man took a gun intending to fight as long as he could, after which he would set his house on fire and flee...* (Serbian Vreme weekly, 14 August 1995, p. 4).

... As we pulled back to Srb and Drvar, we passed though empty villages. There were no dead or wounded civilians or soldiers, just empty houses and livestock. Explosions were occasionally heard, the Serbs were blowing up some facilities lest they should fall into the

hands of the Croats – hospitals, post offices, weapon depots they could not pull out. ...
(Testimony of M.Č., 32, from Obrovac, wounded during the retreat near Srb, transferred for treatment to the Military Medical Academy in Belgrade; reported in the double issue of the "Independent Political Daily" *Naša borba*, 193-194, 12-13 August 1995, p. 9).
Statements by other Serbian refugees also show that buildings and other facilities were set on fire *so as not to leave them to the Croats.* Thus, before leaving Donji Lapac, the Serbs set fire to the Kamensko Hotel, police station, and *at least another 3-4 buildings.*
(The Croatian Helsinki Committee, *Military Operation Storm and its Aftermath*, p. 25, notes 23, 34).

Similarly, a statement made by Dr. I. Kujundžić in Belgrade on 19 July 1996, V.J.K. (born on 8 February 1928), said: *When we joined the column (at Donji Lapac), I saw the house on fire in which I had an apartment, torched by Serbian soldiers before they retreated.*
(Copy of Protocol No. 588 of 19 July 1996, on file at the HMDCDR).

Moving testimonies on the suffering of the Serbian people in the columns whose leaders led them into exile also show that a number of civilians met with disaster, and some houses were torched before Croatian troops reached the formerly occupied areas.

Jagoda, 45, mother of two underage children: *On that day, 4 August, when Krajina fell, I was still working. We were in the barrack in the shelter. We kept hearing stories about one person or another having been killed in the barracks. When things calmed down, I went home. We asked our commander whether we would run and pull out. He said we were not going anywhere. I came home... In the meantime, a man came and said that we had to move. Out of fear, panic, we forgot to take some clothing....* ***Wherever we went, there was just wasteland. Homes were burning by the roadside.*** *My cousin lagged*

behind. They broke the column up and he drove over corpses for 9 kilometers, from Topusko to Dvor na Uni. There the Muslims cut the column in two, slaughtered and killed everybody. My children were scared to death. They formed columns. Some people overtook others who were moving more slowly. But nobody cared for anybody else, for the sick or dying. A relative of mine, a neighbor, died on the way. For a time, her son drove her like that, dead, and then gave up because the children began to panic. He just tipped her over the cart into a roadside ditch, covered her with branches and carried on. Imagine how that man lives today.
(The Women of Krajina – War, Exodus and Exile]; Belgrade, 1996, 127-128).

Neda, born in 1954: *Podgorje is about a mile away from the Municipality of Krnjak; nobody told us anything, but I saw the village burning and women running away... People panicked, we didn't know what to do... Somebody shouted 'let's move' and just as we sat down, I saw a house burning. Groups of Muslims appeared, torched houses, and people began to flee again.* ***We took our personal weapons along because everybody did.*** *People ran into a cornfield, and terrible slaughter ensued.*
(The Women of Krajina – War, Exodus and Exile]; Belgrade, 1996, 262-263).

Desanka, 55: *In the evening, at about 8 p.m. (on 5 August), my husband went to bed, and I followed. Then people from the civil defense came and told us to go to the factory, the 'meeting place.' I called my husband, he said he couldn't go. I grabbed a bag and filled it with the bare essentials. I also took a hunting gun, but no documents because I thought we would be coming back... We stayed in the factory, about thirty of us, infirm people; everything was already burning, in flames. One of the managers called a driver who gave us a bus to take us away. We drove through the burning village. The driver drove with the lights off.*

(The Women of Krajina – War, Exodus and Exile]; Belgrade, 1996, 282-283).

Of course, all this does not lessen the responsibility of individuals on the Croatian side who committed crimes during and after *Storm* (Croatian generals who were in command during the operation had no direct link with those crimes). By September 1999, Croatian authorities brought 3978 charges against persons participating in criminal actions during and immediately after *Storm*. Croatian courts pronounced 1949 verdicts on the basis of the indictments, and 1492 persons of Croatian nationality were handed sentences. By September 1999, of the 26 persons charged with murder, 12 persons were given sentences of one to fifteen years in prison, and 3 individuals received sentences of one and a half to twenty years in prison (from the *White Paper on the Cooperation of the Republic of Croatia with ICTY*, September 1999).

According to data from the State Prosecutor's Office of the Republic of Croatia on criminal offences committed during and immediately after Operation *Storm*, by mid-2011, charges were brought against 4128 known and 2262 unknown persons. Of these, 439 (less than 7%) were members of the Croatian army. Based on these charges, 3728 persons were identified and prosecuted (in 395 cases, or 10%, the prosecution began while the persons involved were still members of the Croatian Armed Forces), and sentences were handed down against 2380 perpetrators. The number of victims on record was 47 in total, of which 33 perpetrators were prosecuted for the murder of 21 persons, while the perpetrators of 26 murders were not identified. At the same time, criminal investigation was carried out for 24 war crimes involving 156 victims. The records of the State Prosecutor's Office of the Republic of Croatia comprised information on a total of 214 killed persons, who were murdered or victims of war crimes committed during or immediately after *Storm*.

Population and Area of the Occupied Parts of the Republic of Croatia

The war and related destruction affected 54% of Croatian territory. During 1991, Serbian forces occupied almost one-third of the territory of the Republic of Croatia (about 17,000 km^2 of a total land area of 56,538 km^2). In early 1992, 1072 settlements in the Republic of Croatia were under Serbian occupation: 123 in the Croatian Danubian area, 58 in Western Slavonia, 245 in Banovina, 227 in Kordun, 179 in Lika, and 240 in Dalmatia (Dražen Živić, "Demographic Scope and Losses", *Creation of the Croatian State and the Homeland War;* 451). The percentage was gradually reduced through the liberation operations of Croatian forces. The following information was presented at the 25th Session of the RSK Government on 29 July 1992. "The Republic of Krajina comprises an area of 13,913 km^2 [probably the UNPAs and pink zones], and consists of two disconnected entities – Northern Dalmatia, Lika, Kordun, Banija and Western Slavonia with a total area of 11,402 km^2, and Eastern Slavonia, Western Srijem and Baranja with a total area of 2511 km^2. As reported at the same session, "about 66,000 fighters" took part in the war, 1021 were killed and 1682 wounded," not including the "28 missing from the Miljevac Plateau" and the "killed and wounded territorial defense members who fought in units of the Ministry of the Interior in northern Bosnia for the corridor to the SRY."

According to the 1991 census, the total population of the areas occupied by the Serbs in autumn 1991 (the area occupied then was larger than the area of the later UNPAs) was 549,083 inhabitants; 287,830 (52.4%) were Serbs, slightly less than one-half (49.5%) of the total number of Serbs in the Republic of Croatia (581,663). However, along with the expelled Croatian and other non-Serbian population, after 1991 a considerable number of Serbs also left the area for existential reasons. (According to Serbian sources, about

100,000 Serbs left the region by the end of 1992, and emigration continued.) According to data from the RSK Refugee Commissariat of July 1994, there were 122,704 refugees and displaced persons living in the RSK, and in late 1994 about 80,000 Serbs from the RSK living in SR Yugoslavia (not including other states) (Barić, 172-173), it can be concluded that at the time, the RSK had less than 300,000 inhabitants, mostly Serbian nationality. Because of political and economic circumstances in the RSK, the emigration of the population from the region did not abate even in 1995, which leads to the conclusion that the figure of 300,000 Serbian refugees in Operation *Storm* (from UNPA Sectors North and South) as mentioned in Serbian sources is greatly overstated.

According to the seemingly overstated data of the General Staff of the Serbian Army of Krajina of June 1993, the population of RSK was 433,595: 91% Serbs, 7% Croats and 2% others, meaning that the number of Croats was about 30,000. The population of the Serbian region of Slavonia, Baranja and Western Srijem was 135,880, of the part of Western Slavonia under Serbian occupation 29,000, and of the occupied parts of Banovina, Kordun, Lika and Northern Dalmatia 268,795. However, these figures are not reliable "because of the continuous migrations in the mentioned areas, as well as the large number of refugees." (Barić, 172).

A more accurate estimate seems to be that there were still about 16,000 Croats at the time of the arrival of UN forces in the RSK area. However, by the end of 1993, 8000 Croats and members of other nationalities were expelled, killed, or forced to leave under various pressures and threats; thus, in 1994 there were less than 8000 Croats in the RSK as compared to the 219,000 living in the area before the war (Barić, 396). By the start of *Storm,* the figure decreased even more.

According to data presented by Slobodan Lang and Branko Čulo in January 1995 in their studies (based also on "official" Yugoslav publications), at the time only 100,000 inhabitants remained in the UNPA zones, and about 278,000 Serbs lived in areas controlled by

Croatian authorities. 252,619 refugees from Croatia were registered in Yugoslavia (198,819 from the UNPA zones and 53,800 from areas controlled by Croatian authorities, including families of JNA officers who had withdrawn from Croatia).

Of course, all these figures need to be taken with a grain of salt, because statistical data on the population of the occupied parts of the Republic of Croatia differ. Among other things, they also depend on whether they refer to the area occupied in the autumn of 1991, or occupied territory included in the UNPAs, with or without the pink zones. They also depend on the accuracy of the figures listed in official publications because the amount of financial and material help from the international community depended on the number of refugees.

The Media and Certain Facts about the Croat-Bosniak (Muslim) Conflict in BH

Croat deputies in the Assembly of Bosnia and Herzegovina took part in voting on a Decision to Hold a Referendum, and the Croatian political and social elite ensured its successful implementation. In spite of that, they were accused of dividing and breaking up Bosnia and Herzegovina. Similarly, some people accused Croatia of having "committed aggression against BH" in order to "create a Greater Croatia." However, the proper question would be what would have happened with BH if the Croats and Croatian forces did not oppose Serbian aggression in that state in 1992, and if they did not (together with the Army of BH) defeat Serbian forces in 1995 and free a considerable part of BH territory. As evidence confirming such an accusation, reference is made to the establishment of the Croatian Community of Herzeg-Bosnia on 18 November 1991, although it was created in order to defend Croats from the impending Serbian aggression. It would be absurd to claim that at the time the Croats in BH had no reason to self-organize when it is known that the BH institutions could not defend either the Croats or other citizens from the attacks of armed Serbian units. Examples such as the incursion of "Martić's Police" from Croatia into BH, and events in areas with a majority Serbian population after June 1991 – after which Alija Izetbegović stated that "at present we cannot deal with the increasingly fierce internal and external aggression" *(Chronology of the 1989-1998 War – Croatia – Bosnia and Herzegovina*, Zagreb, 1998, 65) – and the tribulations of the Croats at Ravno in Herzegovina in October 1991, confirm the impotence of the central Sarajevo authorities to effectively oppose Serbian aggression. Attempts to present Croatia as an aggressor on BH go to extremes. For example, when referring to the "HVO logistical support as proof of Croatian aggression against BH," emphasis is placed on the fact that "wounded HVO members were treated in hospitals in Croatia"

(Smail Čekić, *Aggression against the Republic of Bosnia and Herzegovina – Planning, Preparation, Execution,* Sarajevo, 2004, 1115). Of course, no mention is made of the fact that logistical centers of the Army of BH were also present in Croatia, and that hospitals in Croatia (in Split, Zagreb, Slavonski Brod, Karlovac, Vinkovci, Metković and elsewhere) also simultaneously treated over 10,000 members of the Army of BH and civilian Muslims from BH. (The figure does not include the ill who were healed.) According to the records of Prof. Mihovil Biočić, Ph.D., wartime head of the Split Clinical Center, "in line with our conscience and with Croatian policy in the 1990s, the Split Hospital treated more than 32,000 wounded and sick persons from BH, 40% of whom were Muslims."

Because of the selective publication of transcripts from the President's Office, the general public does not know that it was precisely President Tuđman (imputed with the responsibility of aggression against BH) who concluded at the 56th (closed-door) Session of the Croatian Government on 25 November 1991 (7 days after the proclamation of the Croatian Community of Herzeg-Bosnia), that "in line with Croatia's policy, there can be no changing of borders" so that "the Croats must provide for their interests within that state for as long as its exists." He went on to say that "we must be aware of the fact that the Serbian part of BH is fully under the control of Serbian authorities, armed and serving Greater Serbian policies," and that "Muslims pursue their own policy which, as far as their leadership is concerned, is focused on maintaining Yugoslavia." The statesmanlike moves of President Tuđman with regard to Bosnia and Herzegovina (no change of borders by force, recognition of the sovereignty and independence of BH as a community of three constituent peoples, participation of the Croats in the defense and liberation of BH, etc.), show that the roles of Croatian President Franjo Tuđman and Serbian President Slobodan Milošević cannot be equated, as some persistently try to do, to equate their responsibility for the war in Bosnia and Herzegovina.

As a rule, conflicts between the Croats and Bosniaks/Muslims began in places where the Bosniaks/Muslims (Army of BH) were superior. They spread from central Bosnia via Konjic to Herzegovina, and not the other way round, which refutes the thesis that the Croats provoked and initiated them (Davor Marijan, *Bosnia and Herzegovina 1991-1995, In the Years of the Unfinished War,* Status, No. 3, May/June 2004, 98-110). Owing to the propaganda activity of the Muslim (Bosniak) institutional and extra-institutional structures, the almost generally accepted public view was that the war between the Bosniaks/Muslims and Croats in BH, and the alleged Croatian (RH) aggression against BH began with a conflict in Prozor in October 1992, caused allegedly by the HVO (Croatian Defense Council) and allegedly involving HV (Croatian Army) brigades. However, records have shown that this view is not correct, that the conflict in Prozor began after BH Army troops ambushed and killed one HVO member at Crni Vrh, and that there were no HV units in the area at the time. Contrary to the news published in Sarajevo media that "more than 200 or maybe even 300 Muslims were killed in the ethnic cleansing of Prozor and Rama," the truth is that 9 or 11 Muslims, according to different sources, were killed in the conflict at Prozor (at the same time, five soldiers and civilians were killed and eighteen wounded on the HVO side), and that many Muslims found shelter and protection with Croatian families in villages around Prozor. Naturally, the town suffered damages in the fighting, and unfortunately, some Muslim houses were plundered and torched to the disgrace of the perpetrators of those acts, which was subsequently used by Muslim propaganda to spread the news worldwide that Prozor was "completely razed to the ground." The existence of a secret Muslim hospital in Prozor, and documents of the Muslim political and military leadership found after the conflict, including the so-called Beta Plan for the conflict with the HVO, show that the extremist part of the Muslim leadership in Prozor and the executive committee of the SDA (Party of Democratic Action), had prepared for the conflict with the Croats and that accusing only the Croatian side for the conflict is unsubstantiated.

Sources have shown that the conflict between the HVO and the Army of BH in Prozor did not occur suddenly and unexpectedly, but rather was the result of different local views regarding the momentary political and future arrangement of Bosnia and Herzegovina, that the Army of BH was defeated in the conflict, and that part of the population also withdrew with it from the town. This fact was later used to spread the claim that Prozor was the first town cleansed in a planned way. Having themselves felt the brunt of the Greater Serbian military machine, after the hard summer of 1992 (in which they physically held their ground despite high casualty rates thanks to the military involvement of Croatian troops along the borders and borderland parts of BH), the Muslims launched a process focused on the proclaimed "revival" of Bosnia and Herzegovina. At the time, the process had progressed to the point that led to war with the Croats, who advocated a national and territorial unit in BH. Although that was not the first conflict between the HVO and the Army of BH, Muslim propaganda "turned the clash at Prozor into a symbol of aggression of the Republic of Croatia on their perception of Bosnia and Herzegovina," and was undoubtedly a "sad harbinger" of the war between the Bosniaks/Muslims and the Croats in BH. (Davor Marijan, *The Conflict between the HVO and the Army of BH in Prozor in October 1992,* Journal of Contemporary History, No. 2, Zagreb, 2006)

It is a fact that the armed conflict between the Croats and the Bosniaks/Muslims in BH, also called "a war within a war," cannot be presented in an impartial and comprehensive way without an understanding of its military and sociological aspects. In line with this, the American military historian Charles R. Shrader concluded in his book *Muslim-Croat Civil War in Central Bosnia – A Military History 1992-1994,* (Zagreb, 2004) that "the key facts on the Muslim-Croat conflict in that area were thoroughly distorted because of various ideological, political, social and personal interests." He goes on to say that the few people who wrote or spoke about the conflict, especially journalists, "were sufficiently equipped or prepared to get the facts straight and report accurately about them." His book suggests the conclusion that the only people who can accuse solely Croatia and Croats for the conflict, especially regarding central Bosnia, are those who have no need for a deeper analysis of the event, and rely exclusively on Bosnian government sources from Sarajevo. "Whoever knows anything about military issues (and evidence) would never conclude that the Croats started the conflict in Central Bosnia. There was no major plan for the ethnic cleansing of Muslims in the area, as mistakenly judged by the ICTY. Actually, the case was entirely the opposite."

Shrader claims that very early on, "in the autumn of 1992, the Muslim leadership in Sarajevo brought the strategic decision to launch war against the Croats because they were weaker than the Serbs." Their objective, he believes, was to move the Muslim refugees from eastern Bosnia and Posavina to the Lašva Valley and other areas in which the Croats were traditionally in the majority, and assume control over the defense facilities and plants in Busovača, Vitez, Novi Travnik, Konjic and Bugojno, which were under Croat control. He refers to the statements by the first Chief of the General Staff of the Army of BH (ABH), General Sefer Halilović and his book *Cunning Strategy* (Lukava strategija, Sarajevo, 1997). Of course, Shrader's impartiality and conclusions are open to debate, but one cannot ignore the documents mentioned in the book or data collected "on the field" in talks with participants of the events, especially commanders of the units that fought in BH. One cannot ignore either the data published in books by a Bosniak/Muslim on crimes committed against Croats in central Bosnia and the radicalization of part of the Muslims in BH after the arrival of Islamic volunteers from other countries, e.g., Esad Hećimović, *Garibs – the Mujahedin in Bosnia, 1992-1999* [Garibi-Mudžahedini u Bosni, 1992-1999 Zenica, 2006]. Or the fact that in late 1992 there were at least 70,000 Bosniaks/Muslims, expelled from areas under Serb control in Travnik, Bugojno, Zenica and the Lašva Valley, who had to be provided for and sheltered. (Slobodan Praljak, *Help Provided by the Republic of Croatia to the Muslim/Bosniak People and the Army of BH During 1991-1995*/Pomoć RH muslimansko-bošnjačkom narodu i Armiji BH tijekom 1991.-1995., Zagreb, June 2007, 5.)

According to Shrader, specific reports referring to the events on the ground are deliberately untrue to the disadvantage of the Croats, while the crimes committed against the Croats are downplayed, even though they were no less numerous and widespread. (According to the data of General Slobodan Praljak, "the number of Croatian civilians and captured HV troops killed by 'some' ABH members is at least seven times higher than the number of Muslim/Bosniak civilians and ABH troops killed by 'some' HVO members"; the same ratio is reported for people expelled by either side.) Of course, every crime must be condemned, but the truth is that the crimes committed by Croatian units in Ahmići and Stupni Do, and the detention and banishment of Bosniaks from areas in BH under Croatian control, attracted great attention from political circles, media and the ICTY, as compared to the crimes against the Croats in Grabovica (Municipality of Mostar), the eastern part of Mostar, Trusina and other villages in the Municipality of Konjic, Doljani (Municipality of Jablanica), Gornji Vakuf, Bugojno and surrounding villages (Gračanica, Vučipolje), Dusina, Šušanj and other villages the Municipality of Zenica, Zavidovići, Kiseljak (Žepče), Kiseljak near Sarajevo, Vareš, Kakanj and its surroundings, Vitez and surrounding villages (Križančevo Selo, Buhine Kuće, Brdo-Zabilje, Bobaši), Busočava and its surroundings, Novi Travnik and surrounding villages (Rastovci, Zenepići), Travnik and surrounding villages (Maljine, Čukle, Dolac), Uzdol and Hudutsko (Municipality of Prozor), Gračanica, Fojnica and surrounding villages (Polje Šćitovo, Ostružnica) and other places. (For crimes against the Croats committed by Muslim troops, see: Slobodan Praljak, *Crimes Committed by Some Members of the ABH /Muslim Units/ against Croats in BH 1991-1995* /Zločini koje su počinili neki pripadnici ABH nad Hrvatima u BH 1991.-1995., Zagreb; December 2006).

Similarly, little is known in the Croatian public about the detention and banishment of Croats from areas under Bosniak/Muslim control. According to research by I. Mlivončić, during the war, Bosniak/Muslim authorities set up 331 detention camps and prisons, in which 14,444 Croats were detained: 10,346 were civilians, and 4098 soldiers. Of these, 632 prisoners and detainees were killed, and 50 executed in a ritual manner (Ivica Mlivončić, *Muslim Camps for Croats in Bosnia and Herzegovina*, Muslimanski logori za Hrvate u Bosni i Hercegovini; Naša ognjišta, Mostar, 2008, 249).

At the same time, some media have attempted to blame Croatian policies controlled from Zagreb and President Tuđman for the detention of Bosniak-Muslims in areas under Croatian control in BH, although there is no proof that he was responsible for the establishment of such camps. On the contrary, sources have shown that as soon as they became aware of their existence authorities from Zagreb immediately requested the closing of all camps and release of detainees. This claim is supported by a statement by Andro Vlahušić, current mayor of Dubrovnik (neither during nor after the war was he a member of the ruling party, HDZ), describing the arrival to the Dretelj Camp in 1993, under HVO control. *I felt very badly, because a few hours after leaving Dretelj I had to speak in public about the suffering of the Croats, and present a book in Međugorje entitled* Suffering of the Croats in the 1991-1993 War (Stradanje Hrvata u ratu 1991.-1993.), *which I edited – and an hour or two before that I was a witness of evil deeds committed by members of our people... The camp guards were neither the HVO nor the military police, but Croats who had lost their loved ones in the war against the Bosniaks. From Međugorje we went to Zagreb and reported everything to Mate Granić (Croatian Foreign Minister), who did not know everything about the developments in Herzegovina. (...) The next day, we were summoned to the Office of the President of the*

Republic, where we were received by Vesna Škare Ožbolt, Branimir Jakšić and some other people from the Office who did not know what was happening either. It was a funny feeling, because I thought that we were living in a state with stable authorities and an omnipotent president, and then during those two days in Zagreb, I realized that Tuđman and his advisers, and leading diplomatic and secret service officials, did not have enough knowledge of the developments in Herzegovina. You could see it on their faces. On the same evening, when we visited Pantovčak [President's Office], *one of the first reports on the prime-time evening TV news was Tuđman's letter to Mate Boban asking for the shutting down of all camps and release of detainees.* Three months after the camps were closed, Mate Boban, held as representing the "hard" Herzegovinian line among the Croats in BH (after 1993, President of the Croatian Republic of Herzeg-Bosnia), presented a handgun with a dedication to Andro Vlahušić, and explained that "he helped us close Dretelj" (Pravo na dom, Osijek, 2011, 306).

Along with all that, the media largely presented the various meetings between Croatian and Serbian officials as attempts to partition Bosnia and Herzegovina, ignoring the fact that the representatives of all three constituent BH peoples were meeting and concluding various bilateral agreements, which included Serbian-Muslim agreements (e.g., in early August 1991) or joint declarations. (E.g., on 16 September 1993, on the "cessation of all hostilities and military conflicts between the Army of BH and Army of the Bosnian Serbs.") After all, it is a matter of record that Serbian President S. Milošević spoke with Alija Izetbegović "countless times in Geneva and other places" (minutes of the meeting of the Supreme Defense Council of SR Yugoslavia, August 1994; Slobodna Bosna, 5 May 2011, 29).

The media highlighted in particular negotiations between Serbian General Ratko Mladić and the Croatian leadership in BH as markedly anti-Bosniak. In doing so they ignore the fact that General Mladić and the Serbian leadership, concurrently (in the summer of

1993) talked with Bosniak/Muslim officials (foreign references even mention attempts to "create a Muslim-Orthodox alliance against the Catholics"), and that the then mayor of the Bosniak/Muslim part of Mostar discussed with Mladić a "joint advance to the river Neretva and Neum." (Ivo Lučić, Clash of National Interests as the Basic Cause of the War in Bosnia and Herzegovina; *Sukob nacionalnih interesa kao osnovni uzrok ratnog sukoba u Bosni i Hercegovini*, www.hizbih.info). Similarly, media noted the military cooperation between parts of the HVO and the Army of Republika Srpska in some parts of BH, and ignored the fact that the Muslim/Bosniak Army of BH paid the Serbs for months to shell Croatian targets in Mostar with their artillery. (Šefko Hodžić, Operation Autumn '94/*Operacija jesen '94*, Sarajevo, 2007; archpriest Aleksa Zubac, Vidoslov Journal, No. 3, 1994.) Another fact also ignored is that it was precisely the President of BH Alija Izetbegović who turned down in July and September 1992, and then in December 1992, during an extraordinary meeting of the Organization of the Islamic Conference in Jeddah, Saudi Arabia, where he met with Croatian Foreign Minister Zdenko Škrabalo, President Tuđman's offer concerning integrated joint defense from Serbian aggression with the explanation that "such an alliance would provoke an even greater hostility of the Serbs." President Tuđman was convinced that "Belgrade will not stop, nor would the West ever help either the Muslims or the Croats, which is why they have to turn to each other and defend themselves jointly." (Shrader, 11)

After the conflicts between the Bosniaks/Muslims and Croats in BH continued in April 1993, on 10 May 1993 President Tuđman sent a letter to the President of the Presidency of BH Alija Izetbegović and to the President of the HZ HB Mate Boban. *I am extremely alarmed and concerned because of the continued intensification of conflicts between the Croats and Muslims in some parts of BH. I condemn most strongly the armed conflicts between the Croats and Muslims in BH regardless of who caused them. I call on you to do everything in your power in order to immediately stop the conflicts between the Muslim and Croatian armed units – the Army of BH and the HVO – in the common struggle against the Serbian aggressor. (...) I also call upon all Croats in BH not to be taken in by provocations and to do their best in order to avoid this detrimental conflict.* (S. Praljak, Political and Military Croato/Bosniak Relations 1991-1995, Part I /*Politički i vojni hrvatsko-muslimanski/bošnjački odnosi 1991.-1995, I. dio, 295.*)

The negative perception of Croatia's role in the war in BH was considerably enhanced by extensive misinformation fed to the media by Serbian and Muslim propaganda services. As a consequence, incorrect statements were made even in the Croatian Parliament of the alleged aggression of the Republic of Croatia on Bosnia and Herzegovina, and the partition of BH by Serbia and Croatia. Along with the most frequently mentioned Tuđman-Milošević meeting in Karađorđevo in March 1991, reference is also made to the meeting between Mate Boban (leader of the BH Croats) and Radovan Karadžić (leader of BH Serbs) in Graz. (The report was made public on 6 May 1992.) The meeting discussed the possible Croato-Serbian delimitation in order to "eliminate the reasons for armed conflicts between the Croats and Serbs throughout BH." After that meeting which – it needs to be noted – was one of the meetings of all three parties in BH, the next misinformation fed to the public regarded the Croato-Serbian agreement on relinquishing Bosanska Posavina to the Serbs, and the agreement with the Serbs in the area. The truth is that such an agreement does not exist and that Croatian forces suffered very high casualties in defending Bosanska Posavina from Serbian aggression, especially in the battle for the "Corridor" in 1992 and repelling Serbian attacks in 1995. Despite heavy fighting, Croatian forces succeeded in retaining control over part of the territory. (The Orašje operational zone, including also the 108th HVO Brigade in Brčko which defended the area of the Croatian Municipality of Ravne-Brčko on the other side of the Corridor within the command zone of the 2nd Corps of the Army of BH operating out of Tuzla and other units). It is also true that the withdrawal of HV units from

Bosanska Posavina that took part in the fight against Serbian units in the area was requested by some leading European countries, but also by the highest officials of the Bosniak/Muslim leadership.

A record by Colonel Novica Simić, Commander of the Tactical BH Serbian Force Group in the battle for the Corridor in 1992, shows how hostile propaganda services used the media to provoke the conflict between the Croats and the Muslims. *The Command of the 1st Krajina Corps* [Army of Republika Srpska] *launched misinformation about its intentions through the media. All the misunderstandings, disagreements and diverging interests of Herzeg Bosnia (the Croatian community in BH) and the Muslim leadership in Sarajevo were adroitly harnessed to the purpose. One of the items fed continuously to the public referred to the agreement between Boban and Karadžić signed in Graz, according to which the Serbs were to get a corridor through Posavina. The misinformation about the meeting between the civilian authorities in Osijek with Serb representatives from Posavina and Semberija, with the presence of JNA general Dobrosav Praščević, confused many people. The ensuing official denials, including the denial of General Praščević himself, gave rise to even greater doubts among the Croats and the Muslims that something was 'stirring up' and confirmed their suspicions about 'shady dealings' regarding Bosanska Posavina* (Novica Simić, *Operation Corridor-92*, Operacija Koridor-92; Banja Luka, March 2011, 59).

At the same time, data showing that the Bosniak/Muslim leadership was involved in talks on the partition of Bosnia and Herzegovina have also been ignored. For example, the record by Sefer Halilović, Chief of the General Staff of the Army of BH, that the President of the Presidency of BH Alija Izetbegović had certain schemes in mind after 1992 concerning the partition of BH (S. Halilović, *Cunning Strategy*/Lukava strategija, 18-20). Also according to Halilović, in 1992-1993, Izetbegović's staff had close relations with the envoys of Serbian President S. Milošević, including talks on the exchange of territory, i.e., partition of Bosnia and Herzegovina

(Halilović, 10; Minutes of the Meeting of the Supreme Defense Council of SR Yugoslavia, August 1994; Slobodna Bosna, 5 May 2011, 29). According to Rusmir Mahmutćehajić, Izetbegović accepted the idea about the partition of BH in 1993 (Slobodna Bosna, 2 March 2000, 9).

On 25 February 1992, after his return from negotiations in Lisbon, the President of the Presidency of BH (already the recognized political and religious leader of the Muslim people), convened a closed-door and enlarged session of the Central SDA Committee in Sarajevo, reported on the results of the negotiations, and drew attention to the importance of the forthcoming referendum. He claimed that an "embarrassing proposal had come up about a confederal option for BH," according to which BH would consist of three "states," but that the most important thing now was to "ensure Bosnian independence," and that could only be realized through a referendum. But "if the Croatian community did not participate in the referendum, it would fail!" Izetbegović said that after the agreement in Lisbon the Croats agreed to a referendum and explained: *They* [the Croats] *want to vote now because they think that they will get some kind of sovereignty, national recognition, some regions, etc. in such a Bosnia and Herzegovina, as part of this agreement. The agreement consisted of three items. One, BH remains (...). Two, Bosnia will be transformed by the creation of regions based on the ethnic composition of the population as it is being formulated... And third, that all this would be implemented with the presence and guarantees of the European Community. The first and third points are not an issue, the second is.* (*The Lisbon Secret of Alija Izetbegović,* Lisabonska tajna Alije Izetbegovića, Dani, Sarajevo, 560, 7 March 2008., 30-32; Slobodan Praljak, Political and Military Croato/Bosniak Relations 1991-1995, Part I /*Politički i vojni hrvatsko-muslimanski/bošnjački odnosi 1991.-1995, I. dio*; Zagreb, April 2009, 279-280). The Croats fulfilled their promise. All or almost all Croatian deputies in the BH Assembly voted for the Decision on the Referendum in the early morning hours of 25 January 1992, after the Serbian deputies left the Assembly. Post-referendum events demonstrated to what extent the Bosniak/Muslim side intended to keep their agreement. This also needs to be taken into account when discussing the causes underlying the Croato-Bosniak (Muslim) conflict in BH.

One month after Croatian MPs (largely HDZ members) voted for the referendum, the commander of the Muslim Patriotic League, Sefer Halilović, passed on 25 February 1992 the Directive for the Protection of the Sovereignty of BH. In this Directive, the so-called "extreme HDZ wing" was qualified as a hostile force together with the Serbian Democratic Party and Yugoslav Army, and declared his intention to establish cooperation with the "Croatian people in BH in the fight against the common enemy." In Article 3 of the Directive, he called on the "people of Sandžak, Kosovo and Macedonia to make common cause with our just struggle and embark immediately upon military actions in order to tie down hostile forces and blunt the force of their onslaught on BH" (S. Halilović, *Cunning Strategy*/Lukava strategija, 222-224).

The truth is that it was precisely the Croats who put up a strong resistance to the Serbian aggression against BH. For that matter, Haris Silajdžić, BH Foreign Minister, stated in his letter to UN Security Council President in mid-June 1992, that the HVO was fighting for the freedom and independence of BH as part of the BH defense forces. Immediately after, the Presidency of BH proclaimed a state of war, general mobilization and compulsory work order, whereby Serbia, Montenegro, the former JNA and the extremist part of the SDS were named as aggressors.

Therefore, in order to accurately present the causes of the Croato-Bosniak (Muslim) conflict, due account also needs to be taken of the statements of Muslim officials and their anti-Croatian moves. The fact should also be accepted that there were three sides and three policies in BH, each with their own goals, the implementation of which was at least partly in collision with the policies and goals of the other two parties. The Serbian political elite wanted to preserve Yugoslavia at all costs ("they did not want to leave Yugoslavia").

The Muslims, later Bosniaks, were not against Yugoslavia, they were mainly for it, but they insisted on keeping the integrity of BH. The Croats were for BH, but only if it did not remain in Yugoslavia (Ivo Lučić, Clash of National Interests as the Basic Cause of the War in Bosnia and Herzegovina. *Sukob nacionalnih interesa kao osnovni uzrok ratnog sukoba u Bosni i Hercegovini*, www.hizbih.info). Because of the intransigence of the Serbian policies, which felt superior with the support of JNA, the political struggle for a solution developed into the Serbian aggression against BH and resulted eventually in its partition and high loss of human life, destruction of property, and many crimes against Bosniaks/Muslims and Croats. The Croato-Muslim conflict was also a consequence of that aggression, and involved major human suffering, destruction, and crimes.

According to the 1991 census, the population of BH was 4,364,574 (of which 755,895 or 17.3% Croats). According to some estimates, the population of BH in 2006 was 3,843,000; the number of Croats was 450,000 to 500,000. In late 2010, there were 443,013 Catholics in BH, or 13% of the total; the percentage of the Serbs and Bosniaks/Muslims did not change notably *(How many Croats are there in BH today?* Koliko je Hrvata danas u BH? Crkva na kamenu, 10, October 2008, 17). In 1991, the number of Croats living in the part of BH that is now within Republika Srpska was around 152,000. By 1996, the figure had dropped to approximately 11,900 (Slobodan Praljak, *Help Provided by the Republic of Croatia to the Muslim/Bosniak People and the Army of BH During 1991-1995*/Pomoć RH muslimansko-bošnjačkom narodu i Armiji BH tijekom 1991.-1995., Zagreb, June 2007, 395).

In terms of religious affiliation in BH, by 2010 (as compared to 1991), the number of Catholics dropped from 17.4% to 13%, the number of Orthodox believers increased from 31.2% to 37.1%, the number of Muslims increased from 43.5% to 48%, and the number of "others" decreased from 8.9% to 0.6% of the total. (Darko

Pavičić, *Religious Affiliation in BH 1991 and 2010*, Konfesionalna prisutnost u BH 1991 i 2010, Večernji List, 29 October 2011, 52).

According to some studies, the number of Croats killed in BH during the 1991-1995 war was the following: about 7000 in HVO and HOS (Croatian Defense Forces) units, 436 in the Army of BH, 38 in the JNA and VRS (Army of Republika Srpska), and 3000 in the HV (Croatian Army). 2136 Croatian civilians were also killed in BH (of this figure, Bosniak-Muslim forces killed 930 adults and 121 children). This is in line with the record of 12,637 Croats from BH killed throughout the former Yugoslavia in the period under consideration (Ivica Mlivončić, *Direct Demographic Losses of BH Croats in the 1991-1995 War,* Izravni demografski gubitci b-h Hrvata u ratnim sukobima 1991.-1995., 4. Naša ognjišta, Tomislavgrad, March 2008, 22-23).

According to studies of the Caritas Bishops' Conference of BH in 1999, which rely on the then available records of the Ministry of Welfare, Displaced Persons and Refugees of the Federation of BH, 312,000 Croats (43.5% of the 1991 total) were displaced during the war in BH: 170,000 from areas under Bosniak control and 142,000 from Republika Srpska. The number of displaced persons in BH includes 430,000 (31.7%) Serbs and 485,400 (25.8%) Bosniaks/Muslims. At the same time, 112,000 persons (9.12% of the total for BH) were displaced from areas under Croat control. Altogether 586,400 persons (47.7% of the total number of displaced persons) were displaced from areas under Serbian control, and 529,000 (43.10% of the total) from regions under Bosniak/Muslim control. (Ivo Lučić, *What Bosnia and Herzegovina Was, and Who Were We?* "Što je (bila) Bosna i Hercegovina i tko smo (bili) mi?" Status, No. 14, spring 2010, 131).

Subversive Counterintelligence Activity

(Information Warfare)
(prepared by Gordan Akrap)

Part of the inaccurate information in the media was certainly published within the scope of the propaganda war against Croatia, which was carefully planned immediately after the establishment of the democratically elected government in Croatia at the end of May 1990. It intensified with the start of the overt aggression of Serbia and Montenegro, meaning the JNA – against Croatia in the summer of 1991. A group of Yugoslav military counterintelligence services was very active in Zagreb at the time. They were attached to the Air Force and Air Defense, and colloquially known as KOS; its actual name was the Military Security Agency and Counterintelligence Groups, later publicly known as *Labrador*. It was not the only group operating in the free territory of the Republic of Croatia for the requirements of and under orders of the aggressor. As true members of the "Fifth Column," they collected all kinds of intelligence and reported them to their Yugoslav and/or Serbian case officers, and carried out terrorist acts. (E.g., setting and activating explosive devices on the Jewish cemetery and in front of the door of the Jewish Community Center in Zagreb on 19 August 1991; destruction of monuments commemorating WWII events; etc.). The *Labrador* group was busted in September 1991; most of its members managed to escape to Belgrade, while the captured agents were later exchanged for Croatian POWs.

Upon arrival to Belgrade in early October 1991, agents of the Labrador group joined the newly formed Department of Propaganda War – Air Force and Air Defense Information Service, also known as OPERA, with the following missions:

- pursuit of a propaganda-subversive war and subversive-psychological actions against the Republic of Croatia;

- launching of (mis)information and other views as an independent news agency or through selected reporters;
- provocation of a pro-army and defeatist mood with respect to Croatian and Bosnian authorities;
- promotion of regionalism in Croatia with regard to its real potential for conflicts within Croatia;
- satanization of the Croatian state leadership, emphasizing the nationalist-ustashe orientation and ideology of the Croatian leadership, compromising the entire system and leading persons on a personal level, as well as charges of treason;
- monitoring of all related media in the former Yugoslavia and media following developments in the former Yugoslavia, especially those with correspondents in Belgrade.

Through the activities of *Opera,* lies were continuously launched in local and international media. E.g., the terror against Serbs or the "elimination of Serbs from the Constitution" as the cause of Serbian rebellion against the new Croatian authorities. Systematic crimes committed by Croatian troops against Serbs, especially women and children. Sacrificing Vukovar for the sake of the international recognition of Croatia or in exchange for Herzegovina. The agreed war and partition of Bosnia and Herzegovina between Tuđman and Milošević. The sale of Bosanska Posavina or its exchange for southern Dalmatia, etc. Some of these lies are still present in the general perception of the Croatian public and are often repeated as irrefutable, although there are no serious proofs or indicators supporting such claims.

From the Lecture of Lord David Owen on 27 January 1996

On 27 January 1996, Lord David Owen held a lecture in New York organized by the International Peace Academy for the UN diplomatic corps, attended by more than 50 ambassadors and several UN undersecretaries. Excerpts:

The Republic of Croatia is the greatest victor in this war, while the Croatian Serbs are the greatest losers, mainly because of their own incompetence and obstinacy. Croatia had every right to challenge the Vance Plan because they showed patience and the Serbs were not disarmed. Very few Serbs will return to Croatia, least of all around Knin.

The key to peace is the implementation of the agreement on Eastern Slavonia, which is even more important than the Bosnian peace package. Five thousand troops for Eastern Slavonia is not much, but it is quality that matters. Zagreb and Belgrade are prepared to cooperate on this issue, and it is extremely important for Croatia to demonstrate goodwill towards Serbs who decide to remain in the region. A new, forcible exodus must be avoided, and Serbia needs economic help to look after those Serbs wanting to leave. Reconstruction is the key to the success of a new peace plan, especially in Vukovar. The fact that the transitional administrator is an American is very important. Success in the implementation of the agreement will depend on the continuation of negotiations on Prevlaka.

Croato-Serbian relations are a crucial element of peace in the Balkans (the implicit Muslim issue is secondary). That is why the continuous direct and indirect contacts between Milošević and Tuđman sustained throughout the conflict were particularly important. Tuđman is realistic and quite flexible. He got more than he deserved. But he has problems because he is surrounded by people (Šarinić, Granić, Šušak) of very differing concepts. He is very well represented in the UN. Milošević is not a racist (unlike Karadžić and Krajišnik), but a pragmatist and a politician, and we need him for the implementation of the peace plan.

The Hague Tribunal is important. Certain principal actors need to be brought to justice, primarily Karadžić and Mladić. But one has to understand Milošević's difficulties in delivering them, especially Mladić. Some Croats and Muslims also need to be prosecuted because there will be no reconciliation without that. Nevertheless, a line must be drawn and the "witch hunt" abandoned, because amnesty is more important than tribunals. Even an "isolated pariah" status is sufficient moral and political punishment for some leaders.

For reasons of the balance of forces, the West prevented Tuđman from taking Banja Luka, which he could have done at the time. He agreed to a painful compromise regarding Mrkonjić Grad, but by doing so broke up the Muslims and linked Cazinska Krajina to Croatia. **Let us not fool ourselves – the Dayton package is a partition plan.** The multiculturalism of Bosnia is a myth because it existed only in Sarajevo, Tuzla and some other places.

The BH Federation is essential and we must wish it every success because it is still important for the balance of forces; but if it fails, we shall have three republics in Bosnia and Herzegovina. Mostar is the major test for making or breaking the Federation. The big war is over, but skirmishes between Croats and Muslims are still possible. Most Serbs will not stay in Sarajevo, which will become a predominantly Muslim town – that is the price of their racist policies.

Brčko is a major unsolvable issue, and the arbitration procedure has not been agreed either. The Serbs need to feel the benefits of reconstruction in Bosnia and Eastern Slavonia in order to be cooperative. In military terms, Dayton is an 'exit strategy,' but it will have to be politically and economically present in the region for years to come. Milošević must be given a chance to resolve Kosovo, which will probably end up with its partition between Serbia and

Albania (Serbia getting the mines and the monasteries). Milošević will come out of isolation first through the OSCE, because Kosovo, Prevlaka etc. will be resolved through such mechanisms.

American leadership is extremely important, but America carried on where Europe started. Everybody made mistakes, the EU, US, RF, the negotiators; we all share the blame for ethnic cleansing. The Dayton Agreement will improve future relations between the US and Europe. The United Nations have been criticized too much, but they did what they could with crippled mandates. Instead of the UN, they should have criticized the Security Council and especially its permanent members. (As reported in *Večernji List*, Zagreb, 1996, and *Pravo na dom*, Osijek, 2011)

The lecture confirms that the solutions for ending the war in Bosnia and Herzegovina were imposed by the "great powers." It suggests the guidelines of European and US policies with regard to the territory of the former Yugoslavia and explains everyday issues burdened by developments and apparently deeply unjust decisions. The implementation of these guidelines was partly upset by developments in Kosovo in 1999, when it seemed that Serbia was also being punished for aggression against Croatia and BH. However, after that, in line with Owen's messages that "amnesty is more important than tribunals," that "Croato-Serbian relations are a key element of peace in the Balkans," and that "Tuđman [the Croats] got more than he deserved," emphasis is increasingly being placed on the thesis that the policies of both sides were responsible for the war in Croatia – which is not true. Such a policy, which avoids naming the aggressor in the wars in the former Yugoslavia in the 1990s is not a good foundation for the establishment of Croato-Serbian relations of appropriate quality.

The developments in Kosovo in 1999 and conditions in Bosnia and Herzegovina only prompted some Western political and military officials to reopen the question: should the Croatian and Bosniak/Muslim forces have been given free rein to finally defeat the Serbian army and thwart forever the revival of the Greater

Serbian policy of conquest? Former US ambassador to Croatia Peter Galbraith also expressed this doubt: *I spoke about the situation at the time and speculated what would have happened if we had let the Croats take Banja Luka. I pointed out that the then leadership of the Bosnian Serbs was genocidal and fascistoid, and that, perhaps, it might have been better, for the sake of the stability of the region, if we had permitted the total defeat of the Serbs instead of opting for a compromise. (...) But, if Banja Luka had been captured, we would have had at least 300,000 – 400,000 people in the Posavina corridor, and a very difficult situation. We already had many refugees from Krajina. Their exodus combined with that of the Bosnian Serbs would have occasioned a humanitarian disaster. We could not permit that. We also took into account quite a few other factors.* (As reported in the Portal *Večernji List,* 17 October 2008)

Foreign Volunteers in the Defense of Croatia

During the Homeland War, at least 360,000 conscripts were mobilized in Croatia. Along with Croats, they also included members of other ethnic groups living in Croatia who accepted Croatia as their own state, including 10,000 Serbs and an even greater number of Muslims.

According to the latest data of the Association of Foreign Homeland War Volunteers, more than 500 foreign volunteers (some of them of Croatian origin) fought on the Croatian side: 72 were killed and 90 wounded (most of them severely and several times). They came from the following countries: United Kingdom of Great Britain and Northern Ireland – 149 (15 killed, 25 wounded); France – 73 (7 killed, 21 wounded); Germany 63 (16, 11); Argentina – 3 (2,1); Australia – 15 (1, 2); Austria – 10 (2, 1); Belgium – 4 (1, 2); Bolivia – 2; Bulgaria 3 (2 killed); Czech Republic – 12 (1, 1); Chile – 1 (wounded); Denmark – 6 (2, 2); Estonia – 1 (killed) ; Finland – 2 (1 wounded); Gambia – 1 (killed); Ireland – 10 (1, 2); Italy – 10 (1, 2); Japan – 1; South African Republic – 1; Canada – 9 (3 killed); Lithuania – 1; Hungary – 34 (2, 5); Netherlands – 26 (2, 2); Norway – 3; Poland – 8 (3, 1); Portugal – 2 (1 killed); Russia – 3 (2 killed); USA 19, (3, 1); Slovakia 4 (1 wounded); Spain – 4 (2 wounded); Sweden – 6 (1 wounded); Switzerland – 1; Turkey – 1 (killed); Ukraine – 2 (killed); Zimbabwe – 1.

They came for a variety of personal reasons, especially after photographs from the devastated city of Vukovar were seen all over the world. Some were former soldiers who decided to lend a hand when they saw that Croatia was attacked by a stronger enemy and that its defenses were hampered by an unjust arms embargo. Some came to fight for the freedom of a "small" nation, others out of religious convictions, and some because for them it was a revolution against the communist regime and system. Perhaps the greatest number of all came because of their adventurous spirit, or to get the feel of war, or because of an unhappy love affair, or for who knows what reason. Among them were right-wingers, left-wingers, anarchists and monarchists, revolutionaries, Catholics, Protestants, atheists, Muslims and Jews. Most stayed until the end of the defensive war in Croatia and Bosnia and Herzegovina. In most cases because, as they said, they were on the side of good, on the side of the victims defending themselves from extermination. These reasons were recognized by people who did not know the history of the country to which they came and were not burdened by relations in the former Yugoslavia.

Gaston Besson, one of the foreign volunteers from France, summarizes the gist of the motives guiding those who came to defend Croatia in the following statement: *That was no war, but a treacherous massacre! It was not a conflict between two armies! There was one powerful army, the JNA, which attacked and killed civilians in its stride. (...) Whoever stayed did it for a single reason – and it was not politics, or Catholicism, or pay (which was "peanuts", up to 100 Deutschmarks, the same as Croatian defenders were getting) – but simply because this war was so unjust! It did not matter who was a Croat or a Serb, the only fact was that the stronger party attacked the weaker one, and the former was the one backed by the JNA. (...)*

I don't really want to talk about the Serbs as enemies, because we also had Serbs as comrades-in-arms. We can talk about chetniks, ok? I really have nothing against the Serbs... after all, Serbs also fought with us and for us. Some of our boys were half-Serbian, half-Croatian. So to say that we were fighting against the Serbs is nonsense. If we speak about the enemy then we must refer to them as chetniks and their militias. Those Serbs who called themselves chetniks were ordinary cutthroats. (...) The problem with Serbs, this time I mean all the Serbs and not only the chetniks, is that they are victims of their own propaganda! Their government and their media fed them stories round the clock that we were neo-nazis, fascists, murderers, cutthroats. They were terrified. And those people on the other side thought we were monsters. (...) Yet we never killed a prisoner. (...) Once we got one of them in the woods and found a manual in his backpack titled, "How the Ustashe Kill Serbs." And that stupid fool read that and learned how the ustashe killed and tortured Serbs! I watched him and thought, "This one's crazy!" And I gave him some clothes, even my socks, because it was cold. (...)

I don't remember hating anyone during this war. I don't remember that any of my boys hated anyone either. We were there; we knew there was somebody on the other side. (...) But when you get up in the morning and go into action, you don't say, "Oh, great, I'm now going into action to kill someone!" No, you get up and say, "Shit, I'm going into action, I might get killed!" And you think, if they don't get you, they'll probably get one of your friends. And then, for months after that, you just think how many of your friends got hit, how you carried them from the battlefield, how they screamed when they were wounded. That's what you think about, and not about going somewhere to kill a lot of people. That's that, we are not killers, we were soldiers!

The vast majority of Croatian citizens are deeply grateful to all the Croatian defenders who defended Croatia honorably and fairly, especially those who were not of Croatian nationality but defended Croatia as their own homeland, and those who came from foreign lands and risked their lives to help Croatia in the most trying time of its history.

Course of the International Recognition of the Republic of Croatia Until its Admission to the United Nations

(prepared by Ivan Radoš)

26 June 1991	SLOVENIA[1]
30 July 1991	LITHUANIA[2]
11 December 1991	UKRAINE[3]
14 December 1991	LATVIA
19 December 1991	ICELAND
31 December 1991	ESTONIA
13 January 1992	HOLY SEE
14 January 1992	SAN MARINO

15 January 1992
EEC COUNTRIES[4] (GERMANY[5], DENMARK, ITALY, FRANCE, LUXEMBOURG, UNITED KINGDOM, IRELAND, BELGIUM, GREECE, SPAIN, PORTUGAL, NETHERLANDS), AUSTRIA, MALTA, HUNGARY, NORWAY, BULGARIA, POLAND, SWITZERLAND, CANADA

16 January 1992
SWEDEN, CZECHOSLOVAKIA, CHILE, ARGENTINA, LIECHTENSTEIN, AUSTRALIA, NEW ZEALAND, URUGUAY

17 January 1992	FINLAND
18 January 1992	ROMANIA
21 January 1992	ALBANIA
24 January 1992	BOSNIA AND HERZEGOVINA[6], BRAZIL
27 January 1992	PARAGUAY
29 January 1992	BOLIVIA

The first Asian and Islamic country (other than Turkey) to recognize the Republic of Croatia was Iran (15 March 1992); the first African country to recognize the Republic of Croatia was Egypt (16 April 1992).

By the date of admission of the Republic of Croatia to full UN membership, 22 May 1992, Croatia was recognized among others by the Russian Federation (17 February 1992), Japan (17 March 1992), the United

States of America (7 April 1992; together with Slovenia and Bosnia and Herzegovina), Israel (16 April 1992) and China (27 April 1992).

By the end of 1992, Croatia was recognized by more than 90 countries.

List of Countries which Diplomatically Recognized the Republic of Croatia (According to Records of the Ministry of Foreign Affairs and European Integrations)

7

1	SLOVENIA	26 June 1991
2	LITHUANIA	30 July 1991
3	UKRAINE	11 December 1991
4	LATVIA	14 December 1991
5	ICELAND	19 December 1991
6	GERMANY	19 December 1991
7	ESTONIA	31 December 1991
8	HOLY SEE	13 January 1992
9	SAN MARINO	14 January 1992
10	ITALY	15 January 1991
11	FRANCE	15 January 1992
12	LUXEMBOURG	15 January 1992
13	UNITED KINGDOM	15 January 1992
14	BELGIUM	15 January 1992
15	GREECE	15 January 1992
16	PORTUGAL	15 January 1992
17	SPAIN	15 January 1992
18	NETHERLANDS	15 January 1992
19	IRELAND	15 January 1992
20	DENMARK	15 January 1992
21	AUSTRIA	15 January 1992
22	MALTA	15 January 1992
23	HUNGARY	15 January 1992
24	NORWAY	15 January 1992
25	BULGARIA	15 January 1992
26	POLAND	15 January 1992
27	SWITZERLAND	15 January 1992

28	CANADA	15 January 1992
29	SWEDEN	16 January 1992
30	LIECHTENSTEIN	16 January 1992
31	CZECH REPUBLIC[8]	16 January 1992
32	SLOVAKIA	16 January 1992
33	AUSTRALIA	16 January 1992
34	NEW ZEALAND	16 January 1992
35	CHILE	16 January 1992
36	ARGENTINA	16 January 1992
37	URUGUAY	16 January 1992
38	FINLAND	17 January 1992
39	ROMANIA	18 January 1992
40	ALBANIA	21 January 1992
41	BOSNIA AND HERZEGOVINA	24 January 1992
42	BRAZIL	24 January 1992
43	PARAGUAY	27 January 1992
44	BOLIVIA	29 January 1992
45	TURKEY	6 February 1992
46	MACEDONIA	12 February 1992
47	RUSSIAN FEDERATION	17 February 1992
48	KYRGYZSTAN	26 February 1992
49	COLUMBIA	3 March 1992
50	IRAN	15 March 1992
51	PERU	15 March 1992
52	JAPAN	17 March 1992
53	LIBYA	17 March 1992
54	CYPRUS	27 March 1992
55	TAJIKISTAN	31 March 1992
56	SOUTH AFRICA	2 April 1992
57	UNITED STATES OF AMERICA	7 April 1992
58	SOUTH KOREA	15 April 1992
59	EGYPT	16 April 1992
60	ISRAEL	16 April 1992
61	UNITED ARAB EMIRATES	18 April 1992

62	SUDAN	20 April 1992
63	ALGERIA	24 April 1992
64	TUNISIA	26 April 1992
65	CHINA	27 April 1992
66	MOROCCO	27 April 1992
67	OMAN	28 April 1992
68	THAILAND	2 May 1992
69	PHILIPPINES	5 May 1992
70	VENEZUELA	6 May 1992
71	NORTH KOREA	8 May 1992
72	INDIA	11 May 1992
73	PAKISTAN	11 May 1992
74	SINGAPORE	15 May 1992
75	INDONESIA	16 May 1992
76	JORDAN	17 May 1992
77	BRUNEI DARUSSALAM	21 May 1992
78	GHANA	22 May 1992
79	YEMEN	22 May 1992
80	KENYA	22 May 1992
81	CUBA	22 May 1992
82	MOLDOVA	25 May 1992
83	MEXICO	26 May 1992
84	SRI LANKA	27 May 1995
85	PANAMA	28 May 1992
86	ZAMBIA	1 June 1992
87	MAURITANIA	4 June 1992
88	CAPE VERDE	18 June 1992
89	ARMENIA	21 June 1992
90	LEBANON	7 July 1992
91	JAMAICA	14 August 1992
92	BELARUS	2 September 1992
93	BURKINA FASO	7 October 1992
94	KAZAKHSTAN	10 October 1992
95	ETHIOPIA	6 November 1992

96 TANZANIA 13 November 1992
97 MONGOLIA 19 November 1992
98 QATAR 5 December 1992
99 NIGERIA 21 December 1992
100 GUATEMALA 22 December 1992
101 GEORGIA 13 January 1993
102 BAHRAIN 18 January 1993
103 SAMOA 8 March 1994
104 VIETNAM 5 May 1994
105 SAUDI ARABIA 22 August 1994
106 SAINT VINCENT AND THE GRENADINES 7 October 1994
107 KUWAIT 8 October 1994
108 UZBEKISTAN 6 February 1995
109 ANDORRA 28 April 1995
110 COSTA RICA 19 October 1995
111 BELIZE 23 January 1996
112 ECUADOR 22 February 1996
113 NICARAGUA 29 March 1996
114 SERBIA 23 August 1996
115 MONTENEGRO 12 June 2006
116 KOSOVO 19 March 2008

Along with these states, Croatia currently has diplomatic relations with an additional 58 countries.

1 Croatia and Slovenia recognized each other on 26 June 1991, one day after the Croatian Parliament passed the *Declaration on the Establishment of the Sovereign and Independent Republic of Croatia*, and the Assembly of the Republic of Slovenia proclaimed its independence. EEC countries recognized Slovenia and Croatia on the same day, 15 January 1992.

2 The Baltic States and former Soviet Republics (Lithuania, Latvia and Estonia) were among the first to recognize Croatia. They were admitted to the United Nations on 17 September 1991 (when the recognition of Croatia by Lithuania – 30 July 1991 – became internationally legitimate). The Republic of Latvia, which recognized Croatia on 14 December 1991, was already a UN member on that date.

3 The case of Ukraine, another former Soviet Republic, is specific. After Croatia recognized it on 5 December, Ukraine reciprocated by recognizing Croatia on 11 December 1991. Although Ukraine proclaimed its independence on 24 August 1991, it became independent in December of the same year, after the collapse of the Soviet Union and establishment of the

Commonwealth of Independent States (CIS), when it was finally recognized by Canada, the USA and EEC. However, official UN records declare the date of Ukraine's admission as 24 October 1945, the date of admission of the former USSR. This retroactive acknowledgement of Ukraine's status is the consequence of a letter sent on 24 December 1991 by Boris Yeltsin, then President of the Russian Federation, informing the UN Secretary General that the continuity of the USSR in the United Nations and its bodies would be sustained by the Russian Federation with the support of eleven CIS members. In spite of that, unlike Ukraine or Belarus, some CIS members, e.g., Armenia and Kazakhstan were admitted to the UN singly in 1992.

4 The countries of the European Economic Community decided to jointly recognize the independence and sovereignty of the former Yugoslav republics of Croatia and Slovenia on the basis of the principle of the recognition of new states, accepted on 17 December 1991 by the EEC Ministerial Council.

5 Germany announced its decision regarding recognition already on 19 December 1991, and formally recognized Croatia on 23 December in a letter sent by German President Richard von Weizsäcker to the President of the Republic of Croatia Dr. Franjo Tuđman. The decision entered into force on 15 January 1992, along with the recognition by other EEC members.

6 At the time, the recognition by Bosnia and Herzegovina did not enjoy international legitimacy because BH itself was not recognized as yet (it was recognized on 6 April 1992), nor was it a UN member (admitted on 22 May 1992).

7 The list is taken from the website of the Ministry of Foreign Affairs and European Integrations: http://www.mvpei.hr/MVP.asp?pcpid=1335 (accessed on 22 September 2011).

8 On the date of recognition, 16 January 1992, the Czech Republic and Slovakia were a single state community – the Czech and Slovak Federal Republic. They became independent on 1 January 1993.

From the testimony of S.L. SVK intelligence and army officer, at The Hague Tribunal, VII/28, trial of Slobodan Milošević; transcripts, Fund for Humanitarian Law, Belgrade, 2006, 531-802)

Milošević [Slobodan, Serbian President] had envoys in Krajina, who made sure that all his wishes were fulfilled. Almost with no exception, his representatives were agents of the Serbian State Security Service (SDB). They were present in Krajina from the beginning, and the allegedly "spontaneous" rebellion against Croatian authorities in 1990 was organized from Belgrade. On one occasion, Zimonja [Nikola, agent of the JNA Counterintelligence Service] told me that the log barricades that were put up around Knin in August 1990 were largely manned by paramilitary troops sent from Serbia. Many of these troops were actually from Belgrade, and according to Zimonja, they were getting 100 Deutschmarks to block the roads. That was the first step towards the creation of the Serbian autonomous region around Knin and although it was presented in the Belgrade press as a "spontaneous" action of the local Serbs taken in defense, it was actually planned and initiated by Belgrade. The SDB was by far and large in the forefront of the local population in making such things possible. Its agents provoked incidents, and the press then used them to excite the local population and create a climate of fear necessary to start the war. Milošević's relation with the JNA differed from his relation with the SDB. In a way, certain tension was present, but the army nevertheless cooperated with him and executed his wishes. Under the Constitution, the generals were responsible to the SFRY Presidency, but they were actually accountable to Milošević. That was not to their liking, but they did it all the same. All JNA officers feared his power, especially as most of them had families in Serbia (...)

Whenever the RSK delegation attended a conference abroad, they had to go to Belgrade at least 24 hours before in order to receive instructions from the Serbian government. The RSK government had an office in Belgrade, provided by the SDB. (...) We always knew the subject of the talks abroad in advance because we insisted on getting the agenda beforehand. We told the representatives of the international community that we needed the agenda before the meetings in order to prepare thoroughly for discussion on specific issues. Actually, Belgrade wanted us to send them the agenda 48 hours before our departure so that they could be informed of what was happening. When we attended briefings in Belgrade, we simply received instructions on what exactly to do and what position to take with regard to each issue raised. (...)

Belgrade did not want any solution to the problems dividing the RSK Serbs and Croatian government. For that reason, any contact with the Croats or representatives of the international community was forbidden, because the establishment of any dialogue might have contributed to the peaceful settlement of the conflict. Belgrade was focused on maintaining a high degree of tension in the RSK, and everything we did at international conferences was aligned to that objective. In most cases, they told us not to accept anything. We were told to raise every possible procedural or technical issue in order to delay an agreement. If all our observations were taken care of, and if all other tactical delaying moves were exhausted, we would request a break and someone from the delegation (usually Goran Hadžić) would phone Belgrade and ask for additional instructions. If Belgrade told us that we could accept a suggestion during discussion on a specific subject, it was always done with the understanding that any accepted agreement would subsequently be broken on the ground, usually within 24 hours. (...)

Generally speaking, military agreements served Belgrade's purpose because they could easily be broken. It would be enough to fire a mortar shell onto Croatian territory, and the agreement would be off. By the time we went to Norway, there were 27 military agreements related to Sector North in negotiations between the RSK and Croatia. They were all broken, either on the day they were signed or soon afterwards, probably by the Serbs in 4 out of 5 cases. Whenever that happened, Belgrade would approve the breaking action. As far as political agreements were concerned, Belgrade did not want the solution of any essential points. For example, in Norway the international mediators suggested the setting up, in Krajina, of an experimental village in which a number of its former inhabitants, displaced Croats, would be allowed to return to their homes, thus to demonstrate that Serbs and Croats could live together. The Croatian delegation was absolutely in favor, and the RSK delegation found it hard to find any convincing reason to oppose the suggestion, as we were publicly claiming that Croats were welcome. Having exhausted all possible objections to the plan, Krneta said that we would accept it. In private he told the members of the RSK delegation that the plan could be easily undermined, because on the first night he would send some of his people to the village to kill a couple of Croatian returnees, or even a few Serbs. It was not important who was killed, he said, because that would create a climate of fear anyway, and no Croat would ever even think of coming back. Therefore, if such a political agreement was reached, the RSK could accept it because we knew that it would be easy to prevent its implementation. But Belgrade forbade any agreement of an essential character. (...)

The RSK pursued a continuous policy focused on expelling Croats from Krajina. The RSK government had adopted that policy on orders from Belgrade, and launched a campaign of abuse and violence against all Croats remaining in the region. Every corps of the RSK army had a unit for "dirty missions." However, any initiative of RSK army units had to be approved by Belgrade first. With that objective in mind, a special unit under Ajdinović's command was setup within the 21st Corps. Its responsibility included the elimination of Croatian civilians and the creation of a climate of fear. I am familiar with at least four infamous incidents perpetrated by the unit under Ajdinović's order: the murder of the Serbian mayor in Vrginmost; the planting of an anti-tank mine on the railway track between Vrginmost and Glina, setting of mines round a water tower near Glina, and planting of landmines on a soccer field, also in Glina. The mayor of Vrginmost, Dmitar Obradović, was a moderate Serb, married to a Croat. He was against the RSK idea in general, and favored a peaceful reconciliation with the Croats. The existence of the RSK depended on the conviction of the Serbian population that they could not live at all with the Croats, and anyone opposing that prerequisite, as Obradović did, was considered a threat for the RSK government. They had to hush him up to avoid Serbs questioning the necessity of that special Serbian "state." As a result, he was killed in 1992 under Ajdinović's order. The RSK government blamed "Croatian terrorists" for the murder. (...)

When we saw on television the Croatian flag flying atop Knin on 6 August, we first thought it was a trick, but when everyone realized it was true, rumors began to spread that Belgrade had betrayed us and sold us down the river. People in Topusko panicked when they became aware that nothing could stop Croatian troops. Everybody knew what had happened to the Croats in Krajina in 1991 – hundreds were killed, all their homes and businesses torched, and the entire population forcibly expelled. The general belief was that the Croatian troops, after regaining the region, would launch reprisals. (...) We in the government and RSK military contributed to the process by deliberately sowing panic among the civilian population. Panic is infectious and if people have no time to think things over, they will simply run. If they had time to think about the consequences of leaving their homes and all their property, a much larger number would have stayed, but Belgrade did not want that. Thus, efforts were made to scare the people before they had time to see whether things would proceed as planned. Rumors were spread that the ustashe would kill all the civilians; I know some individuals whose mission was to circulate and tell people that the ustashe were slaughtering children. In such circumstances, nobody wanted to stay and see whether the rumors were true. Everybody simply wanted to leave. I personally made up the story about the civilians massacred by Muslims from the 5th ABiH Corps at Topusko, reported by CNN. There was not a grain of truth in that story. (...)

However, it was not known how everybody would leave Topusko, so my wife suggested we should make a deal with the Croats to take a convoy across Croatian territory, and we did that. We travelled with a Croatian escort through Sisak, then along the highway through Slavonia to Šid in Serbia. There were about 20,000 people in the convoy altogether. I was the last to cross the border of Croatia and enter Serbia. I wore an RSK army officer's uniform the whole time, and had to deliver my hand arms to the Croatian soldiers. While we travelled through Croatia people threw rocks at us, shouted abuse and harassed us. They didn't even search anyone. But when we got to Serbia they treated us like criminals, searched everybody and took away all remaining weapons.

Human Losses

It is estimated that at least 19,500 Croatian citizens were killed or went missing in the Homeland War.

According to incomplete data collected by the end of 2009, about 12,500 citizens were killed (direct demographic losses) on the Croatian side (the free territory of the Republic of Croatia), of which about 50% were civilians, while 1030 are registered as missing. The number of killed civilians includes about 200 children (the figure is not final): over 70% were killed by direct hostile action (shells or mines, plane rockets, snipers etc.), and less than 30% by indirect hostile action (playing with firearms, hand grenades and the like).

Altogether 30,578 persons were wounded (the figure does not include the area occupied during the war): as much as 7169 civilians, 21,959 Croatian defenders, 58 UN force members and 613 enemy soldiers, while no data is available for 779 persons (unknown affiliation), although the majority most probably belonged to hostile units. The number of wounded civilians includes 1044 children; 188 children became disabled from wounds sustained in the war (in 56 cases severe bodily disability, in 92 heavy and in 40 moderate). 5497 children lost one parent, and 74 lost both.

In the same period, about 6239 persons, largely of Serb nationality, were killed in the occupied parts of the Republic of Croatia (of which: 3574 were soldiers, about 1632 civilians, while the status of 1033 is not known), and 646 persons went missing.

According to the figures of Milislav Sekulić, General of the Serb Army of Krajina, between June 1991 and August 1995 Serb casualties amounted to 3496 persons killed and 1857 missing (the source notes that "the actual number is probably higher"). Among those killed (the figures are probably incomplete) there were 54 children (below 18): 25 killed in accidents, 10 committed suicide, the cause of death in 5 cases is unknown, 8 were killed by shelling, 3 were killed in action (on record as “fighters”), 1 was killed and 2 died as a consequence of being wounded.

These figures (which are continuously being updated) were acquired from the Office for Detained and Missing Persons (of the Ministry of the Family, Veterans’ Affairs and Intergenerational Solidarity of the Republic of Croatia), Office for the Protection of the Victims and Participants in the Homeland War (of the Ministry of Health and Welfare of the Republic of Croatia), Medical Corps Headquarters of the Ministry of Health, Croatian Memorial-Documentation Center of the Homeland War, and Milisav Sekulić’s book *Knin je pao u Beogradu* (Knin Fell in Belgrade; Belgrade, 2000).

Mass Graves

Over time, Ovčara has become the symbol of remembrance of the victims of Serbian crimes committed throughout Croatia during the Homeland War, in towns and villages such as Antin, Antunovac, Baćin, Balinci, Beli Manastir, Berak, Bilje, Bogdanovci, Bruška, Bučje, Cerić, Cetingrad, Čakovci, Čanak, Četekovac, Ćelije, Dalj, Donji Čaglić, Drežnik, Drniš, Erdut, Ernestinovo, Ervenik, Glina, Glinsko Novo Selo, Glinska Poljana, Grabovac, Gređane, Hrvatska Kostajnica, Hum, Ilok, Ivanovo Selo, Jankovci (Novi and Stari Jankovci), Jasenice, Joševica, Kijevo, Korlat, Kostrići, Kraljevčani, Kusonje, Lipik, Lisičić, Lovas, Lovinac, Maja, Marinci, Medviđa, Mikluševci, Mohovo, Nadin, Negoslavci, Okučani, Pakrac, Pakrački Vinogradi, Petrinja, Pecki, Petrovci, Plavićevac, Poljanak, Saborsko, Selište, Skela, Smilčić, Smoljanac, Slunj, Sonković, Sotin, Struga, Svinjarevci, Široka Kula, Škabrnja, Šopot, Tenja, Tordinici, Tovarnik, Vaganac, Viduševac, Voćin, Zemunik Donji, and other sites where Croatian defenders and civilians were maltreated and killed. The Croatian public knows very little about these execution sites and the crimes that were committed.

At least 149 mass graves and more than 1200 single graves of the victims of Serbian crimes, mainly Croats, but also members of other ethnic groups that did not support Greater Serbian policies and aggression against Croatia, suggest the conclusion that the killings were planned. The mortal remains of 3782 victims have been exhumed from these graves, and 3217 Croatian defenders and civilians positively identified (Ivan Grujić, *Detainees and Missing Persons in the Homeland War*, Zatočeni i nestali u Domovinskom ratu, Pravo na dom, Osijek, 2001, 289).

In order to avoid generalization, it should be noted that many Serbs in Serbia refused mobilization because they did not want to participate in a war of conquest, and that many who found themselves in the JNA and Serbian-Montenegrin units that attacked

Croatia were there due to a variety of circumstances. For example, the inertia of service or mobilization, or absence of information due to strong anti-Croatian propaganda in the media. Many of them behaved like soldiers and not like criminals. Some even succeeded in saving the lives of Croats that extremist members of Serbian units threatened to kill; some Serbs were even killed while trying to prevent their fellow countrymen from committing crimes against Croats. Unfortunately, there were also many who went on the rampage against Croatia driven by Greater Serbian ideas and hate, the majority of which committed crimes in Croatia and Bosnia and Herzegovina.

Crimes against Croats also provoked outrageous individual reactions on the Croatian side. By the start of Operation *Storm,* citizens of Serbian nationality were killed in places under the control of Croatian authorities such as Gospić, Osijek, Sisak and Paulin Dvor. Other places of retaliation against Serbian civilians include Pakračka Poljana and the Medak Pocket; individual cases of the murders of Serbian civilians were also reported in some other localities. The Croatian public is aware of all these cases, as well as of the murders of citizens of Serbian nationality committed after *Storm* in the hamlets of Grubori, Varivode and Gošić, where a total of 21 persons were killed.

POSTERS

The slab from the Split baptistry with the image of a Croatian king / Poster from the CROATIA UNDER ATTACK! STOP THE DESTRUCTION! series. The slab is believed to be from the basilica of St. Peter

HELP!
STOP
THE
WAR
IN
CROATIA
SUPPORT DEMOCRACY, HUMAN RIGHTS AND FREEDOM
THE AGGRESSORS ARE SERBIA AND THE YUGO COMMUNIST ARMY.
CROATIAN INFORMATION CENTRE

Map with the borders of "Greater Serbia"

Poster of the 14th Congress of the League of Communists of Yugoslavia (SKJ). The Serbian and Montenegrin delegations forcibly asserted their own positions, ignoring and refusing every proposal from the Slovenian delegation, and on January 22 1990 the Slovenian and Croatian delegations walked out

Hrvatska Demokratska Zajednica (HDZ). Croatian Democratic Union

League of Communists of Croatia – Party of Democratic Change (SDP)

Serbian poster: "One people, one will, one state"; along the margins of the "flower" are the names of Croatian and Bosnian cities to be annexed, according to the idea of "Greater Serbia", to Serbia (Beli Manastir, Petrinja, Knin, Banja Luka, Sarajevo, Trebinje…)

Poster from the referendum on the annexation of part of Croatian territory to Serbia: "Serbian people in one state – for annexation"

Poster: "REFERENDUM FOR CROATIA"

The Cathedral of St. James in Šibenik is the most important architectural monument of the Renaissance in Croatia. It was built of stone. Since 2000 it has been on the UNESCO World Heritage list. Early on in the war, on September 17 1991, three mortar bombs hit the square between the cathedral and the Town Hall. The explosions damaged the northern facade of the cathedral and the door. One day later, on September 18, two shells fired from a *PČ 180* of the Yugoslav navy hit the dome of the cathedral and a column between two windows (R. Ivančević, Šibenik Cathedral; Šibenik, 1998; I. Livaković, Šibenik in the September 1991 War; Šibenik, 1992, p.74, 145)

LIVE AND LET LIVE! Author: Ivo Vrtarić. Photograph by Željko Gašparović. Published by War press OGP Novska, 1992. The poster shows Petar Dukarić from Cvetlin, municipality of Bednja. In September 1991 he joined as a volunteer the *Tigers*, the First HV Guards Brigade. The photo was taken in October 1991 in Stari Grabovac on the front line. Owing to the graffito with the name of the world-famous heavy metal act Guns'N'Roses on the wall of the house in the background the photograph was published in many papers round the world and in books on the war against Croatia

VUKOVAR,
A SHAME
FOR EUROPE AND THE WORLD,
ON THE BRINK OF THE 21st CENTURY.
THE AGGRESSORS ARE SERBIA AND THE YUGO COMMUNIST ARMY.

DUBROVNIK, ONCE A FORTRESS OF TREASURE AND BEAUTY, NOW A FORTRESS OF DESTRUCTION, FEAR AND DEATH-IN 1991.

THE AGGRESSORS ARE SERBIA AND THE YUGO COMMUNIST ARMY.

CROATIAN INFORMATION CENTRE
Print: HRVATSKA TISKARA, d.o.o. ZAGREB

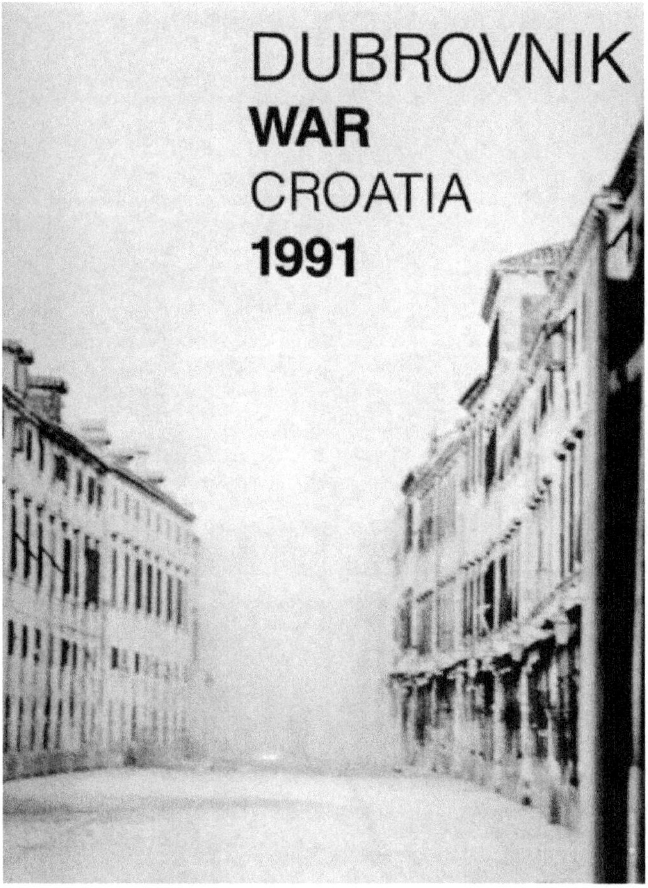

DUBROVNIK/WAR/CROATIA/1991 / Author: Tomislav Gusić, Photograph by: Pavo Urban, Dubrovnik, 1991 The photograph shows stone dust on Stradun, the central street of old Dubrovnik, after the explosion of a shell on December 6 1991. On that day Dubrovnik suffered one of the heaviest attacks. This was one of the last photographs taken by Pavo Urban, who was killed on that day near Orlando's Column by a mortar bomb. (Pavo Urban – The Last Pictures, text by Antun Maračić, Zagreb, 1997) Along with Pavo Urban, the following Croatian newsmen and cameramen were killed during the Homeland War: Gordan Lederer, Žarko Kaić, Živko Krstičević, Tihomir Tunuković, Boris Erdelja, Luka Skračić...

AN APPEAL FOR PEACE IN CROATIA

(BY THE 9th OF DECEMBER, 81 NOBEL LAUREATES HAD SIGNED THIS APPEAL)

During the past several weeks the Yugoslav Army has escalated its war against Croatia. Dozens of villages have been razed. Many historical monuments have been destroyed. Several cities, including Croatia's capital of Zagreb, have been bombed.

The violence and destruction unleashed in Croatia is on a scale unknown in Europe since the Second World War. Innocent civilians are massacred. Hospitals and places of worship are destroyed.

Conscience demands that we raise our voices against this senseless war.

We appeal to the Western and Eastern governments to stop the Yugoslav Army's wanton destruction.

We appeal to all humanitarian organizations to provide aid for all the victims of Yugoslav military brutality.

We appeal to men and women of conscience to speak up against indifference to the plight of Croatian people who are facing not only the danger of total destruction of their country, but also the threat of their own extinction.

THE AGGRESSORS ARE SERBIA AND THE YUGO COMMUNIST ARMY.

CROATIAN INFORMATION CENTRE
Print: HRVATSKA TISKARA, d.o.o. ZAGREB

21.

Abbreviations

A BiH – Armija Bosne i Hercegovine
A BH – Army of Bosnia and Herzegovina
BiH – Bosna i Hercegovina
BH – Bosnia and Herzegovina
EZ – Europska Zajednica / European Community
GBR – Gardijska brigada / Guards brigade
GS (GŠ)– Glavni stožer (štab) / General Staff
HDZ – Hrvatska demokratska zajednica / Croatian Democratic Union
HMDCDR – Hrvatski memorijalno-dokumentacijski centar Domovinskog rata / Croatian Homeland War Memorial and Documentation Centre
HOS – Hrvatske obrambene snage / Croatian Defense Forces
HR HB – Hrvatska Republika Herceg Bosna / Croatian Republic of Herceg Bosna
HV – Hrvatska vojska / Croatian armed forces, Croatian army
HVO – Hrvatsko vijeće obrane / Croatian Defense Council
HZ HB – Hrvatska zajednica Herceg Bosna / Croatian Community of Herceg Bosna
JNA – Jugoslavenska narodna armija / Yugoslav People's Army
MUP – Ministarstvo unutarnjih poslova / Ministry of the Interior
NDH – Nezavisna Država Hrvatska / Independent State of Croatia
OUN – Organizacija Ujedinjenih Naroda / United Nations Organization
RH – Republika Hrvatska / Republic of Croatia
RSK – Republika Srpska Krajina / Republic of Serbian Krajina
SAO –Srpska autonomna oblast / Serbian autonomous region
SDS – Srpska demokratska stranka / Serbian Democratic Party
SFRJ – Socijalistička Federativna Republika Jugoslavija
SFRY – Socialist Federal Republic of Yugoslavia
SKJ – Savez komunista Jugoslavije / League of Communists of Yugoslavia
SRH – Socijalistička Republika Hrvatska / Socialist Republic of Croatia
SUP – Sekretarijat unutarnjih poslova / Ministry of the Interior
SVK – Srpska vojska Krajine / Serbian Army of Krajina
TO – Teritorijalna obrana / Territorial defense
UNCRO – Operacija UN-a za uspostavljanje povjerenja u Hrvatskoj / United Nations Confidence Restoration Operation in Croatia
UNPA – Zaštićeno područje Ujedinjenih naroda / United Nations Protected Area
UNPROFOR – Zaštitne snage Ujedinjenih naroda / United Nations Protection Forces
VO – Vojna oblast / Military district
ZNG – Zbor narodne garde / National Guard Corp

ACKNOWLEDGEMENTS

The book includes some texts and posters from Marijo Reljanović's photo-monograph *The Croatian War Poster* (Hrvatski ratni plakat, Zagreb, 2010), and several pages of photographs from *History of the Croats – Illustrated Chronology* (Povijest Hrvata – Ilustrirana kronologija; Zagreb, Multigraf, 2003).

The sources of the photographs include the Croatian Memorial-Documentation Center of the Homeland War, the Military Museum of the Ministry of the Interior of the Republic of Croatia, photograph files of the Croatian press, Archives of the Croatian Parliament, Croatian Television, the Association of the Homeland War Special Police, photograph files of the *Večernji List* daily (Zagreb), photograph files of the Croatian Historical Museum, and private files of photographers mentioned in the list of photographs.

The author(s) of some photographs are not listed. The possible authors of photographs taken in wartime Vukovar are Andrija Marić, Siniša Jovanov, Stjepan Šustić Štef and Nikola Jurčević, and the names of donors are mentioned in the book.

The photographs were sought or selected by Josipa Maras Kraljević and Danijel Šoštarić.

The working version of the tables in the book was prepared by Nikola Perić.

The advice of many colleagues has been very helpful in my work on this book: Ivo Lučić, Željka Križe Gračanin, Natko Martinić Jerčić, Ivan Radoš...

I would like to thank them all for their cooperation and assistance.

To my parents – Anica and Ante, my wife Anita and my children Ivan, Marta and Ante.

ABOUT THE AUTHOR

Ante Nazor was born on March 15, 1968 in Zagreb. He completed his elementary and high school education in Zagreb as well (1986). Nazor graduated from the Faculty of Philosophy – Humanities and Social Sciences in Zagreb in 1993 (History and Archeology major), and received his Master's Degree in History on July 13, 1999 at the same Faculty. He obtained his PhD on February 16, 2007 (scientific field: Humanities; scientific area: History; branch: National History).

During the period of June-July 1991, Nazor was mobilized in the reserve forces of the National Guard (housed at the Pioneer City in Zagreb and on alert for possible attacks on the barracks). In October and November 1991, he registered as a volunteer on the Eastern Slavonian front and was a member of the 122nd Đakovo "R" Brigade. He then returned to finish his studies until October 1993. From October 22, 1993, until the end of the war, Nazor was employed with the Croatian Military Academy – NCO School of the Croatian Armed Forces in Jastrebarsko.

References

Balkan Battlegrounds: A Military History of the Yugoslav Conflict, 1990-1995, Central Intelligence Agency, Office of Russian and European Analysis, Washington, DC 20505, May 2002

Nikica Barić. *Srpska pobuna u Hrvatskoj 1990.-1995.*, Zagreb, 2005

Nikica Barić. "Prvi hrvatski predsjednik dr. Franjo Tuđman o jugoslavenskom predsjedniku Josipu Brozu Titu", zbornik radova "Dr. Franjo Tuđman u okviru hrvatske historiografije", Zagreb, 2011, p. 313-341

Dušan Bilandžić. *Hrvatska moderna povijest*, Zagreb, 1999

Janko Bobetko. *Sve moje bitke*, Zagreb, 1996

Momir Bulatović. *Pravila ćutanja: istiniti politički triler s poznatim završetkom*, Beograd, 2004

Smail Čekić. *Agresija na Republiku Bosnu i Hercegovinu – planiranje, priprema, izvođenje*, Sarajevo, 2004

Mile Deduković – Alenka Mirković-Nađ – Davor Runtić. *Bitka za Vukovar*, Vinkovci, 1997

Davor Domazet – Lošo. *Hrvatska i veliko ratište*, Zagreb, 2002

Davor Domazet – Lošo. *Hrvatski domovinski rat 1991.-1995. (strateški pogled)*, Zagreb, 2010

Druga bojna Gromovi 108. pješačke brigade HVO Brčko, Brčko, 2011

Bejdo Felić. *Peti korpus 1992.-1995.*, Sarajevo, 2002

Jelena Guskova. Istorija jugoslovenske krize 1990.-2000., Vol. II, Beograd, 2003

Ante Gotovina.*Napadajni bojevi i operacije HV i HVO*, Knin, 1996

Mate Granić. *Vanjski poslovi: Iza kulisa politike*, Zagreb, 2005

Sefer Halilović. *Lukava strategija*, Sarajevo, 1997

Haški tribunal VII/28, suđenje Slobodanu Miloševiću, transkripti, Fond za humanitarno pravo, Beograd, 2006

Esad Hećimović. *Garibi – Mudžahedini u BiH 1992.-1999.*, Zenica, 2006

Šefko Hodžić. "Operacija Jesen 94.", Sarajevo 2007

Richard Holbrooke. *Završiti rat*, Sarajevo, 1998

Hronologija 1990-1995., Banja Luka, 2002

"Izvješće u povodu inicijative Vlade Republike Hrvatske, klasa: 004-01/02-02/12, ur. broj: 5030109-02-2 od 10. listopada 2002. godine", Ustavni sud Republike Hrvatske (predsjednik Suda, dr. sc. Smiljko Sokol), broj: U-X-2271/2002, Zagreb, Nov 12 2002

Borisav Jović. *Poslednji dani SFRJ: Izvodi iz dnevnika.* Beograd, 1995

Hrvoje Kačić. *U službi domovine – Croatia rediviva*, Zagreb, 2006

Veljko Kadijević. *Moje viđenje raspada – vojska bez države*, Beograd, 1993

Kratak pregled vojnih djelovanja u Domovinskom ratu 1991.-1995., Branko Dubravica – Rajko Rakić, Zagreb, 2009

Kronologija rata 1989.-1998. – Hrvatska – Bosna i Hercegovina, Zagreb, 1998

Ivo Lučić. "Što je (bila) Bosna i Hercegovina i tko smo (bili) mi", *Status*, issue 14, Spring 2010

Branko Mamula. *Slučaj Jugoslavija*, Podgorica, 2000

Davor Marijan. *Smrt oklopne brigade*, Zagreb-Sarajevo, 2002

Davor Marijan. "Bosna i Hercegovina 1991.-1995. u godinama nesvršenog rata", *Status*, issue 3, May/June 2004, p. 98-110

Davor Marijan. *Bitka za Vukovar*, Zagreb – Slavonski Brod 2004

Davor Marijan. "Sukob HVO-a i ABiH u Prozoru u listopadu 1992.", *Časopis za suvremenu povijest*, issue 2, Zagreb, 2006

Davor Marijan. "Sukob između HVO-a i Armije BiH u Prozoru u listopadu 1992", *Časopis za suvremenu povijest, 2*, Zagreb, 2006

Davor Marijan. *Oluja*, Zagreb, September 2007

Davor Marijan. *Slom Titove armije – JNA i raspad Jugoslavije 1987.-1992.*, Zagreb, 2008

Ivica Mlivončić. "Izravni demografski gubitci b-h Hrvata u ratnim sukobima 1991.-1995. (4.)", *Naša ognjišta*, Tomislavgrad, March 2008

Ivica Mlivončić. "Muslimanski logori za Hrvate u Bosni i Hercegovini", *Naša ognjišta*, Mostar, 2008

Hasib Mušinbegović, Remzija Šiljak, Kemo Bećirević. *Operacija Vlašić*, Sarajevo, 1999

Mario Nobilo. *Hrvatski feniks: diplomatski procesi iza zatvorenih vrata: 1990.-1997.*, Zagreb 2000

David Owen. *Balkanska odiseja*, Zagreb, 1998

Povijest Hrvata – ilustrirana kronologija, Zoran Ladić – Ante Nazor, Zagreb, 2003

Slobodan Praljak. *Zločini koje su počinili neki pripadnici A BiH (muslimanske postrojbe) nad Hrvatima u BiH 1991.-1995.*, Zagreb, December 2006

Slobodan Praljak. *Procjena ratnih šteta u Hrvatskoj*, Zagreb, December 2006

Slobodan Praljak. *Pomoć Republike Hrvatske Muslimansko-Bošnjačkom narodu i Armiji Bosne i Hercegovine tijekom 1991.-1995.*, Zagreb, June 2007

Slobodan Praljak. *Politički i vojni hrvatsko-muslimanski (bošnjački) odnosi 1991.-1995.*, I. dio, Zagreb, April 2009

Pravo na dom, ed. Slobodan Lang – Branko Pek, Osijek, 2011

Radovan Radinović. "Realna pretnja na delu", *Vojska Krajine*, issue 4-5, July-August 1993

Ranjena crkva u Hrvatskoj, Uništavanje sakralnih objekata u Hrvatskoj 1991.–1995., Zagreb, 1996

Marijo Reljanović. *Hrvatski ratni plakat*, Zagreb, 2010
John Sadikovich. *Tuđman, prva politička biografija*, Zagreb, 2010
Milisav Sekulić. *Knin je pao u Beogradu,*Bad Vilbel, 2001
Charles R. Shrader. *Muslimansko-hrvatski građanski rat u srednjoj Bosni – vojna povijest 1992.-1994.*, Zagreb, 2004
Novica Simić. *Operacija Koridor-92*, Banja Luka, March 2011
Spasimo život (zbrinjavanje napuštenih osoba na oslobođenim područjima Republike Hrvatske), S. Lang – B. Čulo – B. Domazet, Zagreb, 1997
Ivan Stambolić. *Put u bespuća*, Beograd 1995
Ivan Strižić. *Bitka za Slunj*, Slunj-Zagreb, 2007
Stvaranje hrvatske države i Domovinski rat (Zdenko Radelić, Davor Marijan, Nikica Barić, Albert Bing i Dražen Živić), Školska knjiga – Hrvatski institut za povijest, Zagreb, 2006
Hrvoje Šarinić. *Svi moji tajni pregovori sa Slobodanom Miloševićem 1993-95 (98)*, Zagreb, 1999
Miroslav Tuđman,*Istina o Bosni i Hercegovini: dokumenti 1991.-1995.*, Zagreb, 2005
Ustav Republike Hrvatske, *Narodne novine, broj 56*, Dec 22 1990
Ustav SFR Jugoslavije – Ustav SR Hrvatske, ekspoze Jakova Blaževića, Zagreb, 1974
Vojna operacija 'Oluja' i poslije, HHO, Zagreb, 2001
Marko Vrcelj. *Rat za srpsku krajinu 1991.-1995.*, Beograd, 2002
Žene Krajine – rat, egzodus i izbeglištvo, Beograd, 1996
Ozren Žunec. *Goli život – socijetalne dimenzije pobune Srba u Hrvatskoj, I-II*, Zagreb, 2007

Printed in Great Britain
by Amazon

43107745R00169